CHOMSKY ON ANARCHISM

SELECTED AND EDITED BY
BARRY PATEMAN

AK PRESS
EDINBURGH, OAKLAND AND WEST VIRGINIA
2005

Copyright © 1969, 1970, 1976, 1986, 1990,
1995, 1996, 2004, 2005 Noam Chomsky

Chomsky on Anarchism

ISBN: 1-904859-20-8
9781904859260

Library of Congress Control Number: 2005923315

AK Press   AK Press
674 A 23rd Street   PO Box 12766
Oakland CA   Edinburgh, Scotland
94612-1163 USA   EH8 9YE

Interior layout and design: Fran Sendbuehler
Cover design: John Yates
Printed in Canada

Chomsky on Anarchism

PREFACE

I was a teenager when I first learned that Chomsky was an anarchist. The discovery had a powerful effect. This was around 1980 and, while "anarchy" was proclaimed loudly from the stages of some punk rock shows I attended, I felt isolated in my belief that there was something profound, and profoundly *serious*, about the doctrine I had adopted—something beyond easy exhortations to "smash the state," without any suggestion of how, or what to replace it with. I'd read the classics—Proudhon, Bakunin, Kropotkin—but they were hard to find, not to mention dead. Chomsky was not only alive, he was a widely-read, well-respected intellectual, who wrote his first pro-anarchist essay at the age of ten, hung out at anarchist newsstands and bookshops on 4th Avenue in Manhattan as a teenager (not far from my punk stomping grounds), and still maintained his anti-authoritarian beliefs as an adult. Despite the contradiction my peers might have seen in appealing to the authority of such a public figure, I felt validated, and much less alone.

Part of the reason we at AK Press are publishing this book is to inspire that same sense of excitement and discovery. It's much harder to pull off today, of course, at least within the anarchist movement itself. Anarchism is more widespread and visible—validation and community within it much easier to find. Chomsky's version of libertarian socialism is somewhat better known. But perhaps that very familiarity is dangerous. We think we know what anarchism is. We think we know who Chomsky is. And, in that knowing, we miss a lot of nuance and complexity. The essays and interviews collected in this book, written between 1969 and 2004, will hopefully hold surprises and raise productive questions for even the most self-assured anarchist.

We're also publishing this book for the many people out there who don't know what anarchism is, or whose knowledge of it is mostly limited to sensationalist newspaper headlines. For them, we see Chomsky as a bridge to a new set of ideas about the means and ends of social change, to a 150-year tradition of revolutionary thought and practice that has sought social and economic justice without the mediation of bosses, politicians or bureaucrats. Outside the anarchist movement, many are completely unaware of the libertarian socialist roots of Chomsky's work, how they relate not only to his social criticism, but also to his linguistic theory. For them, the surprises in this book will be greater. What, after all, could such a reasonable and intelligent man have to do with people the nightly news tells us are the very antithesis of Reason?

Quite a bit, as this book will make abundantly clear. Chomsky's well-known critiques—of the media, of US foreign policy, of exploitation and oppression in all their forms—don't come out of nowhere. They're based on his fundamental beliefs about what it means to be human: who we are, what we're capable of becoming, how we might organize our lives, and how our potential is stunted and deformed by hierarchical social relationships. Critique without an underlying vision is mere complaint, which is precisely how politicians and Fox News anchors portray all social protest. To understand Chomsky, one must understand his vision—which is to say one must understand anarchism.

If this book serves its purpose, you'll be well on your way. As Barry Pateman suggests in his introduction, there is no single definition of anarchism. Certainly, some anarchists will take issue with different aspects of Chomsky's version—especially, for instance, his refusal to deny the importance of reformist political victories (however clear he is about their limitations). But, whether they know nothing about anarchism or think they know everything, everyone who reads this book will learn something valuable. And then, hopefully, go on to learn more, enough to eventually build the sort of world Chomsky envisions, a world where every person participates directly in the decisions that affect their daily lives and illegitimate authority is consigned to its proper place: a sad historical footnote about the days before we got our act together and set things right.

Charles Weigl
for the AK Press Collective
March 2005

INTRODUCTION

The purpose of this volume is to present some of Noam Chomsky's ideas and thoughts on anarchism. Chomsky is regularly identified by the media as a prominent anarchist/libertarian communist/anarcho-syndicalist (pick as many as you like). More importantly he places *himself* within this political spectrum. Regardless of whether any of these labels fits him perfectly, there can be no doubt that his ideas on social change and the re-structuring of society are worthy of consideration and discussion. We have selected a variety for the reader to consider and, through which, to hopefully gauge both Chomsky's contribution to anarchism and anarchism's contemporary relevance as a means of interpreting and changing the world.

Some of these talks and interviews are published here for the first time and, combined with more familiar material, they reinforce and elaborate Chomsky's sense of what anarchism is and what it could be. Inevitably, there is some repetition among the pieces, specific themes and theorists to which Chomsky often returns. Trying to get the same message across tends to make one repetitive! That said, though, as each idea is revisited, both clarity and nuance are added to some challenging ideas.

Chomsky's introduction to Daniel Guérin's *Anarchism* (1970), which he later revised for publication in *For Reasons of State* (1973) as "Notes on Anarchism," is important in crystallizing his sense of anarchism as both an historical force and a way of bringing about contemporary social change. It was an essay that was criticized by some anarchists. George Woodcock, an anarchist historian, argued that it was one-dimensional. Chomsky, said Woodcock, was a left-wing Marxist (as was Guérin) who wished to use anarchism to soften and clarify his own Marxism. His work was mired in the nineteenth century language of anarchism. At best it was anarcho-syndicalism; at worst simple economic determinism. There was no reference to Kropotkin, Malatesta, Herbert Read. For Woodcock, Chomsky equates anarchist struggle with a single class and fails to see that anarchism appeals to "those people of all classes who seek a society where the potentialities of existence are varied and liberated, a society to be approached by lifestyle rebellion *as well as* economic struggle."

Woodcock's criticisms are interesting and not without their ironies. To be sure, there is in Chomsky's work a certain blurring of terms, as well as the suggestion that left-wing communism, council communism and anarchism have much in common as tools with which to critique state socialism and capitalism. This idea is repeated in varying forms throughout this book. Chomsky remains as equally impressed by Pannekoek as by Rudolph Rocker or Diego Abad de Santillan. In his interview with Barry Pateman in 2004, he argues that there are differences between this left strand of communism and anarchists, but that "they are the kind of differences that ought to exist when people are working together in comradely relationships." Equally important is Chomsky's perception of class as the central tenet of anarchism. It's a theme he will keep returning to and a theme that is out of synch with both Woodcock and some elements of contemporary anarchism. For Chomsky, it is quite straightforward: within modern capitalism we see matters of class arising all the time. To deny or minimize them is nonsensical. Such a position can lead him to harsh criticisms of anarchists like Stirner, primitivists, and all those who cannot see the importance of solidarity and community in a class-based way.

Woodcock and Chomsky are not too far apart however on the central question of how an anarchy can be brought about. Both seem to shy away from the idea of a single revolutionary moment that will overthrow capitalism. Rather, they imagine it could well be a long, drawn-out process. It's an idea shared by other anarchists such as Colin Ward who, in his *Anarchy in Action* (1973), argues that:

> an anarchist society, a society that organizes itself without authority, is always in existence...buried under the weight of the state and its bureaucracy, capitalism and its waste, privilege, religious differences, nationalism and its suicidal loyalties, religious differences and their superstitious separatism.

It is an idea that has always had resonance with some anarchists—Rocker is a notable example—and perhaps allows us to understand some of Chomsky's ideas more clearly. Surely, like Ward, he sees a fundamental human decency in people. A decency that has somehow survived, and will continue to survive, all the weapons that capitalism can throw at it. From this decency comes ways of being that can operate within capitalism and point the way to a future of anarchy. Hence, Chomsky can argue that progressive taxation and Social Security are created by attitudes which, if pushed a little more, would be anarchist. It's a little bit reminiscent of Kropotkin arguing that lifeboatmen were an example of anarchist communism in action, or the syndicalist idea the certain kinds of unions could become the source of a new society—the new in the shell of the old. Such an attitude certainly answers the problem of how we create anarchy in our day-to-day lives. It also explains the myriad of examples Chomsky gives of how to move towards anarchy, many of which implicitly suggest the richness of character and ability to provide mutual aid prevalent in many people. A cynical reader may well want to ask how long one must wait for the state to be eroded by these examples of anarchy in action, or might point out the suppleness and malleability of capitalism in incorporating many of these ideas as its own. But, as Woodcock argues of anarchists: "It is to liberating the great network of human co-operation that even now spreads through all the levels of our lives than to creating or even imagining brave new worlds that they have bent their efforts."

Chomsky's anarchism has always been grounded in history. It might be hard for us now, in an era where there are numerous sympathetic accounts of the anarchist experience in the Spanish revolution, to realize how important his essay "Objectivity and Liberal Scholarship" was in 1969. To be sure, there was Vernon Richard's excellent *Lessons of the Spanish Revolution*, but Chomsky went further. He clinically dissected Gabriel Jackson's *The Spanish Republic and the Civil War:1931–1939* and linked it to the liberal ideology prevalent in America in the 1960s, an ideology that reflects "an antagonism to mass move-ments and to social change that escapes the control of privileged elites," which in Jackson's work reveals itself through a regular use of negative language to describe the actions of the anarchists. Chomsky, using a rich array of historical texts, brought his points to a wide audience and influenced a new generation of researchers and militants, inspiring them to probe deeper and further. In his portrayal of Jackson's work as representing contemporary American liberal thinking on Vietnam, Chomsky impressively linked past and present, making a shrewd and disturbing comment on liberalism in general. In the words of Peter Werbe: "As Chomsky amply and admirably demonstrates, when the major issues of an era are settled in blood, liberalism's pretense to humane ends or means crumbles under the demands of an implacable state."

So here are some key components of Chomsky's anarchism: an awareness of anarchist history and how it still retains a freshness and urgency in the light of today's challenges; a broad and generous definition of anarchism that links left and council communists in its critique of capitalism and sees them as nat-ural allies; the central importance of class in any critique of capitalism and in creating anarchy; and a belief in people's innate goodness, which is reflected in actions and structures that contribute to what Rocker, in *Anarcho-Syndicalism*, calls "a definite trend in the historic development of mankind, which...strives for the free, unhindered unfolding of all the individual and social forces in life." All of this is allied to a flexible methodology through which to accom-plish this unfolding, a willingness to change tactics, to consider a variety of strategies, and a reluctance to speak with too much certainty or rigidity. Chomsky expresses these ideas in clear and straightforward language, arguing strongly against the mystifying nature of much intellectual writing and the feelings of powerlessness caused by unnecessarily complex and elliptical lan-guage.

There are some questions that we can still raise. One has the sense that Chomsky's ideas about class could be a little tighter. Yes, class is manifestly an economic state. It is, however, also a cultural state. To be working class is not just to be part of an hierarchy: it is to be part of an experience, something that is lived. Just what that experience is and how it is realized may well have impli-cations for the anarchism that Chomsky champions. Of course, all writing is a form of shorthand, but one would very much like to see him discuss this rich-er and more complex picture of class at greater length. Secondly, and perhaps more controversially (to anarchists at least), is Chomsky's claim that the state can be used to move towards a more equitable anarchical society. He sees the libertarian movement as sometimes "pursuing doctrine in a rigid fashion without being concerned about the human consequences," when simply opposing the state might mean placing even greater power in the hands of reactionary forces, private (usually corporate) powers that would reinforce inequality and hardship. He goes on, in one interview, to suggest that "protecting the state sector today is a step towards abolishing the state." He also adds that, in the process of pursuing social change though the mechanisms of the state, people will inevitably run up against the inherent limits of such reformist tactics and, eventually, understand that the system itself must be changed.

Such arguments, of course, do challenge accepted anarchist theory. For people like Emma Goldman all states were to be done way with. The "democratic state," she suggested, once it was challenged, would become as oppressive as the most totalitarian state. For Chomsky, the state can maintain "a public arena" where there is still some room in which people can operate and bring about change. It's a position that will spark debate and, in the eyes of some, question his whole conception of anarchism.

More could be said. For instance, Chomsky has a flexible view of voting. He suggests that, like some other anarchists, he does vote on local matters. In terms of national elections, he suggests that if Massachusetts were a swing state he would vote. If not, "there are a variety of possible choices, depending on one's evaluation of the significance." Such flexibility of approach to these matters, which can be interpreted as mere common sense, could also raise the question of what anarchist practice actually is, and how it differs from that of, say, social democrats. Arguments such as these will not go away. Tensions will continue. Attitudes will solidify, shift and change. The consistency between theory and practice will continue to be worked out. Chomsky has much to contribute to that process and there is much for us to admire in both his optimism and his clear sense of the difficult struggles ahead:

> The record of anarchist ideas, and even more, of the inspiring struggles of people who have sought to liberate themselves from oppression and domination must be treasured and preserved, not as a means of freezing thought and conception in some new mold but as a basis for understanding of the social reality and committed work to change it. There is no reason to suppose that history is at an end, that the current structures of authority and domination are graven in stone. It would also be a great error to underestimate the power of social forces that will fight to maintain power and privilege.

Barry Pateman
March 2005

ONE
OBJECTIVITY
AND LIBERAL SCHOLARSHIP
(1969)

I

In a recent essay, Conor Cruise O'Brien speaks of the process of "counterrevolutionary subordination" which poses a threat to scholarly integrity in our own counterrevolutionary society, just as "revolutionary subordination," a phenomenon often noted and rightly deplored, has undermined scholarly integrity in revolutionary situations.[1] He observes that "power in our time has more intelligence in its service, and allows that intelligence more discretion in its methods, than ever before in history," and suggests that this development is not altogether encouraging, since we have moved perceptibly towards the state of "a society maimed through the systematic corruption of its intelligence." He urges that "increased and specific vigilance, not just the elaboration of general principles, is required from the intellectual community toward specific growing dangers to its integrity."

Senator Fulbright has developed a similar theme in an important and perceptive speech.[2] He describes the failure of the universities to form "an effective counterweight to the military-industrial complex by strengthening their emphasis on the traditional values of our democracy." Instead they have "joined the monolith, adding greatly to its power and influence." Specifically, he refers to the failure of the social scientists, "who ought to be acting as responsible and independent critics of the government's policies," but who instead become the agents of these policies. "While young dissenters plead for resurrection of the American promise, their elders continue to subvert it." With "the surrender of independence, the neglect of teaching, and the distortion of scholarship," the university "is not only failing to meet its responsibilities to its students; it is betraying a public trust.

The extent of this betrayal might be argued; its existence, as a threatening tendency, is hardly in doubt. Senator Fullbright mentions one primary cause: the access to money and influence. Others might be mentioned: for example, a highly restrictive, almost universally shared ideology, and the inherent dynamics of professionalization. As to the former, Fulbright has cited elsewhere the observation of De Tocqueville: "I know of no country in which there is so little independence of mind and real freedom of discussion as in America." Free institutions certainly exist, but a tradition of passivity and conformism restricts their use—the cynic might say this is why they continue to exist. The impact of professionalization is also quite clear. The "free-floating intellectual" may occupy himself with problems because of their inherent interest and importance, perhaps to little effect. The professional, however, tends to define his problems on the basis of the technique that he has mastered, and has a natural desire to apply his skills. Commenting on this process, Senator Clark quotes the remarks of Dr. Harold Agnew, director of the Los Alamos Laboratories Weapons Division: "The basis of advanced technology is innovation and nothing is more stifling to innovation than seeing one's product not used or ruled out of consideration on flimsy premises involving public world opinion"[3]—"a shocking statement and a dangerous one," as Clark rightly comments. In much the same way, behavioral scientists who believe themselves to be in possession of certain techniques of control and manipulation will tend to search for problems to which their knowledge and skills might be relevant, defining these as the "important problems"; and it will come as no surprise that they occasionally express their contempt for "flimsy premises involving public world opinion" that restrict the application of these skills. Thus among engineers, there are the "weapons cultists" who construct their bombs and missiles, and among the behavioral scientists, we find the technicians who design and carry out "experiments with population and resources control methods" in Vietnam.[4]

These various factors—access to power, shared ideology, professionalization—may or may not be deplorable in themselves, but there can be no doubt that they interact so as to pose a serious threat to the integrity of scholarship in fields that are struggling for intellectual content and are thus particularly susceptible to the workings of a kind of Gresham's law. What is more, the subversion of scholarship poses a threat to society at large. The danger is particularly great in a society that encourages specialization and stands in awe of technical expertise. In such circumstances, the opportunities are great for the abuse of knowledge and technique—to be more exact, the claim to knowledge and technique. Taking note of these dangers, one reads with concern the claims of some social scientists that their discipline is essential for the training of those to whom they refer as "the mandarins of the future."[5] Philosophy and literature still "have their value," so Ithiel Pool informs us, but it is psychology, sociology, systems analysis, and political science that provide the knowledge by which "men of power are humanized and civilized." In no small measure, the Vietnam war was designed and executed by these new mandarins, and it testifies to the concept of humanity and civilization they are likely to bring to the exercise of power.[6]

Is the new access to power of the technical intelligentsia a delusion or a growing reality? There are those who perceive the "skeletal structure of a new society" in which the leadership will rest "with the research corporation, the industrial laboratories, the experimental stations, and the universities," with "the scientists, the mathematicians, the economists, and the engineers of the new computer technology"—"not only the best talents, but eventually the entire complex of social prestige and social status, will be rooted in the intellectual and scientific communities."[7] A careful look at the "skeletal structure" of this new society, if such it is, is hardly reassuring. As Daniel Bell points out, "it has been war rather than peace that has been largely responsible for the acceptance of planning and technocratic modes in government," and our present "mobilized society" is one that is geared to the "social goal" of "military and war prepared-ness." Bell's relative optimism regarding the new society comes from his assump-tion that the university is "the place where theoretical knowledge is sought, test-ed, and codified in a disinterested way" and that "the mobilized postures of the Cold War and the space race" are a temporary aberration, a reaction to Communist aggressiveness. In contrast, a strong argument can be made that the university has, to a significant degree, betrayed its public trust; that matters of foreign policy are very much "a reflex of internal political forces" as well as of economic institutions (rather than "a judgment about the national interest, involving strategy decisions based on the calculations of an opponent's strength and intentions"); that the mobilization for war is not "irony" but a natural devel-opment, given our present social and economic organization; that the technolo-gists who achieve power are those who can perform a service for existing insti-tutions; and that nothing but catastrophe is to be expected from still further cen-tralization of decision making in government and a narrowing base of corporate affiliates. The experience of the past few years gives little reason to feel optimistic about these developments.

Quite generally, what grounds are there for supposing that those whose claim to power is based on knowledge and technique will be more benign in their exer-cise of power than those whose claim is based on wealth or aristocratic origin? On the contrary, one might expect the new mandarin to be dangerously arro-gant, aggressive, and incapable of adjusting to failure, as compared with his predecessor, whose claim to power was not diminished by honesty as to the lim-itations of his knowledge, lack of work to do, or demonstrable mistakes.[8] In the Vietnam catastrophe, all of these factors are detectable. There is no point in overgeneralizing, but neither history nor psychology nor sociology gives us any particular reason to look forward with hope to the rule of the new mandarins.

In general, one would expect any group with access to power and affluence to construct an ideology that will justify this state of affairs on grounds of the general welfare. For just this reason, Bell's thesis that intellectuals are moving closer to the center of power, or at least being absorbed more fully into the deci-sion-making structure, is to some extent supported by the phenomenon of coun-terrevolutionary subordination noted earlier. That is, one might anticipate that as power becomes more accessible, the inequities of the society will recede from vision, the status quo will seem less flawed, and the preservation of order will become a matter of transcendent importance. The fact is that American intel-lectuals are increasingly achieving the status of a doubly privileged elite: first, as

13

American citizens, with respect to the rest of the world; and second, because of their role in American society, which is surely quite central, whether or not Bell's prediction proves accurate. In such a situation, the dangers of counter-revolutionary subordination, in both the domestic and the international arena, are apparent. I think that O'Brien is entirely correct in pointing to the necessity for "increased and specific vigilance" towards the danger of counterrevolutionary subordination, of which, as he correctly remarks, "we hear almost nothing." I would like to devote this essay to a number of examples.

Several years ago it was enthusiastically proclaimed that "the fundamental political problems of the industrial revolution have been solved," and that "this very triumph of democratic social evolution in the West ends domestic politics for those intellectuals who must have ideologies or utopias to motivate them to social action."[9] During this period of faith in "the end of ideology," even enlightened and informed commentators were inclined to present the most remarkable evaluations of the state of American society. Daniel Bell, for example, wrote that "in the mass consumption economy all groups can easily acquire the outward badges of status and erase the visible demarcations."[10] Writing in *Commentary* in October 1964, he maintained that we have in effect already achieved "the egalitarian and socially mobile society which the 'free floating intellectuals' associated with the Marxist tradition have been calling for during the last hundred years." Granting the obvious general rise in standard of living, the judgment of Gunnar Myrdal seems far more appropriate to the actual situation when he says: "The common idea that America is an immensely rich and affluent country is very much an exaggeration. American affluence is heavily mortgaged. America carries a tremendous burden of debt to its poor people. That this debt must be paid is not only a wish of the do-gooders. Not paying it implies a risk for the social order and for democracy as we have known it."[11] Surely the claim that *all* groups can easily enter the mass-consumption economy and "erase the visible demarcations" is a considerable exaggeration.

Similar evaluations of American society appear frequently in contemporary scholarship. To mention just one example, consider the analysis that Adam Ulam gives of Marx's concept of capitalism: "One cannot blame a contemporary observer like Marx for his conviction that industrial fanaticism and self-righteousness were indelible traits of the capitalist. That the capitalist would grow more humane, that he would slacken in his ceaseless pursuit of accumulation and expansion, were not impressions readily warranted by the English social scene of the 1840's and '50's."[12] Again, granting the important changes in industrial society over the past century, it still comes as a surprise to hear that the capitalist has slackened in his ceaseless pursuit of accumulation and expansion.[13]

Remarks such as these illustrate a failure to come to grips with the reality of contemporary society which may not be directly traceable to the newly found (or at least hopefully sought) access to power and affluence, but which is, nevertheless, what one would expect in the developing ideology of a new privileged elite.

Various strands of this ideology are drawn together in a recent article by Zbigniew Brzezinski,[14] in which a number of the conceptions and attitudes that appear in recent social thought are summarized—I am tempted to say "parodied." Brzezinski too sees a "profound change" taking place in the intellectual community, as "the largely humanist-oriented, occasionally ideologically-minded intellectual-dissenter, who sees his role largely in terms of proffering social critiques, is rapidly being displaced either by experts and specialists, who become involved in special governmental undertakings, or by the generalists-integrators, who become in effect house-ideologues for those in power, providing overall intellectual integration for disparate actions." He suggests that these "organisation-oriented, application-minded intellectuals" can be expected to introduce broader and more relevant concerns into the political system—though there is, as he notes, a danger that "intellectual detachment and the disinterested search for truth" will come to an end, given the new access of the "application-minded intellectuals" to "power, prestige, and the good life." They are a new meritocratic elite, "taking over American life, utilising the universities, exploiting the latest techniques of communications, harnessing as rapidly as possible the most recent technological devices." Presumably, their civilizing impact is revealed by the great progress that has been made, in this new "historical era" that America alone has already entered, with respect to the problems that confounded the bumbling political leaders of past eras—the problems of the cities, of pollution, of waste and destructiveness, of exploitation and poverty. Under the leadership of this "new breed of politicians-intellectuals," America has become "*the* creative society; the others, consciously and unconsciously, are emulative." We see this, for example, in mathematics, the biological sciences, anthropology, philosophy, cinema, music, historical scholarship, and so on, where other cultures, hopelessly outdistanced, merely observe and imitate what America creates. Thus we move towards a new world-wide "'super-culture,' strongly influenced by American life, with its own universal electronic-computer language," with an enormous and growing "psycho-cultural gap" separating America from the rest of the "developed world."

It is impossible even to imagine what Brzezinski thinks a "universal electronic-computer language" may be, or what cultural values he thinks will be created by the new "technologically dominant and conditioned technetron" who, he apparently believes, may prove to be the true "repository of that indefinable quality we call human." It would hardly be rewarding to try to disentangle Brzezinski's confusions and misunderstandings. What is interesting,

15

rather, is the way his dim awareness of current developments in science and technology is used to provide an ideological justification for the "increasing role in the key decision-making institutions of individuals with special intellectual and scientific attainments," the new "organisation-oriented, application-minded intellectuals" based in the university, "the creative eye of the massive communications complex."

Parallel to the assumption that all is basically well at home is the widely articulated belief that the problems of international society, too, would be subject to intelligent management were it not for the machinations of the Communists. One aspect of this complacence is the belief that the Cold War was entirely the result of Russian (later Chinese) aggressiveness. For example, Daniel Bell has described the origins of the Cold War in the following terms: "When the Russians began stirring up the Greek guerrilla EAM in what had been tacitly acknowledged at Teheran as a British sphere of influence, the Communists began their cry against Anglo-American imperialism. Following the rejection of the Marshall Plan and the Communist coup in Czechoslovakia in February, 1948, the Cold War was on in earnest."[15] Clearly, this will hardly do as a balanced and objective statement of the origins of the Cold War, but the distortion it reflects is an inherent element in Bell's optimism about the new society, since it enables him to maintain that our Cold War posture is purely reactive, and that once Communist belligerence is tamed, the new technical intelligentsia can turn its attention to the construction of a more decent society.

A related element in the ideology of the liberal intellectual is the firm belief in the fundamental generosity of Western policy towards the Third World. Adam Ulam again provides a typical example: "Problems of an international society undergoing an economic and ideological revolution seem to defy...the generosity—granted its qualifications and errors—that has characterized the policy of the leading democratic powers of the West."[16] Even Hans Morgenthau succumbs to this illusion. He summarizes a discussion of intervention with these remarks: "We have intervened in the political, military and economic affairs of other countries to the tune of far in excess of $100 billion, and we are at present involved in a costly and risky war in order to build a nation in South Vietnam. Only the enemies of the United States will question the generosity of these efforts, which have no parallel in history."[17] Whatever one may think about the $100 billion, it is difficult to see why anyone should take seriously the professed "generosity" of our effort to build a nation in South Vietnam, any more than the similar professions of benevolence by our many forerunners in such enterprises. Generosity has never been a commodity in short supply among powers bent on extending their hegemony.

Still another strand in the ideology of the new emerging elite is the concern for order, for maintaining the status quo, which is now seen to be quite favorable and essentially just. An excellent example is the statement by fourteen leading political scientists and historians on United States Asian policy, recently distributed by the Freedom House Public Affairs Institute.[18] These scholars designate themselves as "the moderate segment of the academic community." The designation is accurate; they stand midway between the two varieties of extremism, one which demands that we destroy everyone who stands in our path, the other, that we adopt the principles of international behavior we require of every other world power. The purpose of their statement is to "challenge those among us who, overwhelmed by guilt complexes, find comfort in asserting or implying that we are always wrong, our critics always right, and that only doom lies ahead." They find our record in Asia to be "remarkably good," and applaud our demonstrated ability to rectify mistakes, our "capacity for pragmatism and self-examination," and our "healthy avoidance of narrow nationalism," capacities which distinguish us "among the major societies of this era."

The moderate scholars warn that "to avoid a major war in the Asia-Pacific region, it is essential that the United States continue to deter, restrain, and counterbalance Chinese power." True, "China has exercised great prudence in avoiding a direct confrontation with the United States or the Soviet Union" since the Korean War, and it is likely that China will "continue to substitute words for acts while concentrating upon domestic issues." Still, we cannot be certain of this and must therefore continue our efforts to tame the dragon. One of the gravest problems posed by China is its policy of "isolationist fanaticism"—obviously a serious threat to peace. Another danger is the terrifying figure of Mao Tse-tung, a romantic, who refuses to accept the "bureaucratism essential to the ordering of this enormously complex, extremely difficult society." The moderate scholars would feel much more at ease with the familiar sort of technical expert, who is committed to the "triumph of bureaucratism" and who refrains from romantic efforts to undermine the party apparatus and the discipline it imposes.

Furthermore, the moderate scholars announce their support for "our basic position" in Vietnam. A Communist victory in Vietnam, they argue, would "gravely jeopardize the possibilities for a political equilibrium in Asia, seriously damage our credibility, deeply affect the morale—and the policies of our Asian allies and the neutrals." By a "political equilibrium," they do not, of course, refer to the status quo as of 1945–1946 or as outlined by international agreement at Geneva in 1954. They do not explain why the credibility of the United States is more important than the credibility of the indigenous elements in Vietnam who have dedicated themselves to a war of national liberation. Nor do they explain why the morale of the military dictatorships of Thailand and Taiwan must be preserved. They merely hint darkly of the dangers of a third world war, dangers which are real enough and which are increased when advocates of revolutionary change face an external counterrevolutionary force. In principle, such dangers can be lessened by damping revolutionary ardor or by withdrawing the counterrevolutionary force. The latter alternative, however, is unthinkable, irresponsible.

The crucial assumption in the program of the moderate scholars is that we must not encourage "those elements committed to the thesis that violence is the best means of effecting change." It is important to recognize that it is not violence as such to which the moderate scholars object. On the contrary, they approve of our violence in Vietnam, which, as they are well aware, enormously exceeds that of the Vietnamese enemy. To further underline this point, they cite as our greatest triumph in Southeast Asia the "dramatic changes" which have taken place in Indonesia—the most dramatic being the massacre of several hundred thousand people. But this massacre, like our extermination of Vietnamese, is not a use of violence to effect social change and is therefore legitimate. What is more, it may be that those massacred were largely ethnic Chinese and landless peasants, and that the "countercoup" in effect re-established traditional authority more firmly.[19] If so, all the more reason why we should not deplore this use of violence; and in fact, the moderate scholars delicately refrain from alluding to it in their discussion of dramatic changes in Indonesia. We must conclude that when these scholars deplore the use of violence to effect change, it is not the violence but rather steps toward social change that they find truly disturbing. Social change that departs from the course we plot is not to be tolerated. The threat to order is too great.

So great is the importance of stability and order that even reform of the sort that receives American authorization must often be delayed, the moderate scholars emphasize. "Indeed, many types of reform increase instability, however desirable and essential they may be in long-range terms. For people under siege, there is no substitute for security." The reference, needless to say, is not to security from American bombardment, but rather to security from the wrong sorts of political and social change.

The policy recommendations of the moderate scholars are based on their particular ideological bias, namely, that a certain form of stability—not that of North Vietnam or North Korea, but that of Thailand, Taiwan, or the Philippines—is so essential that we must be willing to use our unparalleled means of violence to ensure that it is preserved. It is instructive to see how other mentors of the new mandarins describe the problem of order and reform. Ithiel Pool formulates the central issue as follows:

> In the Congo, in Vietnam, in the Dominican Republic, it is clear that order depends on somehow compelling newly mobilized strata to return to a measure of passivity and defeatism from which they have recently been aroused by the process of modernization. At least temporarily, the maintenance of order requires a lowering of newly acquired aspirations and levels of political activity.[20]

This is what "we have learned in the past thirty years of intensive empirical study of contemporary societies." Pool is merely describing facts, not proposing policy. A corresponding version of the facts is familiar on the domestic scene: workers threaten the public order by striking for their demands, the impatience of the Negro community threatens the stability of the body politic. One can, of course, imagine another way in which order can be preserved in all such cases: namely, by meeting the demands, or at the very least by removing the barriers that have been placed, by force which may be latent and disguised, in the way of attempts to satisfy the "newly acquired aspirations." But this might mean that the wealthy and powerful would have to sacrifice some degree of privilege, and it is therefore excluded as a method for maintenance of order. Such proposals are likely to meet with little sympathy from Pool's new mandarins.

From the doubly privileged position of the American scholar, the transcendent importance of order, stability, and nonviolence (by the oppressed) seems entirely obvious; to others, the matter is not so simple. If we listen, we hear such voices as this, from an economist in India:

> It is disingenuous to invoke "democracy," "due process of law," "non-violence," to rationalise the absence of action. For meaningful concepts under such conditions become meaningless since, in reality, they justify the relentless pervasive exploitation of the masses; at once a denial of democracy and a more sinister form of violence perpetrated on the overwhelming majority through contractual forms.[21]

Moderate American scholarship does not seem capable of comprehending these simple truths.

It would be wrong to leave the impression that the ideology of the liberal intelligentsia translates itself into policy as a rain of cluster bombs and napalm. In fact, the liberal experts have been dismayed by the emphasis on military means in Vietnam and have consistently argued that the key to our efforts should be social restructuring and economic assistance. Correspondingly, I think that we can perceive more clearly the attitudes that are crystallizing among the new mandarins by considering the technical studies of pacification, for example, the research monograph of William Nighswonger, cited earlier (see note 4). The author, now a professor of political science, was senior United States civilian representative of the Agency for International Development in Quang Nam Province from 1962 to 1964. As he sees the situation, "the knotty problems of pacification are intricately intertwined with the issues of political development and they necessitate—at this time in history—intimate American involvement." Thus Americans must ask some "basic questions of value and obligation—questions that transcend the easy legalisms of 'self-determination' and 'nonintervention.'" These easy legalisms have little relevance to a world in which the West is challenged by "the sophisticated methodology and quasi-religious motivation of Communist insurgency." It is our duty, in the interest of democracy and freedom, to apply our expertise to these twin goals: "to isolate the enemy and destroy his influence and control over the rural population, and to win the peasant's willing support through effective local administration and programs of rural improvement." "An underlying assumption is that insurgency ought to be defeated—for the sake of human rights...." Despite the "remarkable achievements in economic and social development" in Russia and China, "The South Vietnamese peasant deserves something better," and we must give it to him—as we have in Latin America and the Philippines—even if this requires abandoning the easy legalisms of the past and intervening with military force.

Of course, it won't be easy. The enemy has enormous advantages. For one thing, "as in China, the insurgents in Vietnam have exploited the Confucian tenets of ethical rule both by their attacks on government corruption and by exemplary Communist behavior"; and "the Viet-Cong inherited, after Geneva, much of the popular support and sympathies previously attached to the Viet-Minh in the South." After the fall of Diem, matters became still worse: "...vast regions that had been under government control quickly came under the influence of the Viet-Cong." By late 1964 the pacification of Quang Nam Province had become "all but impossible," and the worst of it is that "the battle for Quang Nam was lost by the government to Viet-Cong forces recruited for the most part from within the province."[22] By 1966, the Vietcong seem so well entrenched in rural areas that "only a highly imaginative and comprehensive counterinsurgency campaign, with nearly perfect execution and substantial military support, would be capable of dislodging such a powerful and extensive insurgent apparatus."

A major difficulty we face is the "progressive social and economic results" shown by the Vietcong efforts. An AID report in March 1965 explains the problem. Comparing "our 'new life hamlets'" to the Vietcong hamlets, the report comments as follows:

> The basic differences are that the VC hamlets are well organized, clean, economically self supporting and have an active defense system. For example, a cottage industry in one hamlet was as large as has been previously witnessed anywhere in Chuong Thien province. New canals are being dug and pineapples are under cultivation. The VC also have a relocation program for younger families. These areas coincide with the areas just outside the planned GVN sphere of interest. Unless the USOM/GVN activities exhibit a more qualitative basis [sic], there is little likelihood of changing the present attitudes of the people. For example, in one area only five kilometers from the province capital, the people refused medical assistance offered by ARVN medics.

However, all is not lost. Even though "the Viet-Cong strength in the country-side has made a 'quantum leap' from its position of early 1962," there is a compensating factor, namely, "the counterinsurgent military capability was revolutionized by substantial American troop inputs." This allows us entirely new options. For example, we can implement more effectively some of the "experiments with population and resources control methods" that were tried by the USOM and the National Police as early as 1961, though with little success. Given the new possibilities for "material and human resources control," we may even recapture some of the population—a serious matter; "Given the enormous numbers of South Vietnamese citizens presently allied with the Viet-Cong (for whatever reason), the recovery of these peasants for the national cause must be made one of the central tasks of the pacification enterprise."

If we are going to succeed in implementing "material and human resources control," we must moderate ARVN behavior somehow. Thus, according to an AID report of February 1965, "A high incident rate of stealing, robbing, raping and obtaining free meals in the rural areas has not endeared the population towards ARVN or Regional Forces." Nor did it improve matters when many civilians witnessed a case in which an ARVN company leader killed a draft dodger, disemboweled him, "took his heart and liver out and had them cooked at a restaurant," after which "the heart and liver were eaten by a number of soldiers." Such acts cause great difficulties, especially in trying to combat an enemy so vile as to practice "exemplary Communist behavior."

More generally, "the success of pacification requires that there be survivors to be pacified," and given "the sheer magnitude of American, Korean, Australian and indigenous Vietnamese forces," which has so severely "strained the economic and social equilibrium of the nation," it is sometimes difficult to ensure this minimal condition.

There are other problems, for example, "the difficulty of denying food to the enemy" in the Mekong Delta; "the hunger for land ownership," which, for some curious reason, is never satisfied by our friends in Saigon; the corruption; occasional bombing of the "wrong" village; the pervasive "Viet-Cong infiltration of military and civilian government organization"; the fact that when we relocate peasants to new hamlets, we often leave "the fox still in the henhouse," because of inadequate police methods; and so on.

Still, we have a good "pacification theory," which involves three steps: "elimination of the Viet-Cong by search-and-destroy operations, protection and control of the population and its resources by police and military forces, and preparing and arming the peasants to defend their own communities." If we rarely reach the third stage, this is because we have not yet learned to "share the sense of urgency of the revolutionary cause," or "to nourish these attitudes" among our "Vietnamese associates." Thus *we* understand that the "real revolution" is the one we are implementing, "in contrast to the artificially stimulated and controlled revolution of Diem and the Communists," but we have difficulties in communicating this fact to the Vietnamese peasant or to our "Vietnamese associates." What is needed, clearly, is better training for American officials, and of course, true national dedication to this humanitarian task.

A grave defect in our society, this political scientist argues, is our tendency to avoid "an active American role in the fostering of democratic institutions abroad." The pacification program in Vietnam represents an attempt to meet our responsibility to foster democratic institutions abroad, through rational methods of material and human resources control. Refusal to dedicate ourselves to this task might be described as "a policy more selfish and timid than it was broad and enlightened"[23] to use the terminology of an earlier day.

When we strip away the terminology of the behavioral sciences, we see revealed, in such work as this, the mentality of the colonial civil servant, persuaded of the benevolence of the mother country and the correctness of its vision of world order, and convinced that he understands the true interests of the backward peoples whose welfare he is to administer. In fact, much of the scholarly work on Southeast Asian affairs reflects precisely this mentality. As an example, consider the August 1967 issue of *Asian Survey*, fully devoted to a Vietnam symposium in which a number of experts contribute their thoughts on the success of our enterprise and how it can be moved forward.

22   The introductory essay by Samuel Huntington, chairman of the department of government at Harvard, is entitled "Social Science and Vietnam." It emphasizes the need "to develop scholarly study and understanding of Vietnam" if our "involvement" is to succeed, and expresses his judgment that the papers in this volume "demonstrate that issues and topics closely connected to policy can be presented and analyzed in scholarly and objective fashion."

Huntington's own contribution to "scholarly study and understanding of Vietnam" includes an article in the *Boston Globe*, February 17, 1968. Here he describes the "momentous changes in Vietnamese society during the past five years," specifically, the process of urbanization. This process "struck directly at the strength and potential appeal of the Viet Cong." "So long as the overwhelming mass of the people lived in the countryside, the VC could win the war by winning control of those people—and they came very close to doing so in both 1961 and 1964. But the American sponsored urban revolution undercut the VC rural revolution." The refugees fleeing from the rural areas found not only security but also "prosperity and economic well-being." "While wartime urban prosperity hurt some, the mass of the poor people benefitted from it."

The sources of urbanization have been described clearly many times, for example, by this American spokesman in Vietnam: "There have been three choices open to the peasantry. One, to stay where they are; two, to move into the areas controlled by us; three, to move off into the interior towards the

Vietcong.... Our operations have been designed to make the first choice impossible, the second attractive, and to reduce the likelihood of anyone choosing the third to zero."[24] The benefits accruing to the newly urbanized elements have also been amply described in the press, for example, by James Doyle of the *Globe*, February 22, 1968: Saigon "is a rich city, the bar owners, B-girls, money changers and black marketeers all making their fortunes while it lasts. It is a poor city, with hundreds of thousands of refugees crammed into thatched huts and tin-roofed shacks, more than two million people shoe-horned into 21 square miles." Or Neil Sheehan, in a classic and often-quoted article (*New York Times*, October 9, 1966):

> A drive through Saigon demonstrates another fashion in which the social system works. Virtually all the new construction consists of luxury apartments, hotels and office buildings financed by Chinese businessmen or affluent Vietnamese with relatives or connections within the regime. The buildings are destined to be rented to Americans. Saigon's workers live, as they always have, in fetid slums on the city's outskirts.... Bars and bordellos, thousands of young Vietnamese women degrading themselves as bar girls and prostitutes, gangs of hoodlums and beggars and children selling their older sisters and picking pockets have become ubiquitous features of urban life.

Many have remarked on the striking difference between the way in which the press and the visiting scholar describe what they see in Vietnam. It should occasion no surprise. Each is pursuing his own craft. The reporter's job is to describe what he sees before his eyes; many have done so with courage and even brilliance. The colonial administrator, on the other hand, is concerned to justify what he has done and what he hopes to do, and—if an "expert" as well—to construct an appropriate ideological cover, to show that we are just and righteous in what we do, and to put nagging doubts to rest. One sees moral degradation and fetid slums; the other, prosperity and well-being—and if kindly old Uncle Sam occasionally flicks his ashes on someone by mistake, that is surely no reason for tantrums.

Returning to the collection of scholarly and objective studies in *Asian Survey*, the first, by Kenneth Young, president of the Asia Society, describes our difficulties in "transferring innovations and institutions to the Vietnamese" and calls for the assistance of social scientists in overcoming these difficulties. Social scientists should, he feels, study "the intricacies that effectively inhibit or transfer what the Americans, either by government policy or by the technician's action, want to introduce into the mind of a Vietnamese or into a Vietnamese organization." The problem, in short, is one of communication. For this objective scholar, there is no question of our right to "transfer innovations and institutions to the Vietnamese," by force if necessary, or of our superior insight into the needed innovations or appropriate institutions. In just the same way, Lord Cornwallis understood the necessity of "transferring the institution" of a squirearchy to India—as any reasonable person could see, this was the only civilized form of social organization.

The "scholarly objectivity" that Huntington lauds is further demonstrated in the contribution by Milton Sacks, entitled "Restructuring Government in South Vietnam." As Sacks perceives the situation, there are two forces in South Vietnam, the "nationalists" and the "Communists." The "Communists" are the Vietminh and the NLF; among the "nationalists," he mentions specifically the VNQDD and the Dai Viet (and the military). The "nationalists" have a few problems; for example, they "were manipulated by the French, by the Japanese, by the communists and latterly by the Americans," and "too many of South Vietnam's leading generals fought with the French against the Vietnamese people."[25] Our problem is the weakness of the nationalists, although there was some hope during General Khanh's government, "a most interesting effort because it was a genuine coalition of representatives of all the major political groups in South Vietnam." Curiously, this highly representative government was unable to accept or even to consider "a proposal for what appeared to be an authentic coalition government" coming from the National Liberation Front in mid-1964.[26] According to Douglas Pike, the proposal could not be seriously considered because none of the "non-Communists" in South Vietnam, "with the possible exception of the Buddhists, thought themselves equal in size and power to risk entering into a coalition, fearing that if they did the whale would swallow the minnow." Thus, he continues, "coalition government with a strong NLF could not be sold within South Vietnam," even to the government which, as Sacks informs us, was "a genuine coalition" of "all the major political groups in South Vietnam." Rather, the GVN and its successors continued to insist that the NLF show their sincerity by withdrawing "their armed units and their political cadres from South Vietnamese territory" (March 1, 1965).

According to Sacks, "the problem which presents itself is to devise an institutional arrangement that will tend to counteract the factors and forces which are conducive to that instability" that now plagues Vietnamese political life. This problem, of course, is one that presents itself to *us*. And, Sacks feels, it is well on its way to solution, with the new constitution and the forthcoming (September 1967) elections, which "will provide spokesmen who claim legitimacy through popular mandate and speak with authority on the issues of war and peace for their constituency." Although this "free election...will still leave unrepresented those who are fighting under the banner of the South Vietnam National Liberation Front and those whose candidates were not permitted to stand in the elections," we must, after all, understand that no institution in the real world can be perfect. The important thing, according to Sacks, is that for the first time since the fall of Diem, there will be elections that are not seen by the government in power simply "as a means of legitimating the power they already had, using the governmental machinery to underwrite themselves." Putting aside the remarkable naiveté regarding the forthcoming elections, what is striking is the implicit assumption that we have a right to continue our efforts to restructure the South Vietnamese government, in the interests of what we determine to be Vietnamese nationalism. In just the same way, the officers of the Kwantung Army sought to support "genuine Manchurian nationalism," thirty-five years ago.

To understand more fully what is implied by the judgment that we must defend the "nationalists" against the "Communists," we can turn again to Pike's interesting study. The nationalist groups mentioned by Sacks are the VNQDD and the Dai Viet. The former, after its virtual destruction by the French, was revived by the Chinese Nationalists in 1942. "It supported itself through banditry. It executed traitors with a great deal of publicity, and its violent acts in general were carefully conceived for their psychological value." Returning to Vietnam "with the occupying Chinese forces following World War II," it "was of some importance until mid-1946, when it was purged by the Vietminh." "The VNQDD never was a mass political party in the Western sense. At its peak of influence it numbered, by estimates of its own leaders, less than 1,500 persons. Nor was it ever particularly strong in either Central or South Vietnam. It had no formal structure and held no conventions or assemblies." As to the Dai Viet, "Dai Viet membership included leading Vietnamese figures and governmental officials who viewed Japan as a suitable model for Vietnam [N. B. fascist Japan]. The organization never made any particular obeisance either to democracy or to the rank-and-file Vietnamese. It probably never numbered more than 1,000 members and did not consider itself a mass-based organization. It turned away from Western liberalism, although its economic orientation was basically socialist, in favor of authoritarianism and blind obedience." During World War II, "it was at all times strongly pro-Japanese."

In contrast to these genuine nationalists, we have the Vietminh, whose "war was anticolonial, clearly nationalistic, and concerned *all* Vietnamese," and the NLF, which regarded the rural Vietnamese not "simply as a pawn in a power struggle but as the active element in the thrust," which "maintained that its contest with the GVN and the United States should be fought out at a political level and that the use of massed military might was in itself illegitimate," until forced by the Americans and the GVN "to use counterforce to survive." In its internal documents as well as its public pronouncements the NLF insisted, from its earliest days, that its goal must be to "set up a democratic national coalition administration in South Vietnam; realize independence, democratic freedoms, and improvement of the people's living conditions; safeguard peace; and achieve national reunification on the basis of independence and democracy." "Aside from the NLF there has never been a truly mass-based political party in South Vietnam." It organized "the rural population through the instrument of self-control—victory by means of the organizational weapon," setting up a variety of self-help "functional liberation associations" based on "associational discipline" coupled with "the right of freedom of discussion and secret vote at association meetings," and generating "a sense of community, first, by developing a pattern of political thought and behavior appropriate to the social problems of the rural Vietnamese village in the midst of sharp social change and, second, by providing a basis for group action that allowed the individual villager to see that his own efforts could have meaning and effect" (obviously, a skilled and treacherous enemy). This was, of course, prior to "the advent of massive American aid, and the GVN's strategic hamlet program." With the American takeover of the war, the emphasis shifted to military rather than political action, and ultimately, North Vietnamese involvement and perhaps control; "beginning in 1965, large numbers of regular army troops from North Vietnam were sent into South Vietnam."

In short, what we see is a contrast between the Dai Viet and VNQDD, representing South Vietnamese nationalism, and the NLF, an extrinsic alien force. One must bear in mind that Sacks would undoubtedly accept Pike's factual description as accurate, but, like Pike, would regard it as demonstrating nothing, since we are the ultimate arbiters of what counts as "genuine Vietnamese nationalism."

An interesting counterpoint to Sacks' exposition of nationalist versus Communist forces is provided in David Wurfel's careful analysis, in the same issue of *Asian Survey*, of the "Saigon political elite." He argues that "this elite has not substantially changed its character in the last few years" (i.e., since 1962), though there may be a few modifications: "Formerly, only among the great landlords were there those who held significant amounts of both political and economic power; grandiose corruption may have allowed others to attain that distinction in recent years." Continuing, "the military men in post-Diem cabinets all served under Bao Dai and the French in a civil or military capacity." Under the French, "those who felt most comfortable about entering the civil service were those whose families were already part of the bureaucratic-intellectual elite. By the early 1950's they saw radicalism, in the form of the Viet Minh, as a threat to their own position. The present political elite is the legacy of these developments." Although, he observes, things might change, "the South Vietnamese cabinets and perhaps most of the rest of the political elite have been constituted by a highly westernized intelligentsia. Though the people of South Vietnam seem to be in a revolutionary mood, this elite is hardly revolutionary." The NLF constitutes a "counter-elite," less Westernized: of the NLF Central Committee members, "only 3 out of 27 report studying in France."

The problem of "restructuring government" is further analyzed by Ithiel Pool, along lines that parallel Sacks's contribution to this collection of "scholarly, objective studies." He begins by formulating a general proposition: "I rule

26

out of consideration here a large range of viable political settlements," namely, those that involve "the inclusion of the Viet Cong in a coalition government or even the persistence of the Viet Cong as a legal organization in South Vietnam." Such arrangements "are not acceptable"—to us, that is. The only acceptable settlement is one "imposed by the GVN despite the persisting great political power of the Viet Cong."

There is, of course, a certain difficulty: "...the Viet Cong is too strong to be simply beaten or suppressed." It follows, then, that we must provide inducements to the Vietcong activists to join our enterprise. This should not prove too difficult, he feels. The Vietcong leadership consists basically of bureaucratic types who are on the make. Cognitive dissonance theory suggests that this "discontented leadership" has "the potential for making a total break when the going gets too rough." We must therefore provide them with "a political rationalization for changing sides." The problem is ideological. We must induce a change in the "image of reality" of the Vietcong cadres, replacing their "naive ideology," which sees the GVN as "American puppets and supporters of exploiters, the tax collectors, the merchants, the big landlords, the police, and the evil men in the villages," by a more realistic conception. We can do this by emphasizing hamlet home rule and preventing the use of military forces to collect rents, a suggestion which will be greeted with enthusiasm in Saigon, no doubt. The opportunity to serve as functionaries for a central government which pursues such policies will attract the Vietcong cadres and thus solve our problem, that of excluding from the political process the organization that contains the effective political leaders.

Others have expressed a rather different evaluation of the human quality and motivation of these cadres. For example, Joseph Buttinger contrasts the inability of the Diem regime to mobilize support with the success of the NLF: "...that people willing to serve their country were to be found in Vietnam no one could doubt. The Vietminh had been able to enlist them by the tens of thousands and to extract from them superhuman efforts and sacrifices in the struggle for independence."[27] Military reports by the dozens relate the amazing heroism and dedication of the guerrillas. Throughout history, however, colonial administrators have had their difficulties in comprehending or coming to grips with this phenomenon.

In the course of his analysis of our dilemma in Vietnam, Pool explains some of the aspects of our culture that make it difficult for us to understand such matters clearly. We live in "a guilt culture in which there is a tradition of belief in equality." For such reasons, we find it hard to understand the true nature of Vietcong land redistribution, which is primarily "a patronage operation" in which "dissatisfied peasants band together in a gang to despoil their neighbors" and "then reward the deserving members of the cabal."

This terminology recalls Franz Borkenau's description of the "streak of moral indifference" in the history of Russian revolutionism, which permitted such atrocities as the willingness "to 'expropriate,' by means of robbery, the individual property of individual bourgeois."[28] Our side, in contrast, adheres to the "tradition of belief in equality" when we implement land reform. For example, the *New York Times*, December 26, 1967, reports a recent conference of experts studying the "Taiwan success in land reform," one of the real success stories of American intervention. "The Government reimbursed the former landlords in part (30 per cent) with shares of four large public enterprises taken over from the Japanese. The remainder was paid in bonds.... Many speakers at the conference singled out the repayment as the shrewdest feature of the Taiwan program. It not only treated the landlords fairly, they said, but it also redirected the landlords' energies and capital towards industry," thus advancing the "wholesale restructuring of society" in the only healthy and humane direction.

In a side remark, Pool states that "in lay public debates now going on one often hears comments to the effect that Vietnamese communism, because it is anti-Chinese, would be like Yugoslav communism." It would, of course, be ridiculous to argue such a causal connection, and, in fact, I have never heard it proposed in "lay public debate" or anywhere else. Rather, what has been maintained by such laymen as Hans Morgenthau, General James Gavin, and others is that Vietnamese Communism is likely to be Titoist, in the sense that it will strive for independence from Chinese domination. Thus they reject the claim that by attacking Vietnamese Communism we are somehow "containing Chinese Communism"—a claim implied, for example, in the statement of the "Citizens Committee for Peace with Freedom in Vietnam," in which Ithiel Pool, Milton Sacks, and others, speaking for "the understanding, independent and responsible men and women who have consistently opposed rewarding international aggressors from Adolf Hitler to Mao Tse-tung," warn that if we "abandon Vietnam," then "Peking and Hanoi, flushed with success, [will] continue their expansionist policy through many other 'wars of liberation.'" By misstating the reference to Titoist tendencies, Pool avoids the difficulty of explaining how an anti-Chinese North Vietnam is serving as the agent of Hitlerian aggression from Peking; by referring to "lay public debate," he hopes, I presume, to disguise the failure of argument by a claim to expertise.

Returning again to the *Asian Survey* Vietnam symposium, the most significant contribution is surely Edward Mitchell's discussion of his RAND Corporation study on "the significance of land tenure in the Vietnamese insurgency." In a study of twenty-six provinces, Mitchell has discovered a significant correlation between "inequality of land tenure" and "extent of Government [read: American] control." In brief, "greater inequality implies greater control." "Provinces seem to be more secure when the percentage of owner-operated land is low (tenancy is high); inequality in the distribution of farms by size is great; large, formerly French-owned estates are present; and no land redistribution has taken place." To explain this phenomenon, Mitchell turns to history and behavioral psychology. As he notes, "in a number of historical cases it has been the better-to-do peasant who has revolted while his poorer brothers actively supported or passively accepted the existing order." The "behavioral explanation" lies "in the relative docility of poorer peasants and the firm authority of landlords in the more 'feudal' areas...the landlord can exercise considerable influence over his tenant's behavior and readily discourage conduct inconsistent with his own interests."

In an interview with the *New York Times* (October 15, 1967) Mitchell adds an additional explanation for the fact that the most secure areas are those that remain "essentially feudal in social structure": when the feudal structure is eliminated, "there's a vacuum and that is ideal for the Vietcong because they've got an organization to fill the vacuum." This observation points to a difficulty that has always plagued the American effort. As Joseph Buttinger points out, the Diem regime too was unable to experiment with "freely constituted organizations" because these "would have been captured by the Vietminh."[29]

Mitchell's informative study supports an approach to counterinsurgency that has been expressed by Roger Hilsman, who explains that in his view, modernization "cannot help much in a counterguerrilla program," because it "inevitably uproots established social systems [and] produces political and economic dislocation and tension." He therefore feels that popularity of governments, reform, and modernization may be "important ingredients," but that their role in counterinsurgency "must be measured more in terms of their contributions to physical security."[30]

Before leaving this symposium on social science and Vietnam, we should take note of the scholarly detachment that permits one *not* to make certain comments or draw certain conclusions. For example, John Bennett discusses the important matter of "geographic and job mobility": "Under the dual impact of improved opportunities elsewhere and deteriorating security at home, people are willing to move to a hitherto unbelievable extent." No further comment on this "willingness," which provides such interesting new opportunities for the restructuring of Vietnamese society. John Donnell discusses the unusual success of pacification in Binh Dinh Province, particularly in the areas controlled by the Koreans, who "have tended to run their own show with their own methods and sometimes have not allowed the RD teams sent from Saigon all the operational leeway desired," and who have been "extremely impressive in eliminating NLF influence." Again, no comment is given on these methods; amply reported in the press,[31] or on the significance of the fact that Koreans are eliminating NLF influence from Vietnamese villages, and not allowing the Vietnamese government cadres the leeway desired.

Mitchell draws no policy conclusions from his study, but others have seen the point: recall the remarks of the moderate scholars on the dangers of social reform. Other scholars have carried the analysis much further. For example, Charles Wolf, senior economist of the RAND Corporation, discusses the matter in a recent book.[32] Wolf considers two "theoretical models" for analyzing insurgency problems. The first is the approach of the hearts-and-minds school of counterinsurgency, which emphasizes the importance of popular support. Wolf agrees that it is no doubt "a desirable goal" to win "popular allegiance to a government that is combating an insurgent movement," but this objective, he argues, is not appropriate "as a conceptual framework for counterinsurgency programs." His alternative approach has as its "unifying theme" the concept of "influencing *behavior*, rather than attitudes." Thus, "confiscation of chickens, razing of houses, or destruction of villages have a place in counterinsurgency efforts, but only if they are done for a strong reason: namely, to penalize those who have assisted the insurgents...whatever harshness is meted out by government forces [must be] unambiguously recognizable as deliberately imposed because of behavior by the population that contributes to the insurgent movement." Furthermore, it must be noted that "policies that would increase rural income by raising food prices, or projects that would increase agricultural productivity through distribution of fertilizer or livestock, may be of negative value during an insurgency...since they may actually facilitate guerrilla operations by increasing the availability of inputs that the guerrillas need." More generally: "In setting up economic and social improvement programs, the crucial point is to connect such programs with the kind of population behavior the government wants to promote." The principle is to reward the villages that cooperate and to provide penalties for the behavior that the government is trying to discourage. "At a broad, conceptual level, the main concern of counterinsurgency efforts should be to influence the behavior of the population rather than their loyalties and attitudes"; "the primary consideration should be whether the proposed measure is likely to increase the cost and difficulties of insurgent operations and help to disrupt the insurgent organization, rather than whether it wins popular loyalty and support, or whether it contributes to a more productive, efficient, or equitable use of resources."

Other scholars have elaborated on the advantages of Wolf's "alternative approach," which concerns itself with control of behavior rather than the mystique of popular support. For example, Morton H. Halperin, of the Harvard Center for International Affairs, writes that in Vietnam, the United States "has been able to prevent any large-scale Vietcong victories, regardless of the loyalties of the people." Thus we have an empirical demonstration of a certain principle of behavioral science, as Halperin notes:

> The events in Vietnam also illustrate the fact that most people
> tend to be motivated, not by abstract appeals, but rather by their
> perception of the course of action that is most likely to lead to
> their own personal security and to the satisfaction of their economic,
> social, and psychological desires. Thus, for example,
> large-scale American bombing in South Vietnam may have
> antagonized a number of people; but at the same time it demon-

strated to these people that the Vietcong could not guarantee their security as it had been able to do before the bombing and that the belief in an imminent victory for the Vietcong might turn out to be dangerously false.[33]

In short, along with "confiscation of chickens, razing of houses, or destruction of villages," we can also make effective use of 100 pounds of explosives per person, 12 tons per square mile, as in Vietnam, as a technique for controlling behavior, relying on the principle, now once again confirmed by experiment, that satisfaction of desires is a more important motivation in human behavior than abstract appeals to loyalty. Surely this is extremely sane advice. It would, for example, be absurd to try to control the behavior of a rat by winning its loyalty rather than by the proper scheduling of reinforcement.

An added advantage of this new, more scientific approach is that it will "modify the attitudes with which *counter*insurgency efforts are viewed in the United States"[34] (when we turn to the United States, of course, we are concerned with people whose attitudes must be taken into account, not merely their behavior). It will help us overcome one of the main defects in the American character, the "emotional reaction" that leads us to side with "crusaders for the common man" and against a "ruthless, exploitative tyrant" ("that there may be reality as well as appearance in this role-casting is not the point"). This sentimentality "frequently interferes with a realistic assessment of alternatives, and inclines us instead toward a carping righteousness in our relations with the beleaguered government we are ostensibly supporting"; it may be overcome by concentration on control of behavior rather than modification of attitudes or the winning of hearts and minds. Hence the new approach to counterinsurgency should not only be effective in extending the control of American-approved governments, but it may also have a beneficial effect on us. The possibilities are awe-inspiring. Perhaps in this way we can even escape the confines of our "guilt culture in which there is a tradition of belief in equality."

It is extremely important, Wolf would claim, that we develop a rational understanding of insurgency, for "insurgency is probably the most likely type of politico-military threat in the third world, and surely one of the most complex and challenging problems facing United States policies and programs." The primary objective of American foreign policy in the Third World must be "the *denial* of communist control," specifically, the support of countries that are defending their "independence from external and internal communist domination." The latter problem, defending independence from internal Communist domination, is the crucial problem, particularly in Latin America. We must counter the threat by a policy of promoting economic growth and modernization (making sure, however, to avoid the risks inherent in these processes—cf. Mitchell), combined with "a responsible use of force." No question is raised about the appropriateness of our use of force in a country threat-

31

ened by insurgency. The justification, were the question raised, is inherent in the assumption that we live "in a world in which loss of national independence is often synonymous with communist control, and communism is implicitly considered to be irreversible." Thus, by Orwellian logic, we are actually defending national independence when we intervene with military force to protect a ruling elite from internal insurgency.[35]

Perhaps the most interesting aspect of scholarly work such as this is the way in which behavioral-science rhetoric is used to lend a vague aura of respectability. One might construct some such chain of associations as this. Science, as everyone knows, is responsible, moderate, unsentimental, and otherwise good. Behavioral science tells us that we can be concerned only with behavior and control of behavior. Therefore we *should* be concerned only with behavior and control of behavior;[36] and it is responsible, moderate, unsentimental, and otherwise good to control behavior by appropriately applied reward and punishment. Concern for loyalties and attitudes is emotional and unscientific. As rational men, believers in the scientific ethic, we should be concerned with manipulating behavior in a desirable direction, and not be deluded by mystical notions of freedom, individual needs, or popular will.

Let me make it clear that I am not criticizing the behavioral sciences because they lend themselves to such perversion. On other grounds, the "behavioral persuasion" seems to me to lack merit; it seriously mistakes the method of science and imposes pointless methodological strictures on the study of man and society, but this is another matter entirely. It is, however, fair to inquire to what extent the popularity of this approach is based on its demonstrated achievements, and to what extent its appeal is based on the ease with which it can be refashioned as a new coercive ideology with a faintly scientific tone. (In passing, I think it is worth mention that the same questions can be raised outside of politics, specifically, in connection with education and therapy.)

The assumption that the colonial power is benevolent and has the interests of the natives at heart is as old as imperialism itself. Thus the liberal Herman Merivale, lecturing at Oxford in 1840, lauded the "British policy of colonial enlightenment" which "stands in contrast to that of our ancestors," who cared little "about the internal government of their colonies, and kept them in subjection in order to derive certain supposed commercial advantages from them," whereas we "give them commercial advantages, and tax ourselves for their benefit, in order to give them an interest in remaining under our supremacy, that we may have the pleasure of governing them."[37] And our own John Hay in 1898 outlined "a partnership in beneficence" which would bring freedom and civilization to Cuba, Hawaii, and the Philippines, just as the Pax Britannica had brought these benefits to India, Egypt, and South Africa.[38] But although the benevolence of imperialism is a familiar refrain, the idea that the issue of benevolence is irrelevant, an improper, sentimental consideration, is something of an innovation in imperialist rhetoric, a contribution of the sort one might perhaps expect from "the new mandarins" whose claim to power is based on knowledge and technique.

Going a step beyond, notice how perverse is the entire discussion of the "conceptual framework" for counterinsurgency. The idea that we must choose between the method of "winning hearts and minds" and the method of shaping behavior presumes that we have the right to choose at all. This is to grant us a right that we would surely accord to no other world power. Yet the overwhelming body of American scholarship accords us this right. For example, William Henderson, formerly associate executive director and Far Eastern specialist for the Council on Foreign Relations, proposes that we must "prosecute a constructive, manipulative diplomacy" in order to deal with "internal subversion, particularly in the form of Communist-instigated guerrilla warfare or insurgency"—"internal aggression," as he calls it, in accordance with contemporary usage.[39] Our "historic tasks," he proclaims, are "nothing less than to assist purposefully and constructively in the processes of modern nation building in Southeast Asia, to deflect the course of a fundamental revolution into channels compatible with the long range interests of the United States." It is understood that true "nation building" is that path of development compatible with our interests; hence there is no difficulty in pursuing these historic tasks in concert. There are, however, two real stumbling-blocks in the way of the required manipulative diplomacy. The first is "a great psychological barrier." We must learn to abandon "old dogma" and pursue a "new diplomacy" that is "frankly interventionist," recognizing "that it goes counter to all the traditional conventions of diplomatic usage." Some may ask whether "we have the moral right to interfere in the properly autonomous affairs of others," but Henderson feels that the Communist threat fully justifies such interference and urges that we be ready to "use our 'special forces' when the next bell rings," with no moral qualms or hesitation. The second barrier is that "our knowledge is pitifully inadequate." He therefore calls on the academic community, which will be only too willing to oblige, to supply "the body of expertise and the corps of specialists," the knowledge, the practitioners, and the teachers, to enable us to conduct such a "resourceful diplomacy" more effectively.

Turning to the liberal wing, we find that Roger Hilsman has a rather similar message in his study of the diplomacy of the Kennedy administration, *To Move a Nation.* He informs us that the most divisive issue among the "hardheaded and pragmatic liberals" of the Kennedy team was how the United States should deal with the problem of "modern guerrilla warfare, as the Communists practice it." The problem is that this "is *internal* war, an ambiguous aggression that avoids direct and open attack violating international frontiers" (italics his). Apparently, the hardheaded and pragmatic liberals were never divided on the issue of our right to violate international frontiers in reacting to such "internal war." As a prime example of the "kind of critical,

33

searching analysis" that the new, liberal, revitalized State Department was trying to encourage, Hilsman cites a study directed to showing how the United States might have acted more effectively to overthrow the Mossadegh government in Iran. Allen Dulles was "fundamentally right," according to Hilsman, in judging that Mossadegh in Iran (like Arbenz in Guatemala) had come to power (to be sure, "through the usual processes of government") with "the intention of creating a Communist state"—a most amazing statement on the part of the State Department chief of intelligence; and Dulles was fundamentally right in urging support from the United States "to loyal anti-Communist elements" in Iran and Guatemala to meet the danger, even though "no invitation was extended by the *government* in power," obviously. Hilsman expresses the liberal view succinctly in the distinction he draws between the Iranian subversion and the blundering attempt at the Bay of Pigs: "It is one thing...to help the Shah's supporters in Iran in their struggle against Mossadegh and his Communist allies, but it is something else again to sponsor a thousand-man invasion against Castro's Cuba, where there was no effective internal opposition." The former effort was admirable; the latter, bound to fail, "is something else again" from the point of view of pragmatic liberalism.

In Vietnam liberal interventionism was not properly conducted, and the situation got out of hand. We learn more about the character of this approach to international affairs by studying a more successful instance. Thailand is a case in point, and a useful perspective on liberal American ideology is given by the careful and informative work of Frank C. Darling, a Kennedy liberal who was a CIA analyst for Southeast Asia and is now chairman of the political science department at DePauw University.[40]

The facts relevant to this discussion, as Darling outlines them, are briefly as follows. At the end of World War II the former British minister, Sir Josiah Crosby, warned that unless the power of the Thai armed forces was reduced, "the establishment of a constitutional government would be doomed and the return of a military dictatorship would be inevitable." American policy in the postwar period was to support and strengthen the armed forces and the police, and Gosby's prediction was borne out.

There were incipient steps towards constitutional government in the immediate postwar period. However, a series of military coups established Phibun Songkhram, who had collaborated with the Japanese during the war, as premier in 1948, aborting these early efforts. The American reaction to the liberal governments had been ambiguous and "temporizing." In contrast, Phibun was immediately recognized by the United States. Why? "Within this increasingly turbulent region Thailand was the only nation that did not have a Communist insurrection within its borders and it was the only country that remained relatively stable and calm. As the United States considered measures to deter Communist aggression in Southeast Asia, a conservative and anti-Communist regime in Thailand became increasingly attractive regardless of its internal policies or methods of achieving power." Phibun got the point. In August 1949, "he stated that foreign pressure had become 'alarming' and that internal Communist activity had 'vigorously increased.'" In 1950, Truman approved a $10 million grant for military aid.

The new rulers made use of the substantial American military aid to convert the political system into "a more powerful and ruthless form of authoritarianism," and to develop an extensive system of corruption, nepotism, and profiteering that helped maintain the loyalty of their followers. At the same time, "American corporations moved in, purchasing large quantities of rubber and tin...shipments of raw materials now went directly to the United States instead of through Hong Kong and Singapore."[41] By 1958, "the United States purchased 90 per cent of Thailand's rubber and most of its tin." American investment, however, remained low, because of the political instability as well as "the problems caused by more extensive public ownership and economic planning." To improve matters, the Sarit dictatorship (see below) introduced tax benefits and guarantees against nationalization and competition from government-owned commercial enterprises, and finally banned trade with China and abolished all monopolies, government or private, "in an attempt to attract private foreign capital."

American influence gave "material and moral support" to the Phibun dictatorship and "discouraged the political opposition." It strengthened the executive power and "encouraged the military leaders to take even stronger measures in suppressing local opposition, using the excuse that all anti-government activity was Communist-inspired." In 1954, Pridi Phanomyong, a liberal intellectual who had been the major participant in the overthrow of the absolute monarchy in 1932, had led the Free Thai underground during the war, and had been elected in 1946 when Thai democracy reached "an all-time high," appeared in Communist China; the United States was supporting Phibun, "who had been an ally of the Japanese, while Pridi, who had courageously assisted the OSS, was in Peking cooperating with the Chinese Communists." This was "ironic."

It is difficult to imagine what sort of development towards a constitutional, parliamentary system might have taken place had it not been for American-supported subversion. The liberals were extremely weak in any event, in particular because of the domination of the economy by Western and Chinese enterprises linked with the corrupt governmental bureaucracy. The Coup Group that had overthrown the government "was composed almost entirely of commoners, many of whom had come from the peasantry or low-ranking military and civil service families," and who now wanted their share in corruption and authoritarian control. The opposition "Democrats" were, for the most part, "members of the royal family or conservative landowners who wanted to preserve their role in the government and their personal wealth." Whatever opportunities might have existed for the development of some more equitable society disappeared once the American presence became dominant, however. Surely any Thai liberal reformer must have been aware of this by 1950, in the wake of the coups, the farcical rigged elections, the murder and torture of leaders of the Free Thai anti-Japanese underground, the takeover by the military of the political and much of the commercial system—particularly when he listened to the words of American Ambassador Stanton as he signed a new aid agreement: "The American people fully support this program of aid to Thailand because of their deep interest in the Thai people whose devotion to the ideals of freedom and liberty and wholehearted support of the UN have won the admiration of the American people."

"A notable trend throughout this period was the growing intimacy between the Thai military leaders and the top-level military officials from the United States," who helped them obtain "large-scale foreign aid which in turn bolstered their political power." The head of the American military mission, Colonel Charles Sheldon, stated that Thailand was "threatened by armed aggression by people who do not believe in democracy, who do not believe in freedom or the dignity of the individual man as do the people of Thailand and my country." Adlai Stevenson, in 1953, warned the Thai leaders "that their country was the real target of the Vietminh," and expressed his hope that they "fully appreciate the threat." Meanwhile, United States assistance had built a powerful army and supplied the police with tanks, artillery, armored cars, an air force, naval patrol vessels, and a training school for paratroopers. The police achieved one of the highest ratios of policemen to citizens in the world—about 1 to 400. The police chief meanwhile relied on "his monopoly of the opium trade and his extensive commercial enterprises for the income he needed to support his personal political machine," while the army chief "received an enormous income from the national lottery."

It was later discovered that the chief of police had committed indescribable atrocities; "the extent of the torture and murder committed by the former police chief will probably never be known." What is known is what came to light after Sarit, the army chief, took power in a new coup in 1957. Sarit "stressed the need to maintain a stable government and intensify the suppression of local Communists to 'ensure continued American trust, confidence and aid.'" The Americans were naturally gratified, and the official reaction was very favorable. When Sarit died in 1963 it was discovered that his personal fortune reached perhaps $137 million. Both Darling and Roger Hilsman refer to him as a "benevolent" dictator, perhaps because he "realized that Communism could not be stopped solely by mass arrests, firing squads, or threats of brutal punishment, and launched a development project in the Northeast regions," along with various other mild reforms—without, however, ceasing the former practices, which he felt might "impress the Americans again with the need for more military and economic aid to prevent 'Communist' subversion." He also imposed rigid censorship, abolished trade organizations and labor unions and punished suspected "Communists" without mercy, and, as noted earlier, took various steps to attract foreign investment.

By 1960, "twelve percent of American foreign aid to Thailand since the beginning of the cold war had been devoted to economic and social advancement." The effect of the American aid was clear. "The vast material and diplomatic support provided to the military leaders by the United States helped to prevent the emergence of any competing groups who might check the trend toward absolute political rule and lead the country *back* to a more modern form of government" (italics mine). In fiscal 1963, the Kennedy administration tried to obtain from Congress $50 million in military aid for Thailand, perhaps to commemorate these achievements. The Kennedy administration brought "good intentions and well-founded policy proposals," but otherwise "made no significant modifications in the military-oriented policy in Thailand."

These excerpts give a fair picture of the American impact on Thailand, as it emerges from Darling's account. Naturally, he is not too happy about it. He is disturbed that American influence frustrated the moves towards constitutional democracy and contributed to an autocratic rule responsible for atrocities that sometimes "rivaled those of the Nazis and the Communists." He is also disturbed by our failure to achieve real control (in his terms, "security and stability") through these measures. Thus when Sarit took power in the 1957 coup, "the Americans had no assurance that he would not orient a new regime towards radical economic and social programs as Castro, for example, had done in Cuba.... At stake was an investment of about $300 million in military equipment and a gradually expanding economic base which could have been used against American interests in Southeast Asia had it fallen into unfriendly hands." Fortunately, these dire consequences did not ensue, and in place of radical economic and social programs there was merely a continuation of the same old terror and corruption. The danger was real, however.

What conclusions does Darling draw from this record? As he sees it,[42] there are four major alternatives for American foreign policy.

The first would be to "abolish its military program and withdraw American troops from the country." This, however, would be "irrational," because throughout the non-Communist world "respect for American patience and tolerance in dealing with nondemocratic governments would decline"; furthermore, "Thailand's security and economic progress would be jeopardized." To the pragmatic liberal, it is clear that confidence in our commitment to military dictatorships such as that in Thailand must be maintained, as in fact was implied by the moderate scholars' document discussed earlier; and it would surely be unfortunate to endanger the prospects for further development along the lines that were initiated in such a promising way under American influence, and that are now secured by some 40,000 American troops.

A second alternative would be neutralization of Thailand and other nations in Southeast Asia. This also is irrational. For one thing, "the withdrawal of the American military presence would not be matched by the removal of any Communist forces"—there being no nonindigenous Communist forces—and therefore we would gain nothing by this strategy. Furthermore, we could never be certain that there would not be "infiltration of Communist insurgents in the future." And finally, "the Thai leaders have decided to cooperate with the United States," for reasons that are hardly obscure.

A third alternative would be to use our power in Thailand to "push political and economic reforms." But this policy alternative would "do great damage to American strategy in Thailand and other non-Communist nations." And what is more, "extensive interference in the domestic affairs of other nations, no matter how well intentioned, is contrary to American traditions," as our postwar record in Thailand clearly demonstrates.[43]

Therefore, we must turn to the fourth alternative, and maintain our present policy. "This alternative is probably the most rational and realistic. The military policy can be enhanced if it is realized that only American military power is capable of preventing large-scale overt aggression in Southeast Asia, and the proper role for the Thai armed forces is to be prepared to cope with limited guerrilla warfare."

This exposition of United States policy in Thailand and the directions it should take conforms rather well to the general lines of pragmatic liberalism as drawn by Hilsman, among others. It also indicates clearly the hope that we offer today to the countries on the fringes of Asia. Vietnam may be an aberration. Our impact on Thailand, however, can hardly be attributed to the politics of inadvertence.

An interesting sidelight is Darling's explanation in *Thailand and the United States* of how, in an earlier period, "the Western concept of the rule of law" was disseminated through American influence. "Evidence that some officials were obtaining an understanding of the rule of law was revealed" by the statement of a Thai minister who pointed out that "it is essential to the prosperity of a nation that it should have fixed laws, and that nobles should be restrained from oppressing the people, otherwise the latter were like chickens, who instead of being kept for their eggs, were killed off." In its international behavior as well, the Thai government came to understand the necessity for the rule of law: "A growing respect for law was also revealed in the adherence of the Thai government to the unequal restrictions contained in the treaties with the Western nations in spite of the heavy burden they imposed on the finances of the kingdom." This is all said without irony. In fact, the examples clarify nicely what the "rule of law" means to weak nations, and to the exploited in any society.

Darling, Hilsman, and many others whom I have been discussing represent the moderate liberal wing of scholarship on international affairs. It may be useful to sample some of the other views that appear in American scholarship. Consider, for example, the proposals of Thomas R. Adam, professor of political science at New York University.[44]

Adam begins by outlining an "ideal solution" to American problems in the Pacific, towards which we should bend our efforts. The ideal solution would have the United States recognized as "the responsible military protagonist of all Western interests in the area" with a predominant voice in a unified Western policy. United States sovereignty over some territorial base in the area would give us "ideal conditions for extending power over adjoining regions." Such a base would permit the formation of a regional organization, under our dominance, that would make possible "direct intervention in Korea, Vietnam, Laos and Cambodia" without the onus of unilateral intervention ("in the face of brazen communist aggression, it is not the fact of intervention as such that constitutes the issue but rather its unilateral character").

We must understand that for the preservation of Western interests, there is no reasonable alternative to the construction of such a base of power in territories over which we possess direct sovereignty. We cannot maintain the "historic connection" between Asia and the West unless we participate in Asian affairs "through the exercise of power and influence." We must accept "the fact that we are engaged in a serious struggle for cultural survival that involves that continuous presence of Western-oriented communities" in Asia. It is an illusion to believe that we can retreat from Asia and leave it to its own devices, for our own Western culture must be understood as "a minority movement of recent date in the evolution of civilization," and it cannot be taken for granted that Asia will remain incapable of intervening in our affairs." Thus to defend ourselves, we must intervene with force in the affairs of Asia. If we fail to establish "our industrial enterprise system" universally, we will have to "defend our privileges and gains by means of the continuing, brutalizing, and costly exercise of superior force in every corner of the globe."

Why are we justified in forceful intervention in the affairs of Asia? "One obvious justification for United States intervention in Asian affairs lies in our leadership of the world struggle against communism. Communist political and economic infiltration among a majority of the world's peoples appears to American political leadership to be fatal to our safety and progress; this attitude is supported almost unanimously by public opinion." Pursuing this logic a few steps further, we will soon have the same "obvious justification" for taking out China with nuclear weapons—and perhaps France as well, for good measure.

Further justification is that the defense of our western seaboard "requires that the North Pacific be controlled as a virtual American lake," a fact which "provides one basis for United States intervention in power struggles throughout the region," to preserve the security of this *mare nostrum*. Our "victory over Japan left a power vacuum in Southeast Asia and the Far East that was tempting to communist aggression; therefore, we had to step in and use our military power." "Island possessions, such as Guam, those of the strategic trust territories, and probably Okinawa, remain indispensable, if not to the narrow defense of our shores, certainly to the military posture essential to our total security and world aims."[45] Apart from the magnificent scope of this vision, rarely equaled by our forerunners, the terminology is not unfamiliar.

There are, to be sure, certain restraints that we must observe as we design our policy of establishing an "operational base" for exercise of power in the Far East; specifically, "policy must rest on political and social objectives that are acceptable to, or capable of being imposed upon, all participating elements." Obviously, it would not be pragmatic to insist upon policies that are not capable of being imposed upon the participating elements in our new dominions.

These proposals are buttressed with a brief sketch of the consequences of Western dominion in the past, for example, the "Indian success story," in which "enterprise capital proved a useful incentive to fruitful social change in the subcontinent of India and its environs," a development flawed only by the passivity shown by "traditional Asian social systems" as they imitated "the industrial ideology of their colonial tutor." An important lesson to us is the success of the "neutral Pax Britannica" in imposing order, so that "commerce could flourish and its fruits compensate for vanished liberties."

40   Adam spares us the observation that the ungrateful natives sometimes fail to appreciate these centuries of solicitude. Thus to a left-wing member of the Congress party in India: "The story is that the British, in the process of their domination over India, kept no limits to brutality and savagery which man is capable of practicing. Hitler's depredations, his Dachaus and Belsens...pale into insignificance before this imperialist savagery...."[46] Such a reaction to centuries of selfless and tender care might cause some surprise, until we realize that it is probably only an expression of the enormous guilt felt by the beneficiary of these attentions.

A generation ago, there were other political leaders who feared the effect of Communist gains on their safety and progress, and who, with the almost unanimous support of public opinion, set out to improve the world through forceful intervention—filling power vacuums, establishing territorial bases essential to their total security and world aims, imposing political and social objectives on participating elements. Professor Adam has little to tell us that is new.

II

The examples of counterrevolutionary subordination that I have so far cited have for the most part been drawn from political science and the study of international, particularly Asian, affairs—rather dismal branches of American scholarship, by and large, and so closely identified with American imperial goals that one is hardly astonished to discover the widespread abandonment of civilized norms. In opening this discussion, however, I referred to a far more general issue. If it is plausible that ideology will in general serve as a mask for self-interest, then it is a natural presumption that intellectuals, in interpreting history or formulating policy, will tend to adopt an elitist position, condemning popular movements and mass participation in decision making, and emphasizing rather the necessity for supervision by those who possess the knowledge and understanding that is required (so they claim) to manage society and control social change. This is hardly a novel thought. One major element in the anarchist critique of Marxism a century ago was the prediction that, as Bakunin formulated it:

> According to the theory of Mr. Marx, the people not only must not destroy [the state] but must strengthen it and place it at the complete disposal of their benefactors, guardians, and teachers—the leaders of the Communist party, namely Mr. Marx and his friends, who will proceed to liberate [mankind] in their own way. They will concentrate the reins of government in a strong hand, because the ignorant people require an exceedingly firm guardianship; they will establish a single state bank, concentrating in its hands all commercial, industrial, agricultural and even scientific production, and then divide the masses into two armies—industrial and agricultural—under the direct command of the state engineers, who will constitute a new privileged scientific-political estate.[47]

One cannot fail to be struck by the parallel between this prediction and that of Daniel Bell, cited earlier—the prediction that in the new postindustrial society, "not only the best talents, but eventually the entire complex of social prestige and social status, will be rooted in the intellectual and scientific communities."[48] Pursuing the parallel for a moment, it might be asked whether the left-wing critique of Leninist elitism can be applied, under very different conditions, to the liberal ideology of the intellectual elite that aspires to a dominant role in managing the welfare state.

Rosa Luxemburg, in 1918, argued that Bolshevik elitism would lead to a state of society in which the bureaucracy alone would remain an active element in social life—though now it would be the "red bureaucracy" of that State Socialism that Bakunin had long before described as "the most vile and terrible lie that our century has created."[49] A true social revolution requires a "spiritual transformation in the masses degraded by centuries of bourgeois class rule";[50] "it is only by extirpating the habits of obedience and servility to the last root that the working class can acquire the understanding of a new form of discipline, self-discipline arising from free consent."[51] Writing in 1904, she predicted that Lenin's organizational concepts would "enslave a young labor

41

movement to an intellectual elite hungry for power...and turn it into an automaton manipulated by a Central Committee."[52] In the Bolshevik elitist doctrine of 1918 she saw a disparagement of the creative, spontaneous, self-correcting force of mass action, which alone, she argued, could solve the thousand problems of social reconstruction and produce the spiritual transformation that is the essence of a true social revolution. As Bolshevik practice hardened into dogma, the fear of popular initiative and spontaneous mass action, not under the direction and control of the properly designated vanguard, became a dominant element of so-called "Communist" ideology.

Antagonism to mass movements and to social change that escapes the control of privileged elites is also a prominent feature of contemporary liberal ideology.[53] Expressed as foreign policy, it takes the form described earlier. To conclude this discussion of counterrevolutionary subordination, I would like to investigate how, in one rather crucial case, this particular bias in American liberal ideology can be detected even in the interpretation of events of the past in which American involvement was rather slight, and in historical work of very high caliber.

In 1966, the American Historical Association gave its biennial award for the most outstanding work on European history to Gabriel Jackson, for his study of Spain in the 1930s.[54] There is no question that of the dozens of books on this period, Jackson's is among the best, and I do not doubt that the award was well deserved. The Spanish Civil War is one of the crucial events of modern history, and one of the most extensively studied as well. In it, we find the interplay of forces and ideas that have dominated European history since the industrial revolution. What is more, the relationship of Spain to the great powers was in many respects like that of the countries of what is now called the Third World. In some ways, then, the events of the Spanish Civil War give a foretaste of what the future may hold, as Third World revolutions uproot traditional societies, threaten imperial dominance, exacerbate great-power rivalries, and bring the world perilously close to a war which, if not averted, will surely be the final catastrophe of modern history. My reason for wanting to investigate an outstanding liberal analysis of the Spanish Civil War is therefore twofold: first, because of the intrinsic interest of these events; and second, because of the insight that this analysis may provide with respect to the underlying elitist bias which I believe to be at the root of the phenomenon of counterrevolutionary subordination.

In his study of the Spanish Republic, Jackson makes no attempt to hide his own commitment in favor of liberal democracy, as represented by such figures as Azaña, Casares Quiroga, Martínez Barrio,[55] and the other "responsible national leaders." In taking this position, he speaks for much of liberal scholarship; it is fair to say that figures similar to those just mentioned would be supported by American liberals, were this possible, in Latin America, Asia, or

Africa. Furthermore, Jackson makes little attempt to disguise his antipathy towards the forces of popular revolution in Spain, or their goals.

It is no criticism of Jackson's study that his point of view and sympathies are expressed with such clarity. On the contrary, the value of this work as an interpretation of historical events is enhanced by the fact that the author's commitments are made so clear and explicit. But I think it can be shown that Jackson's account of the popular revolution that took place in Spain is misleading and in part quite unfair, and that the failure of objectivity it reveals is highly significant in that it is characteristic of the attitude taken by liberal (and Communist) intellectuals towards revolutionary movements that are largely spontaneous and only loosely organized, while rooted in deeply felt needs and ideals of dispossessed masses. It is a convention of scholarship that the use of such terms as those of the preceding phrase demonstrates naiveté and muddle-headed sentimentality. The convention, however, is supported by ideological conviction rather than history or investigation of the phenomena of social life. This conviction is, I think, belied by such events as the revolution that swept over much of Spain in the summer of 1936.

The circumstances of Spain in the 1930s are not duplicated elsewhere in the underdeveloped world today, to be sure. Nevertheless, the limited information that we have about popular movements in Asia, specifically, suggests certain similar features that deserve much more serious and sympathetic study than they have so far received.[56] Inadequate information makes it hazardous to try to develop any such parallel, but I think it is quite possible to note long-standing tendencies in the response of liberal as well as Communist intellectuals to such mass movements.

As I have already remarked, the Spanish Civil War is not only one of the critical events of modern history but one of the most intensively studied as well. Yet there are surprising gaps. During the months following the Franco insurrection in July 1936, a social revolution of unprecedented scope took place throughout much of Spain. It had no "revolutionary vanguard" and appears to have been largely spontaneous, involving masses of urban and rural laborers in a radical transformation of social and economic conditions that persisted, with remarkable success, until it was crushed by force. This predominantly anarchist revolution and the massive social transformation to which it gave rise are treated, in recent historical studies, as a kind of aberration, a nuisance that stood in the way of successful prosecution of the war to save the bourgeois regime from the Franco rebellion. Many historians would probably agree with Eric Hobsbawm[57] that the *failure* of social revolution in Spain "was due to the anarchists," that anarchism was "a disaster," a kind of "moral gymnastics" with no "concrete results," at best "a profoundly moving spectacle for the student of popular religion." The most extensive historical study of the anarchist revolution[58] is relatively inaccessible, and neither its author, now living in southern France, nor the many refugees who will never write memoirs but who might

43

provide invaluable personal testimony have been consulted, apparently, by writers of the major historical works.[59] The one published collection of documents dealing with collectivization[60] has been published only by an anarchist press and hence is barely accessible to the general reader, and has also rarely been consulted—it does not, for example, appear in Jackson's bibliography, though Jackson's account is intended to be a social and political, not merely a military, history. In fact, this astonishing social upheaval seems to have largely passed from memory. The drama and pathos of the Spanish Civil War have by no means faded; witness the impact a few years ago of the film *To Die in Madrid*. Yet in this film (as Daniel Guérin points out) one finds no reference to the popular revolution that had transformed much of Spanish society.

I will be concerned here with the events of 1936–1937,[61] and with one particular aspect of the complex struggle involving Franco Nationalists, Republicans (including the Communist party), anarchists, and socialist workers' groups. The Franco insurrection in July 1936 came against a background of several months of strikes, expropriations, and battles between peasants and Civil Guards. The left-wing Socialist leader Largo Caballero had demanded in June that the workers be armed, but was refused by Azaña. When the coup came, the Republican government was paralyzed. Workers armed themselves in Madrid and Barcelona, robbing government armories and even ships in the harbor, and put down the insurrection while the government vacillated, torn between the twin dangers of submitting to Franco and arming the working classes. In large areas of Spain effective authority passed into the hands of the anarchist and socialist workers who had played a substantial, generally dominant role in putting down the insurrection.

The next few months have frequently been described as a period of "dual power." In Barcelona, industry and commerce were largely collectivized, and a wave of collectivization spread through rural areas, as well as towns and villages, in Aragon, Castile, and the Levant, and to a lesser but still significant extent in many parts of Catalonia, Asturias, Estremadura, and Andalusia. Military power was exercised by defense committees; social and economic organization took many forms, following in main outlines the program of the Saragossa Congress of the anarchist CNT in May 1936. The revolution was "apolitical," in the sense that its organs of power and administration remained separate from the central Republican government and, even after several anarchist leaders entered the government in the autumn of 1936, continued to function fairly independently until the revolution was finally crushed between the fascist and Communist-led Republican forces. The success of collectivization of industry and commerce in Barcelona impressed even highly unsympathetic observers such as Borkenau. The scale of rural collectivization is indicated by these data from anarchist sources: in Aragon, 450 collectives with half a million members; in the Levant, 900 collectives accounting for about half the agricultural production and 70 percent of marketing in this, the richest agricultural region of Spain; in Castile, 300 collectives with about 100,000 members.[62] In Catalonia, the bourgeois government headed by Companys retained nominal authority, but real power was in the hands of the anarchist-dominated committees.

The period of July through September may be characterized as one of spontaneous, widespread, but unconsummated social revolution.[63] A number of anarchist leaders joined the government; the reason, as stated by Federica Montseny on January 3, 1937, was this: "...the anarchists have entered the government to prevent the Revolution from deviating and in order to carry it further beyond the war, and also to oppose any dictatorial tendency, from wherever it might come."[64] The central government fell increasingly under Communist control—in Catalonia, under the control of the Communist-dominated PSUC—largely as a result of the valuable Russian military assistance. Communist success was greatest in the rich farming areas of the Levant (the government moved to Valencia, capital of one of the provinces), where prosperous farm owners flocked to the Peasant Federation that the party had organized to protect the wealthy farmers; this federation "served as a powerful instrument in checking the rural collectivization promoted by the agricultural workers of the province."[65] Elsewhere as well, counterrevolutionary successes reflected increasing Communist dominance of the Republic.

The first phase of the counterrevolution was the legalization and regulation of those accomplishments of the revolution that appeared irreversible. A decree of October 7 by the Communist Minister of Agriculture, Vicente Uribe, legalized certain expropriations—namely, of lands belonging to participants in the Franco revolt. Of course, these expropriations had already taken place, a fact that did not prevent the Communist press from describing the decree as "the most profoundly revolutionary measure that has been taken since the military uprising."[66] In fact, by exempting the estates of landowners who had not directly participated in the Franco rebellion, the decree represented a step backward, from the standpoint of the revolutionaries, and it was criticized not only by the CNT but also by the Socialist Federation of Land Workers, affiliated with the UGT. The demand for a much broader decree was unacceptable to the Communist-led ministry, since the Communist party was "seeking support among the propertied classes in the anti-Franco coup" and hence "could not afford to repel the small and medium proprietors who had been hostile to the working class movement before the civil war."[67] These "small proprietors," in fact, seem to have included owners of substantial estates. The decree compelled tenants to continue paying rent unless the landowners had supported Franco, and by guaranteeing former landholdings, it prevented distribution of land to the village poor. Ricardo Zabalza, general secretary of the Federation of Land Workers, described the resulting situation as one of "galling injustice"; "the sycophants of the former political bosses still enjoy a privileged position

45

at the expense of those persons who were unable to rent even the smallest parcel of land, because they were revolutionaries."[68]

To complete the stage of legalization and restriction of what had already been achieved, a decree of October 24, 1936, promulgated by a CNT member who had become Councilor for Economy in the Catalonian Generalitat, gave legal sanction to the collectivization of industry in Catalonia. In this case too, the step was regressive, from the revolutionary point of view. Collectivization was limited to enterprises employing more than a hundred workers, and a variety of conditions were established that removed control from the workers' committees to the state bureaucracy.[69]

The second stage of the counterrevolution, from October 1936 through May 1937, involved the destruction of the local committees, the replacement of the militia by a conventional army, and the re-establishment of the prerevolutionary social and economic system, wherever this was possible. Finally, in May 1937, came a direct attack on the working class in Barcelona (the May Days).[70] Following the success of this attack, the process of liquidation of the revolution was completed. The collectivization decree of October 24 was rescinded and industries were "freed" from workers' control. Communist-led armies swept through Aragon, destroying many collectives and dismantling their organizations and, generally, bringing the area under the control of the central government. Throughout the Republican-held territories, the government, now under Communist domination, acted in accordance with the plan announced in *Pravda* on December 17, 1936: "So far as Catalonia is concerned, the cleaning up of Trotzkyist and Anarcho-Syndicalist elements there has already begun, and it will be carried out there with the same energy as in the U.S.S.R."[71]—and, we may add, in much the same manner.

In brief, the period from the summer of 1936 to 1937 was one of revolution and counterrevolution: the revolution was largely spontaneous with mass participation of anarchist and socialist industrial and agricultural workers; the counterrevolution was under Communist direction, the Communist party increasingly coming to represent the right wing of the Republic. During this period and after the success of the counterrevolution, the Republic was waging a war against the Franco insurrection; this has been described in great detail in numerous publications, and I will say little about it here. The Communist-led counterrevolutionary struggle must, of course, be understood against the background of the ongoing antifascist war and the more general attempt of the Soviet Union to construct a broad anti-fascist alliance with the Western democracies. One reason for the vigorous counterrevolutionary policy of the Communists was their belief that England would never tolerate a revolutionary triumph in Spain, where England had substantial commercial interests, as did France and to a lesser extent the United States.[72] I will return to this matter below. However, I think it is important to bear in mind that there were undoubtedly other factors as well. Rudolf Rocker's comments are, I believe, quite to the point:

> ...the Spanish people have been engaged in a desperate struggle against a pitiless foe and have been exposed besides to the secret intrigues of the great imperialist powers of Europe. Despite this the Spanish revolutionaries have not grasped at the disastrous expedient of dictatorship, but have respected all honest convictions. Everyone who visited Barcelona after the July battles, whether friend or foe of the C.N.T., was surprised at the freedom of public life and the absence of any arrangements for suppressing the free expression of opinion.
>
> For two decades the supporters of Bolshevism have been hammering it into the masses that dictatorship is a vital necessity for the defense of the so-called proletarian interests against the assaults of the counter-revolution and for paving the way for Socialism. They have not advanced the cause of Socialism by this propaganda, but have merely smoothed the way for Fascism in Italy, Germany and Austria by causing millions of people to forget that dictatorship, the most extreme form of tyranny, can never lead to social liberation. In Russia, the so-called dictatorship of the proletariat has not led to Socialism, but to the domination of a new bureaucracy over the proletariat and the whole people....
>
> What the Russian autocrats and their supporters fear most is that the success of libertarian Socialism in Spain might prove to their blind followers that the much vaunted "necessity of a dictatorship" is nothing but one vast fraud which in Russia has led to the despotism of Stalin and is to serve today in Spain to help the counter-revolution to a victory over the revolution of the workers and peasants.[73]

After decades of anti-Communist indoctrination, it is difficult to achieve a perspective that makes possible a serious evaluation of the extent to which Bolshevism and Western liberalism have been united in their opposition to popular revolution. However, I do not think that one can comprehend the events in Spain without attaining this perspective.

With this brief sketch—partisan, but I think accurate—for background, I would like to turn to Jackson's account of this aspect of the Spanish Civil War (see note 54).

Jackson presumes (p. 259) that Soviet support for the Republican cause in Spain was guided by two factors: first, concern for Soviet security; second, the hope that a Republican victory would advance "the cause of worldwide 'people's revolution' with which Soviet leaders hoped to identify themselves." They did not press their revolutionary aims, he feels, because "for the moment it was essential not to frighten the middle classes or the Western governments."

As to the concern for Soviet security, Jackson is no doubt correct. It is clear that Soviet support of the Republic was one aspect of the attempt to make common cause with the Western democracies against the fascist threat. However, Jackson's conception of the Soviet Union as a revolutionary power—hopeful that a Republican victory would advance "the interrupted movement toward world revolution" and seeking to identify itself with "the cause of the worldwide 'people's revolution'"—seems to me entirely mistaken. Jackson presents no evidence to support this interpretation of Soviet policy, nor do I know of any. It is interesting to see how differently the events were interpreted at the time of the Spanish Civil War, not only by anarchists like Rocker but also by such commentators as Gerald Brenan and Franz Borkenau, who were intimately acquainted with the situation in Spain. Brenan observes that the counterrevolutionary policy of the Communists (which he thinks was "extremely sensible") was

> the policy most suited to the Communists themselves. Russia is a totalitarian regime ruled by a bureaucracy: the frame of mind of its leaders, who have come through the most terrible upheaval in history, is cynical and opportunist: the whole fabric of the state is dogmatic and authoritarian. To expect such men to lead a social revolution in a country like Spain, where the wildest idealism is combined with great independence of character, was out of the question. The Russians could, it is true, command plenty of idealism among their foreign admirers, but they could only harness it to the creation of a cast-iron bureaucratic state, where everyone thinks alike and obeys the orders of the chief above him.[74]

He sees nothing in Russian conduct in Spain to indicate any interest in a "people's revolution." Rather, the Communist policy was to oppose "even such rural and industrial collectives as had risen spontaneously and flood the country with police who, like the Russian Ogpu, acted on the orders of their party rather than those of the Ministry of the Interior." The Communists were concerned to suppress altogether the impulses towards "spontaneity of speech or action," since "their whole nature and history made them distrust the local and spontaneous and put their faith in order, discipline and bureaucratic uniformity"—hence placed them in opposition to the revolutionary forces in Spain. As Brenan also notes, the Russians withdrew their support once it became clear that the British would not be swayed from the policy of appeasement, a fact which gives additional confirmation to the thesis that only considerations of Russian foreign policy led the Soviet Union to support the Republic.

Borkenau's analysis is similar. He approves of the Communist policy, because of its "efficiency," but he points out that the Communists "put an end to revolutionary social activity, and enforced their view that this ought not to be a revolution but simply the defence of a legal government...communist policy in Spain was mainly dictated not by the necessities of the Spanish fight but by the interests of the intervening foreign power, Russia," a country "with a revolutionary past, not a revolutionary present." The Communists acted "not with the aim of transforming chaotic enthusiasm into disciplined enthusiasm [which Borkenau feels to have been necessary], but with the aim of substituting disciplined military and administrative action for the action of the masses and getting rid of the latter entirely." This policy, he points out, went "directly against the interests and claims of the masses" and thus weakened popular support. The now apathetic masses would not commit themselves to the defense of a Communist-run dictatorship, which restored former authority and even "showed a definite preference for the police forces of the old regime, so hated by the masses." It seems to me that the record strongly supports this interpretation of Communist policy and its effects, though Borkenau's assumption that Communist "efficiency" was necessary to win the anti-Franco struggle is much more dubious—a question to which I return below.[75]

It is relevant to observe, at this point, that a number of the Spanish Communist leaders were reluctantly forced to similar conclusions. Bolloten cites several examples,[76] specifically, the military commander "El Campesino" and Jesus Hernandez, a minister in the Caballero government. The former, after his escape from the Soviet Union in 1949, stated that he had taken for granted the "revolutionary solidarity" of the Soviet Union during the Civil War—a most remarkable degree of innocence—and realized only later "that the Kremlin does not serve the interests of the peoples of the world, but makes them serve its own interests; that, with a treachery and hypocrisy without parallel, it makes use of the international working class as a pawn in its political intrigues." Hernandez, in a speech given shortly after the Civil War, admits that the Spanish Communist leaders "acted more like Soviet subjects than sons of the Spanish people." "It may seem absurd, incredible," he adds, "but our education under Soviet tutelage had deformed us to such an extent that we were completely denationalized; our national soul was torn out of us and replaced by a rabidly chauvinistic internationalism, which began and ended with the towers of the Kremlin."

Shortly after the Third World Congress of the Communist International in 1921, the Dutch "ultra-leftist" Hermann Gorter wrote that the congress "has decided the fate of the world revolution for the present. The trend of opinion that seriously desired world revolution...has been expelled from the Russian International. The Communist Parties in western Europe and throughout the world that retain their membership of the Russian International will become nothing more than a means to preserve the Russian Revolution and the Soviet Republic."[77] This forecast has proved quite accurate. Jackson's conception that the Soviet Union was a revolutionary power in the late 1930s, or even that the

Soviet leaders truly regarded themselves as identified with world revolution, is without factual support. It is a misinterpretation that runs parallel to the American Cold War mythology that has invented an "international Communist conspiracy" directed from Moscow (now Peking) to justify its own interventionist policies.

Turning to events in revolutionary Spain, Jackson describes the first stages of collectivization as follows: the unions in Madrid, "as in Barcelona and Valencia, abused their sudden authority to place the sign *incautado* [placed under workers' control] on all manner of buildings and vehicles" (p. 219). Why was this an *abuse* of authority? This Jackson does not explain. The choice of words indicates a reluctance on Jackson's part to recognize the reality of the revolutionary situation, despite his account of the breakdown of Republican authority. The statement that the workers "abused their sudden authority" by carrying out collectivization rests on a moral judgment that recalls that of Ithiel Pool, when he characterizes land reform in Vietnam as a matter of "despoiling one's neighbors," or of Franz Borkenau, when he speaks of expropriation in the Soviet Union as "robbery," demonstrating "a streak of moral indifference."

Within a few months, Jackson informs us, "the revolutionary tide began to ebb in Catalonia" after "accumulating food and supply problems, and the experience of administering villages, frontier posts, and public utilities, had rapidly shown the anarchists the unsuspected complexity of modern society" (pp. 13–14). In Barcelona, "the naive optimism of the revolutionary conquests of the previous August had given way to feelings of resentment and of somehow having been cheated," as the cost of living doubled, bread was in short supply, and police brutality reached the levels of the monarchy. "The POUM and the anarchist press simultaneously extolled the collectivizations and explained the failures of production as due to Valencia policies of boycotting the Catalan economy and favoring the *bourgeoisie*. They explained the loss of Málaga as due in large measure to the low morale and the disorientation of the Andalusian proletariat, which saw the Valencia government evolving steadily toward the right" (p. 368). Jackson evidently believes that this left-wing interpretation of events was nonsensical, and that in fact it was anarchist incompetence or treachery that was responsible for the difficulties: "In Catalonia, the CNT factory committees dragged their heels on war production, claiming that the government deprived them of raw materials and was favoring the *bourgeoisie*" (p. 365).

In fact, "the revolutionary tide began to ebb in Catalonia" under a middle-class attack led by the Communist party, not because of a recognition of the "complexity of modern society." And it was, moreover, quite true that the Communist-dominated central government attempted, with much success, to hamper collectivized industry and agriculture and to disrupt the collectivization of commerce. I have already referred to the early stages of counterrevolution. Further investigation of the sources to which Jackson refers and others shows that the anarchist charges were not baseless, as Jackson implies. Bolloten cites a good deal of evidence in support of his conclusion that

> In the countryside the Communists undertook a spirited defence of the small and medium proprietor and tenant farmer against the collectivizing drive of the rural wage-workers, against the policy of the labour unions prohibiting the farmer from holding more land than he could cultivate with his own hands, and against the practices of revolutionary committees, which requisitioned harvests, interfered with private trade, and collected rents from tenant farmers.[78]

The policy of the government was clearly enunciated by the Communist Minister of Agriculture: "We say that the property of the small farmer is sacred and that those who attack or attempt to attack this property must be regarded as enemies of the regime."[79] Gerald Brenan, no sympathizer with collectivization, explains the failure of collectivization as follows (p. 321):

> The Central Government, and especially the Communist and Socialist members of it, desired to bring [the collectives] under the direct control of the State: they therefore failed to provide them with the credit required for buying raw materials: as soon as the supply of raw cotton was exhausted the mills stopped working...even [the munitions industry in Catalonia] were harassed by the new bureaucratic organs of the Ministry of Supply.[80]

He quotes the bourgeois President of Catalonia, Companys, as saying that "workers in the arms factories in Barcelona had been working 56 hours and more each week and that no cases of sabotage or indiscipline had taken place," until the workers were demoralized by the bureaucratization—later, militarization—imposed by the central government and the Communist party.[81] His own conclusion is that "the Valencia Government was now using the P.S.U.C. against the C.N.T.—but not...because the Catalan workers were giving trouble, but because the Communists wished to weaken them before destroying them."

The cited correspondence from Companys to Prieto, according to Vernon Richards (p. 47), presents evidence showing the success of Catalonian war industry under collectivization and demonstrating how "much more could have been achieved had the means for expanding the industry not been denied them by the Central Government." Richards also cites testimony by a spokesman for the subsecretariat of munitions and armament of the Valencia government admitting that "the war industry of Catalonia had produced ten times more than the rest of Spanish industry put together and [agreeing]...that this output could have been quadrupled as from beginning of September* if

---

*The quoted testimony is from September 1, 1937; presumably, the reference is to September 1936.

Catalonia had had access to the necessary means for purchasing raw materials that were unobtainable in Spanish territory." It is important to recall that the central government had enormous gold reserves (soon to be transmitted to the Soviet Union), so that raw materials for Catalan industry could probably have been purchased, despite the hostility of the Western democracies to the Republic during the revolutionary period (see below). Furthermore, raw materials had repeatedly been requested. On September 24, 1936, Juan Fabregas, the CNT delegate to the Economic Council of Catalonia who was in part responsible for the collectivization decree cited earlier, reported that the financial difficulties of Catalonia were created by the refusal of the central government to "give any assistance in economic and financial questions, presumably because it has little sympathy with the work of a practical order which is being carried out in Catalonia"[82]—that is, collectivization. He "went on to recount that a Commission which went to Madrid to ask for credits to purchase war materials and raw materials, offering 1,000 million pesetas in securities lodged in the Bank of Spain, met with a blank refusal. It was sufficient that the new war industry in Catalonia was controlled by the workers of the C.N.T. for the Madrid Government to refuse any unconditional aid. Only in exchange for government control would they give financial assistance."[83]

Broué and Témime take a rather similar position. Commenting on the charge of "incompetence" leveled against the collectivized industries, they point out that "one must not neglect the terrible burden of the war." Despite this burden, they observe, "new techniques of management and elimination of dividends had permitted a lowering of prices" and "mechanisation and rationalization, introduced in numerous enterprises...had considerably augmented production. The workers accepted the enormous sacrifices with enthusiasm because, in most cases, they had the conviction that the factory belonged to them and that at last they were working for themselves and their class brothers. A truly new spirit had come over the economy of Spain with the concentration of scattered enterprises, the simplification of commercial patterns, a significant structure of social projects for aged workers, children, disabled, sick and the personnel in general" (pp. 150–51). The great weakness of the revolution, they argue, was the fact that it was not carried through to completion. In part this was because of the war; in part, a consequence of the policies of the central government. They too emphasize the refusal of the Madrid government, in the early stages of collectivization, to grant credits or supply funds to collectivized industry or agriculture—in the case of Catalonia, even when substantial guarantees were offered by the Catalonian government. Thus the collectivized enterprises were forced to exist on what assets had been seized at the time of the revolution. The control of gold and credit "permitted the government to restrict and prevent the function of collective enterprises at will" (p. 144).

According to Broué and Témime, it was the restriction of credit that finally destroyed collectivized industry. The Companys government in Catalonia refused to create a bank for industry and credit, as demanded by the CNT and POUM, and the central government (relying, in this case, on control of the banks by the socialist UGT) was able to control the flow of capital and "to reserve credit for private enterprise." All attempts to obtain credit for collectivized industry were unsuccessful, they maintain, and "the movement of collectivization was restricted, then halted, the government remaining in control of industry through the medium of the banks...[and later] through its control of the choice of managers and directors," who often turned out to be the former owners and managers, under new titles. The situation was similar in the case of collectivized agriculture (pp. 204 f.).

The situation was duly recognized in the West. *The New York Times*, in February 1938, observed: "The principle of State intervention and control of business and industry, as against workers' control of them in the guise of collectivization, is gradually being established in loyalist Spain by a series of decrees now appearing. Coincidentally there is to be established the principle of private ownership and the rights of corporations and companies to what is lawfully theirs under the Constitution."[84]

Morrow cites (pp. 64–65) a series of acts by the Catalonian government restricting collectivization, once power had shifted away from the new institutions set up by the workers' revolution of July 1936. On February 3, the collectivization of the dairy trade was declared illegal.[85] In April, "the Generalidad annulled workers' control over the customs by refusing to certify workers' ownership of material that had been exported and was being tied up in foreign courts by suits of former owners; henceforth the factories and agricultural collectives exporting goods were at the mercy of the government." In May, as has already been noted, the collectivization decree of October 24 was rescinded, with the argument that the decree "was dictated without competency by the Generalidad," because "there was not, nor is there yet, legislation of the [Spanish] state to apply" and "article 44 of the Constitution declares expropriation and socialization are functions of the State." A decree of August 28 "gave the government the right to intervene in or take over any mining or metallurgical plant." The anarchist newspaper *Solidaridad Obrera* reported in October a decision of the department of purchases of the Ministry of Defense that it would make contracts for purchases only with enterprises functioning "on the basis of their old owners" or "under the corresponding intervention controlled by the Ministry of Finance and Economy."[86]

Returning to Jackson's statement that "In Catalonia, the CNT factory committees dragged their heels on war production, claiming that the government deprived them of raw materials and was favoring the *bourgeoisie*," I believe one must conclude that this statement is more an expression of Jackson's bias in favor of capitalist democracy than a description of the historical acts. At the very least, we can say this much: Jackson presents no evidence to support his conclusion; there is a factual basis for questioning it. I have cited a number of sources that the liberal historian would regard, quite correctly, as biased in favor of the revolution. My point is that the failure of objectivity, the deep-seated bias of liberal historians, is a matter much less normally taken for granted, and that there are good rounds for supposing that this failure of objectivity has seriously distorted the judgments that are rather brashly handed down about the nature of the Spanish revolution.

Continuing with the analysis of Jackson's judgments, unsupported by any cited evidence, consider his remark, quoted above, that in Barcelona "the naive optimism of the revolutionary conquests of the previous August had given way to feelings of resentment and of somehow having been cheated." It is a fact that by January 1937 there was great disaffection in Barcelona. But was this simply a consequence of "the unsuspected complexity of modern society?" Looking into the matter a bit more closely, we see a rather different picture. Under Russian pressure, the PSUC was given substantial control of the Catalonian government, "putting into the Food Ministry [in December 1936] the man most to the Right in present Catalan politics, Comorera"[87]—by virtue of his political views, the most willing collaborator with the general Communist party position. According to Jackson, Comorera "immediately took steps to end barter and requisitioning, and became a defender of the peasants against the revolution" (p. 314); he "ended requisition, restored money payments, and protected the Catalan peasants against further collectivization" (p. 361). This is all that Jackson has to say about Juan Comorera.

We learn more from other sources: for example, Borkenau, who was in Barcelona for the second time in January 1937—and is universally recognized as a highly knowledgeable and expert observer, with strong anti-anarchist sentiments. According to Borkenau, Comorera represented "a political attitude which can best be compared with that of the extreme right wing of the German social-democracy. He had always regarded the fight against anarchism as the chief aim of socialist policy in Spain.... To his surprise, he found unexpected allies for his dislike [of anarchist policies] in the communists."[88] It was impossible to reverse collectivization of industry at that stage in the process of counterrevolution; Comorera did succeed, however, in abolishing the system by which the provisioning of Barcelona had been organized, namely, the village committees, mostly under CNT influence, which had cooperated (perhaps, Borkenau suggests, unwillingly) in delivering flour to the towns. Continuing, Borkenau describes the situation as follows:

> ...Comorera, starting from those principles of abstract liberalism which no administration has followed during the war, but of which right-wing socialists are the last and most religious admirers, did not substitute for the chaotic bread committees a centralized administration. He restored private commerce in bread,

simply and completely. There was, in January, not even a system of rationing in Barcelona. Workers were simply left to get their bread, with wages which had hardly changed since May, at increased prices, as well as they could. In practice it meant that the women had to form queues from four o'clock in the morning onwards. The resentment in the working-class districts was naturally acute, the more so as the scarcity of bread rapidly increased after Comorera had taken office.[89]

In short, the workers of Barcelona were not merely giving way to "feelings of resentment and of somehow having been cheated" when they learned of "the unsuspected complexity of modern society." Rather, they had good reason to believe that they *were* being cheated, by the old dog with the new collar.

George Orwell's observations are also highly relevant:

> Everyone who has made two visits, at intervals of months, to Barcelona during the war has remarked upon the extraordinary changes that took place in it. And curiously enough, whether they went there first in August and again in January, or, like myself, first in December and again in April, the thing they said was always the same: that the revolutionary atmosphere had vanished. No doubt to anyone who had been there in August, when the blood was scarcely dry in the streets and militia were quartered in the small hotels, Barcelona in December would have seemed bourgeois; to me, fresh from England, it was liker to a workers' city than anything I had conceived possible. Now [in April] the tide had rolled back. Once again it was an ordinary city, a little pinched and chipped by war, but with no outward sign of working-class predominance.... Fat prosperous men, elegant women, and sleek cars were everywhere.... The officers of the new Popular Army, a type that had scarcely existed when I left Barcelona, swarmed in surprising numbers...[wearing] an elegant khaki uniform with a tight waist, like a British Army officer's uniform, only a little more so. I do not suppose that more than one in twenty of them had yet been to the front, but all of them had automatic pistols strapped to their belts; we, at the front, could not get pistols for love or money....* A deep change had come over the town. There were two facts that were the keynote of all else. One was that the people—the civil population—had lost much of their interest in the war; the other was that the normal division of society into rich and poor, upper class and lower class, was reasserting itself.[90]

---

*Orwell had just returned from the Aragon front, where he had been serving with the POUM militia in an area heavily dominated by left-wing (POUM and anarchist) troops.

Whereas Jackson attributes the ebbing of the revolutionary tide to the discovery of the unsuspected complexity of modern society, Orwell's firsthand observations, like those of Borkenau, suggest a far simpler explanation. What calls for explanation is not the disaffection of the workers of Barcelona but the curious constructions of the historian.

Let me repeat, at this point, Jackson's comments regarding Juan Comorera: Comorera "immediately took steps to end barter and requisitioning, and became a defender of the peasants against the revolution"; he "ended requisitions, restored money payments, and protected the Catalan peasants against further collectivization." These comments imply that the peasantry of Catalonia was, as a body, opposed to the revolution and that Comorera put a stop to the collectivization that they feared. Jackson nowhere indicates any divisions among the peasantry on this issue and offers no support for the implied claim that collectivization was in process at the period of Comorera's access to power. In fact, it is questionable that Comorera's rise to power affected the course of collectivization in Catalonia. Evidence is difficult to come by, but it seems that collectivization of agriculture in Catalonia was not, in any event, extensive, and that it was not extending in December, when Comorera took office. We know from anarchist sources that there had been instances of forced collectivization in Catalonia,[91] but I can find no evidence that Comorera "protected the peasantry" from forced collectivization. Furthermore, it is misleading, at best, to imply that the peasantry *as a whole* was opposed to collectivization. A more accurate picture is presented by Bolloten (p. 56), who points out that "if the individual farmer viewed with dismay the swift and widespread development of collectivized agriculture, the farm workers of the Anarchosyndicalist CNT and the Socialist UGT saw in it, on the contrary, the commencement of a new era." In short, there was a complex class struggle in the countryside, though one learns little about it from Jackson's oversimplified and misleading account. It would seem fair to suppose that this distortion again reflects Jackson's antipathy towards the revolution and its goals. I will return to this question directly, with reference to areas where agricultural collectivization was much more extensive than in Catalonia.

The complexities of modern society that baffled and confounded the unsuspecting anarchist workers of Barcelona, as Jackson enumerates them, were the following: the accumulating food and supply problems and the administration of frontier posts, villages, and public utilities. As just noted, the food and supply problems seem to have accumulated most rapidly under the brilliant leadership of Juan Comorera. So far as the frontier posts are concerned, the situation, as Jackson elsewhere describes it (p. 368), was basically as follows: "In Catalonia the anarchists had, ever since July 18, controlled the customs stations at the French border. On April 17, 1937, the reorganized carabineros, acting on orders of the Finance Minister, Juan Negrín, began to reoccupy the frontier. At least eight anarchists were killed in clashes with the carabineros." Apart from this difficulty, admittedly serious, there seems little reason to suppose that the problem of manning frontier posts contributed to the ebbing of the revolutionary tide. The available records do not indicate that the problems of administering villages or public utilities were either "unsuspected" or too complex for the Catalonian workers—a remarkable and unsuspected development, but one which nevertheless appears to be borne out by the evidence available to us. I want to emphasize again that Jackson presents no evidence to support his conclusions about the ebbing of the revolutionary tide and the reasons for the disaffection of the Catalonian workers. Once again, I think it fair to attribute his conclusions to the elitist bias of the liberal intellectual rather than to the historical record.

Consider next Jackson's comment that the anarchists "explained the loss of Málaga as due in large measure to the low morale and the disorientation of the Andalusian proletariat, which saw the Valencia government evolving steadily toward the right." Again, it seems that Jackson regards this as just another indication of the naivete and unreasonableness of the Spanish anarchists. However, here again there is more to the story. One of the primary sources that Jackson cites is Borkenau, quite naturally, since Borkenau spent several days in the area just prior to the fall of Málaga on February 8, 1937. But Borkenau's detailed observations tend to bear out the anarchist "explanation," at least in part. He believed that Málaga might have been saved, but only by a "fight of despair" with mass involvement, of a sort that "the anarchists might have led." But two factors prevented such a defense: first, the officer assigned to lead the defense, Lieutenant Colonel Villalba, "interpreted this task as a purely military one, whereas in reality he had no military means at his disposal but only the forces of a popular movement"; he was a professional officer, "who in the secrecy of his heart hated the spirit of the militia" and was incapable of comprehending the "political factor."[92] A second factor was the significant decline, by February, of political consciousness and mass involvement. The anarchist committees were no longer functioning and the authority of the police and Civil Guards had been restored. "The nuisance of hundreds of independent village police bodies had disappeared, but with it the passionate interest of the village in the civil war.... The short interlude of the Spanish Soviet system was at an end" (p. 212). After reviewing the local situation in Málaga and the conflicts in the Valencia government (which failed to provide support or arms for the militia defending Málaga), Borkenau concludes (p. 228): "The Spanish republic paid with the fall of Málaga for the decision of the Right wing of its camp to make an end of social revolution and of its Left wing not to allow that." Jackson's discussion of the fall of Málaga refers to the terror and political rivalries within the town but makes no reference to the fact that Borkenau's description, and the accompanying interpretation, do support the belief that the defeat was due in large measure to low morale and to the incapacity, or unwillingness, of the Valencia government to fight a popular war. On the contrary, he concludes that Colonel Villalba's lack of means for "controlling the bitter political rivalries" was one factor that prevented him from carrying out the essential military tasks. Thus he seems to adopt the view that Borkenau condemns, that the task was a "purely military one." Borkenau's eyewitness account appears to me much more convincing.

In this case too Jackson has described the situation in a somewhat misleading fashion, perhaps again because of the elitist bias that dominates the liberal-Communist interpretation of the Civil War. Like Lieutenant Colonel Villalba, liberal historians often reveal a strong distaste for "the forces of a popular movement" and "the spirit of the militia." And an argument can be given that they correspondingly fail to comprehend the "political factor."

In the May Days of 1937, the revolution in Catalonia received the final blow. On May 3, the councilor for public order, PSUC member Rodriguez Salas, appeared at the central telephone building with a detachment of police, without prior warning or consultation with the anarchist ministers in the government, to take over the telephone exchange. The exchange, formerly the property of IT&T, had been captured by Barcelona workers in July and had since functioned under the control of a UGT-CNT committee, with a governmental delegate, quite in accord with the collectivization decree of October 24, 1936. According to the London *Daily Worker* (May 11, 1937), "Salas sent the armed republican police to disarm the employees there, most of them members of the CNT unions." The motive, according to Juan Comorera, was "to put a stop to an abnormal situation," namely, that no one could speak over the telephone "without the indiscreet ear of the controller knowing it."[93] Armed resistance in the telephone building prevented its occupation. Local defense committees erected barricades throughout Barcelona. Companys and the anarchist leaders pleaded with the workers to disarm. An uneasy truce continued until May 6, when the first detachments of Assault Guards arrived, violating the promises of the government that the truce would be observed and military forces withdrawn. The troops were under the command of General Pozas, formerly commander of the hated Civil Guard and now a member of the Communist party. In the fighting that followed, there were some five hundred killed and over a thousand wounded. "The May Days in reality sounded the death-knell of the revolution, announcing political defeat for all and death for certain of the revolutionary leaders."[94]

These events—of enormous significance in the history of the Spanish revolution—Jackson sketches in bare outline as a marginal incident. Obviously the historian's account must be selective; from the left-liberal point of view that Jackson shares with Hugh Thomas and many others, the liquidation of the revolution in Catalonia was a minor event, as the revolution itself was merely a kind of irrelevant nuisance, a minor irritant diverting energy from the struggle to save the bourgeois government. The decision to crush the revolution by force is described as follows:

On May 5, Companys obtained a fragile truce, on the basis of which the PSUC councilors were to retire from the regional government, and the question of the Telephone Company was left to future negotiation. That very night, however, Antonio Sesé, a UGT official who was about to enter the reorganized cabinet, was murdered. In any event, the Valencia authorities were in no mood to temporize further with the Catalan Left. On May 6 several thousand *asaltos* arrived in the city, and the Republican Navy demonstrated in the port.[95]

What is interesting about this description is what is left unsaid. For example, there is no comment on the fact that the dispatch of the *asaltos* violated the "fragile truce" that had been accepted by the Barcelona workers and the anarchist and the POUM troops nearby, and barely a mention of the bloody consequences or the political meaning of this unwillingness "to temporize further with the Catalan Left." There is no mention of the fact that along with Sesé, Berneri and other anarchist leaders were murdered, not only during the May Days but in the weeks preceding.[96] Jackson does not refer to the fact that along with the Republican navy, British ships also "demonstrated" in the port.[97] Nor does he refer to Orwell's telling observations about the Assault Guards, as compared to the troops at the front, where he had spent the preceding months. The Assault Guards "were splendid troops, much the best I had seen in Spain.... I was used to the ragged, scarcely-armed militia on the Aragon front, and I had not known that the Republic possessed troops like these.... The Civil Guards and Carabineros, who were not intended for the front at all, were better armed and far better clad than ourselves. I suspect it is the same in all wars—always the same contrast between the sleek police in the rear and the ragged soldiers in the line."[98] (See page 61 below.)

The contrast reveals a good deal about the nature of the war, as it was understood by the Valencia government. Later, Orwell was to make this conclusion explicit: "A government which sends boys of fifteen to the front with rifles forty years old and keeps its biggest men and newest weapons in the rear is manifestly more afraid of the revolution than of the fascists. Hence the feeble war policy of the past six months, and hence the compromise with which the war will almost certainly end."[99] Jackson's account of these events, with its omissions and assumptions, suggests that he perhaps shares the view that the greatest danger in Spain would have been a victory of the revolution.

Jackson apparently discounts Orwell's testimony, to some extent, commenting that "the readers should bear in mind Orwell's own honest statement that he knew very little about the political complexities of the struggle." This is a strange comment. For one thing, Orwell's analysis of the "political complexities of the struggle" bears up rather well after thirty years; if it is defective, it is probably in his tendency to give too much prominence to the POUM in comparison with the anarchists—not surprising, in view of the fact that he was with the POUM militia. His exposure of the fatuous nonsense that was appearing at the time in the Stalinist and liberal presses appears quite accurate, and later discoveries have given little reason to challenge the basic facts that he reported or the interpretation that he proposed in the heat of the conflict. Orwell does, in fact, refer to his own "political ignorance." Commenting on the final defeat of the revolution in May, he states: "I realized—though owing to my political ignorance, not so clearly as I ought to have done—that when the Government felt more sure of itself there would be reprisals." But this form of "political ignorance" has simply been compounded in more recent historical work.

Shortly after the May Days, the Caballero government fell and Juan Negrín became premier of Republican Spain. Negrín is described as follows, by Broué and Témime: "...he is an unconditional defender of capitalist property and resolute adversary of collectivization, whom the CNT ministers find blocking all of their proposals. He is the one who solidly reorganized the carabineros and presided over the transfer of the gold reserves of the Republic to the USSR. He enjoyed the confidence of the moderates...[and] was on excellent terms with the Communists."

The first major act of the Negrín government was the suppression of the POUM and the consolidation of central control over Catalonia. The government next turned to Aragon, which had been under largely anarchist control since the first days of the revolution, and where agricultural collectivization was quite extensive and Communist elements very weak. The municipal councils of Aragon were coordinated by the Council of Aragon, headed by Joaquín Ascaso, a well-known CNT militant, one of whose brothers had been killed during the May Days. Under the Caballero government, the anarchists had agreed to give representation to other antifascist parties, including the Communists, but the majority remained anarchist. In August the Negrín government announced the dissolution of the Council of Aragon and dispatched a division of the Spanish army, commanded by the Communist officer Enrique Lister, to enforce the dissolution of the local committees, dismantle the collectives, and establish central government control. Ascaso was arrested on the charge of having been responsible for the robbery of jewelry—namely, the jewelry "robbed" by the Council for its own use in the fall of 1936. The local anarchist press was suppressed in favor of a Communist journal, and in general local anarchist centers were forcefully occupied and closed. The last anarchist stronghold was captured, with tanks and artillery, on September 21. Because of government-imposed censorship, there is very little of a direct record of these events, and the major histories pass over them quickly.[100] According to Morrow, "the official CNT press...compared the assault on Aragon with the subjection of Asturias by Lopez Ochoa in October 1934"—the latter, one of the bloodiest acts of repression in modern Spanish history. Although this is an exaggeration, it is a fact that the popular organs of administration were wiped out by Lister's legions, and the revolution was now over, so far as Aragon was concerned.

About these events, Jackson has the following comments:

> On August 11 the government announced the dissolution of the *Consejo de Aragón*, the anarchist-dominated administration which had been recognized by Largo Caballero in December, 1936. The peasants were known to hate the Consejo, the anarchists had deserted the front during the Barcelona fighting, and the very existence of the Consejo was a standing challenge to the authority of the central government. For all these reasons Negrín did not hesitate to send in troops, and to arrest the anarchist officials. Once their authority had been broken, however, they were released.[101]

These remarks are most interesting. Consider first the charge that the anarchists had deserted the front during the May Days. It is true that elements of certain anarchist and POUM divisions were prepared to march on Barcelona, but after the "fragile truce" was established on May 5, they did not do so; no anarchist forces even approached Barcelona to defend the Barcelona proletariat and its institutions from attack. However, a motorized column of 5,000 Assault Guards was sent from the front by the government to break the "fragile truce."[102] Hence the only forces to "desert the front" during the Barcelona fighting were those dispatched by the government to complete the job of dismantling the revolution, by force. Recall Orwell's observations quoted above, page 59.

What about Jackson's statement that "the peasants were known to hate the Consejo?" As in the other cases I have cited, Jackson gives no indication of any evidence on which such a judgment might be based. The most detailed investigation of the collectives is from anarchist sources, and they indicate that Aragon was one of the areas where collectivization was most widespread and successful.[103] Both the CNT and the UGT Land Workers' Federation were vigorous in their support for collectivization, and there is no doubt that both were mass organizations. A number of nonanarchists, observing collectivization in Aragon firsthand, gave very favorable reports and stressed the voluntary character of collectivization.[104] According to Gaston Leval, an anarchist observer who carried out detailed investigation of rural collectivization, "in Aragon 75 percent of small proprietors have voluntarily adhered to the new order of things," and others were not forced to involve themselves in collectives.[105] Other anarchist observers—Augustin Souchy in particular—gave detailed observations of the functioning of the Aragon collectives. Unless one is willing to assume a fantastic degree of falsification, it is impossible to reconcile their descriptions with the claim that "the peasants were known to hate the Consejo"—unless, of course, one restricts the term "peasant" to "individual

61

farm owner," in which case it might very well be true, but would justify disbanding the Council only on the assumption that the rights of the individual farm owner must predominate, not those of the landless worker. There is little doubt that the collectives were economically successful,[106] hardly likely if collectivization were forced and hated by the peasantry.

I have already cited Bolloten's general conclusion, based on very extensive documentary evidence, that while the individual farmer may have viewed the development of collectivized agriculture with dismay, "the farm workers of the Anarchosyndicalist CNT and the Socialist UGT saw in it, on the contrary, the commencement of a new era." This conclusion seems quite reasonable, on the basis of the materials that are available. With respect to Aragon, specifically, he remarks that the "debt-ridden peasants were strongly affected by the ideas of the CNT and FAI, a factor that gave a powerful spontaneous impulse to collective farming," though difficulties are cited by anarchist sources, which in general appear to be quite honest about failures. Bolloten cites two Communist sources, among others, to the effect that about 70 percent of the population in rural areas of Aragon lived in collectives (p. 71); he adds that "many of the region's 450 collectives were largely voluntary," although "the presence of militiamen from the neighbouring region of Catalonia, the immense majority of whom were members of the CNT and FAI" was "in some measure" responsible for the extensive collectivization. He also points out that in many instances peasant proprietors who were not compelled to adhere to the collective system did so for other reasons: "...not only were they prevented from employing hired labour and disposing freely of their crops...but they were often denied all benefits enjoyed by members" (p. 72). Bolloten cites the attempt of the Communists in April 1937 to cause dissension in "areas where the CNT and UGT had established collective farms by mutual agreement" (p. 195), leading in some cases to pitched battles and dozens of assassinations, according to CNT sources.[107]

Bolloten's detailed analysis of the events of the summer of 1937 sheds considerable light on the question of peasant attitudes towards collectivization in Aragon:

> It was inevitable that the attacks on the collectives should have had an unfavorable effect upon rural economy and upon morale, for while it is true that in some areas collectivization was anathema to the majority of peasants, it is no less true that in others collective farms were organized spontaneously by the bulk of the peasant population. In Toledo province, for example, where even before the war rural collectives existed, 83 per cent of the peasants, according to a source friendly to the Communists, decided in favour of the collective cultivation of the soil. As the campaign against the collective farms reached its height just before the summer harvest [1937]...a pall of dismay and apprehension

descended upon the agricultural labourers. Work in the fields was abandoned in many places or only carried on apathetically, and there was danger that a substantial portion of the harvest, vital for the war effort, would be left to rot. [p. 196]

It was under these circumstances, he points out, that the Communists were forced to change their policy and—temporarily—to tolerate the collectives. A decree was passed legalizing collectives *"during the current agricultural year"* (his italics) and offering them some aid. This "produced a sense of relief in the countryside during the vital period of the harvest." Immediately after the crops had been gathered, the policy changed again to one of harsh repression. Bolloten cites Communist sources to the effect that "a short though fierce campaign at the beginning of August" prepared the way for the dissolution of the Council of Aragon. Following the dissolution decree, "the newly appointed Governor General, José Ignacio Mantecón, a member of the Left Republican Party, but a secret Communist sympathizer [who joined the party in exile, after the war]...ordered the break-up of the collective farms." The means: Lister's division, which restored the old order by force and terror. Bolloten cites Communist source conceding the excessive harshness of Lister's methods. He quotes the Communist general secretary of the Institute of Agrarian Reform, who admits that the measures taken to dissolve the collectives were "a very grave mistake, and produced tremendous disorganization in the countryside," as "those persons who were discontented with the collectives...took them by assault, carrying away and dividing up the harvest and farm implements without respecting the collectives that had been formed without violence or pressure, that were prosperous, and that were a model of organization.... As a result, labour in the fields was suspended almost entirely, and a quarter of the land had not been prepared at the time for sowing" (p. 200). Once again, it was necessary to ameliorate the harsh repression of the collectives, to prevent disaster. Summarizing these events, Bolloten describes the resulting situation as follows:

> But although the situation in Aragon improved in some degree, the hatreds and resentments generated by the break-up of the collectives and by the repression that followed were never wholly dispelled. Nor was the resultant disillusionment that sapped the spirit of the Anarchosyndicalist forces on the Aragon front ever entirely removed, a disillusionment that no doubt contributed to the collapse of that front a few months later...after the destruction of the collective farms in Aragon, the Communist Party was compelled to modify its policy, and support collectives also in other regions against former owners who sought the return of confiscated land.... [pp. 200–201]

Returning to Jackson's remarks, I think we must conclude that they seriously misrepresent the situation.[108] The dissolution of the Council of Aragon and the large-scale destruction of the collectives by military force was simply another stage in the eradication of the popular revolution and the restoration of the old order. Let me emphasize that I am not criticizing Jackson for his negative attitude towards the social revolution, but rather for the failure of objectivity when he deals with the revolution and the ensuing repression.

Among historians of the Spanish Civil War, the dominant view is that the Communist policy was in essentials the correct one—that in order to consolidate domestic and international support for the Republic it was necessary to block and then reverse the social revolution. Jackson, for example, states that Caballero "realized that it was absolutely necessary to rebuild the authority of the Republican state and to work in close co-operation with the middle-class liberals." The anarchist leaders who entered the government shared this view, putting their trust in the good faith of liberals such as Companys and believing—naively, as events were to show—that the Western democracies would come to their aid.

A policy diametrically opposed to this was advocated by Camillo Berneri. In his open letter to the anarchist minister Federica Montseny[109] he summarizes his views in the following way: "The dilemma, war or revolution, no longer has meaning. *The only dilemma is this: either victory over Franco through revolutionary war, or defeat*" (his italics). He argued that Morocco should be granted independence and that an attempt should be made to stir up rebellion throughout North Africa. Thus a revolutionary struggle should be undertaken against Western capitalism in North Africa and, simultaneously, against the bourgeois regime in Spain, which was gradually dismantling the accomplishments of the July revolution. The primary front should be political. Franco relied heavily on Moorish contingents, including a substantial number from French Morocco. The Republic might exploit this fact, demoralizing the Nationalist forces and perhaps even winning them to the revolutionary cause by political agitation based on the concrete alternative of pan-Islamic—specifically, Moroccan—revolution. Writing in April 1937, Berneri urged that the army of the Republic be reorganized for the defense of the revolution, so that it might recover the spirit of popular participation of the early days of the revolution. He quotes the words of his compatriot Louis Bertoni, writing from the Huesca front:

> The Spanish war, deprived of all new faith, of any idea of a social transformation, of all revolutionary grandeur, of any universal meaning, is now merely a national war of independence that must be carried on to avoid the extermination that the international plutocracy demands. There remains a terrible question of life or death, but no longer a war to build a new society and a new humanity.

In such a war, the human element that might bring victory over fascism is lost.

In retrospect, Berneri's ideas seem quite reasonable. Delegations of Moroccan nationalists did in fact approach the Valencia government asking for arms and matériel, but were refused by Caballero, who actually proposed territorial concessions in North Africa to France and England to try to win their support. Commenting on these facts, Broué and Témime observe that these policies deprived the Republic of "the instrument of revolutionary defeatism in the enemy army," and even of a possible weapon against Italian intervention. Jackson, on the other hand, dismisses Berneri's suggestion with the remark that independence for Morocco (as for that matter, even aid to the Moroccan nationalists) was "a gesture that would have been highly appreciated in Paris and London." Of course it is correct that France and Britain would hardly have appreciated this development. As Berneri points out, "it goes without saying that one cannot simultaneously guarantee French and British interests in Morocco and carry out an insurrection." But Jackson's comment does not touch on the central issue, namely, whether the Spanish revolution could have been preserved, both from the fascists at the front and from the bourgeois-Communist coalition within the Republic, by a revolutionary war of the sort that the left proposed—or, for that matter, whether the Republic might not have been saved by a political struggle that involved Franco's invading Moorish troops, or at least eroded their morale. It is easy to see why Caballero was not attracted by this bold scheme, given his reliance on the eventual backing of the Western democracies. On the basis of what we know today, however, Jackson's summary dismissal of revolutionary war is much too abrupt.

Furthermore, Bertoni's observations from the Huesca front are borne out by much other evidence, some of it cited earlier. Even those who accepted the Communist strategy of discipline and central control as necessary concede that the repressions that formed an ineliminable part of this strategy "tended to break the fighting spirit of the people."[110] One can only speculate, but it seems to me that many commentators have seriously underestimated the significance of the political factor, the potential strength of a popular struggle to defend the achievements of the revolution. It is perhaps relevant that Asturias, the one area of Spain where the system of CNT-UGT committees was not eliminated in favor of central control, is also the one area where guerrilla warfare continued well after Franco's victory. Broué and Témime observe[111] that the resistance of the partisans of Asturias "demonstrates the depth of the revolutionary élan, which had not been shattered by the reinstitution of state authority, conducted here with greater prudence." There can be no doubt that the revolution was both widespread and deeply rooted in the Spanish masses. It seems quite possible that a revolutionary war of the sort advocated by Berneri would have been successful, despite the greater military force of the fascist armies. The idea that men can overcome machines no longer seems as romantic or naive as it may have a few years ago.

Furthermore, the trust placed in the bourgeois government by the anarchist leaders was not honored, as the history of the counterrevolution clearly shows. In retrospect, it seems that Berneri was correct in arguing that they should not have taken part in the bourgeois government, but should rather have sought to replace this government with the institutions created by the revolution.[112] The anarchist minister García Oliver stated that "we had confidence in the word and in the person of a Catalan democrat and retained and supported Companys as President of the Generalitat,"[113] at a time when in Catalonia, at least, the workers' organizations could easily have replaced the state apparatus and dispensed with the former political parties, as they had replaced the old economy with an entirely new structure. Companys recognized fully that there were limits beyond which he could not cooperate with the anarchists. In an interview with H. E. Kaminski, he refused to specify these limits, but merely expressed his hope that "the anarchist masses will not oppose the good sense of their leaders," who have "accepted the responsibilities incumbent upon them"; he saw his task as "directing these responsibilities in the proper path," not further specified in the interview, but shown by the events leading up to the May Days.[114] Probably, Companys' attitude towards this willingness of the anarchist leaders to cooperate was expressed accurately in his reaction to the suggestion of a correspondent of the *New Statesman and Nation*, who predicted that the assassination of the anarchist mayor of Puigcerdá would lead to a revolt: "[Companys] laughed scornfully and said the anarchists would capitulate as they always had before."[115] As has already been pointed out in some detail, the liberal-Communist Party coalition had no intention of letting the war against Franco take precedence over the crushing of the revolution. A spokesman for Comorera put the matter clearly: "This slogan has been attributed to the P.S.U.C.: 'Before taking Saragossa, it is necessary to take Barcelona.' This reflects the situation exactly...."[116] Comorera himself had, from the beginning, pressed Companys to resist the CNT.[117] The first task of the antifascist coalition, he maintained, was to dissolve the revolutionary committees.[118] I have already cited a good deal of evidence indicating that the repression conducted by the Popular Front seriously weakened popular commitment and involvement in the antifascist war. What was evident to George Orwell was also clear to the Barcelona workers and the peasants in the collectivized villages of Aragon: the liberal-Communist coalition would not tolerate a revolutionary transformation of Spanish society; it would commit itself fully to the anti-Franco struggle only after the old order was firmly re-established, by force, if necessary.[119]

There is little doubt that farm workers in the collectives understood quite well the social content of the drive towards consolidation and central control. We learn this not only from anarchist sources but also from the socialist press in the spring of 1937. On May 1, the Socialist party newspaper *Adelante* had the following to say:

At the outbreak of the Fascist revolt the labor organizations and the democratic elements in the country were in agreement that the so-called Nationalist Revolution, which threatened to plunge our people into an abyss of deepest misery, could be halted only by a Social Revolution. The Communist Party, however, opposed this view with all its might. It had apparently completely forgotten its old theories of a "workers' and peasants' republic" and a "dictatorship of the proletariat." From its constant repetition of its new slogan of the parliamentary democratic republic it is clear that it has lost all sense of reality. When the Catholic and conservative sections of the Spanish bourgeoisie saw their old system smashed and could find no way out, the Communist Party instilled new hope into them. It assured them that the democratic bourgeois republic for which it was pleading put no obstacles in the way of Catholic propaganda and, above all, that it stood ready to defend the class interests of the bourgeoisie.[120]

That this realization was widespread in the rural areas was underscored dramatically by a questionnaire sent by *Adelante* to secretaries of the UGT Federation of Land Workers, published in June 1937.[121] The results are summarized as follows:

67

The replies to these questions revealed an astounding unanimity. Everywhere the same story. The peasant collectives are today most vigorously opposed by the Communist Party. The Communists organize the well-to-do farmers who are on the lookout for cheap labor and are, for this reason, outspokenly hostile to the cooperative undertakings of the poor peasants.

It is the element which before the revolution sympathized with the Fascists and Monarchists which, according to the testimony of the trade-union representatives, is now flocking into the ranks of the Communist Party. As to the general effect of Communist activity on the country, the secretaries of the U.G.T. had only one opinion, which the representative of the Valencia organization put in these words: "It is a misfortune in the fullest sense of the word."[122]

It is not difficult to imagine how the recognition of this "misfortune" must have affected the willingness of the land workers to take part in the antifascist war, with all the sacrifices that this entailed.

The attitude of the central government to the revolution was brutally revealed by its acts and is attested as well in its propaganda. A former minister describes the situation as follows:

> The fact that is concealed by the coalition of the Spanish Communist Party with the left Republicans and right wing Socialists is that there has been a successful social revolution in half of Spain. Successful, that is, in the collectivization of factories and farms which are operated under trade union control, and operated quite efficiently. During the three months that I was director of propaganda for the United States and England under Alvarez del Vayo, then Foreign Minister for the Valencia Government, I was instructed not to send out one word about this revolution in the economic system of loyalist Spain. Nor are any foreign correspondents in Valencia permitted to write freely of the revolution that has taken place.[123]

In short, there is much reason to believe that the will to fight Franco was significantly diminished, perhaps destroyed, by the policy of authoritarian centralization undertaken by the liberal-Communist coalition, carried through by force, and disguised in the propaganda that was disseminated among Western intellectuals[124] and that still dominates the writing of history. To the extent that this is a correct judgment, the alternative proposed by Berneri and the left "extremists" gains in plausibility.

As noted earlier, Caballero and the anarchist ministers accepted the policy of counterrevolution because of their trust in the Western democracies, which they felt sure would sooner or later come to their aid. This feeling was perhaps understandable in 1937. It is strange, however, that a historian writing in the 1960s should dismiss the proposal to strike at Franco's rear by extending the revolutionary war to Morocco, on grounds that this would have displeased Western capitalism (see page 65 above).

Berneri was quite right in his belief that the Western democracies would not take part in an antifascist struggle in Spain. In fact, their complicity in the fascist insurrection was not slight. French bankers, who were generally pro-Franco, blocked the release of Spanish gold to the loyalist government, thus hindering the purchase of arms and, incidentally, increasing the reliance of the Republic on the Soviet Union.[125] The policy of "nonintervention," which effectively blocked Western aid for the loyalist government while Hitler and Mussolini in effect won the war for Franco, was also technically initiated by the French government—though apparently under heavy British pressure.[126]

As far as Great Britain is concerned, the hope that it would come to the aid of the Republic was always unrealistic. A few days after the Franco coup, the foreign editor of *Paris-Soir* wrote: "At least four countries are already taking active interest in the battle—France, which is supporting the Madrid Government, and Britain, Germany and Italy, each of which is giving discreet but nevertheless effective assistance to one group or another among the insurgents."[127] In fact, British support for Franco took a fairly concrete form at the very earliest stages of the insurrection. The Spanish navy remained loyal to the

Republic,* and made some attempt to prevent Franco from ferrying troops from Morocco to Spain. Italian and German involvement in overcoming these efforts is well documented;[128] the British role has received less attention, but can be determined from contemporary reports. On August 11, 1936, the *New York Times* carried a front-page report on British naval actions in the Straits of Gibraltar, commenting that "this action helps the Rebels by preventing attacks on Algeciras, where troops from Morocco land." (A few days earlier, loyalist warships had bombarded Algeciras, damaging the British consulate.) An accompanying dispatch from Gibraltar describes the situation as it appeared from there:

> Angered by the Spanish factions' endangering of shipping and neutral Gibraltar territory in their fighting, Great Britain virtually blockaded Gibraltar Harbor last night with the huge battleship Queen Elizabeth in the center of the entrance, constantly playing searchlights on nearby waters.

> Many British warships patrolled the entire Strait today, determined to prevent interference with Britain's control over the entrance to the Mediterranean, a vital place in the British "lifeline to the East."

> This action followed repeated warnings to the Spanish Government and yesterday's decree that no more fighting would be permitted in Gibraltar Harbor. The British at Gibraltar had become increasingly nervous after the shelling of Algeciras by the Loyalist battleship Jaime I.

> *Although British neutrality is still maintained, the patrol of the Strait and the closing of the harbor will aid the military Rebels because Loyalist warships cannot attempt to take Algeciras, now in Rebel hands, and completely isolate the Rebels from Morocco. The Rebels now can release some troops, who were rushed back to Algeciras, for duty further north in the drive for Madrid.*

> It was reported in Gibraltar tonight that the Rebels had sent a transport across the Strait and had landed more troops from Morocco for use in the columns that are marching northward from headquarters at Seville.

> This was the second time this year that Britain warned a power when she believed her measure of Mediterranean control was threatened, and it remains to be seen whether the Madrid Government will flout the British as the Italians did. If it attempts to do so, the British gunners of the Gibraltar fort have

69

*To be more precise, pro-Franco officers were killed, and the seamen remained loyal to the Republic, in many instances.

authority to fire warning shots. What will happen if such shots go unheeded is obvious.

All the British here refer to the Madrid Government as the "Communists" and there is no doubt where British sympathies now lie, encouraged by the statement of General Francisco Franco, leader of the Rebels, that he is not especially cooperating with Italy.

The British Government has ordered Spaniards here to cease plotting or be expelled and has asked Britons "loyally to refrain from either acting or speaking publicly in such a manner as to display marked partiality or partisanship."

The warning, issued in the official Gibraltar Gazette, was signed by the British Colonial Secretary here.

The warning was issued after reports of possible Communist troubles here had reached official ears and after strong complaints that Spanish Rebels were in Gibraltar. It was said Rebels were making headquarters here and entering La Linea to fight. [Italics mine]

I have quoted this dispatch in full because it conveys rather accurately the character of British "neutrality" in the early stages of the war and thenceforth. In May 1938, the British ambassador to Spain, Sir Henry Chilton, "expressed the conviction that a Franco victory was necessary for peace in Spain; that there was not the slightest chance that Italy and/or Germany would dominate Spain; and that even if it were possible for the Spanish Government to win (which he did not believe) he was convinced that a victory for Franco would be better for Great Britain."[129] Churchill, who was at first violently opposed to the Republic, modified his position somewhat after the crushing of the revolution in the summer of 1937. What particularly pleased him was the forceful repression of the anarchists and the militarization of the Republic (necessary when "the entire structure of civilization and social life is destroyed," as it had been by the revolution, now happily subdued).[130] However, his good feelings towards the Republic remained qualified. In an interview of August 14, 1938, he expressed himself as follows: "Franco has all the right on his side because he loves his country. Also Franco is defending Europe against the Communist danger—if you wish to put it in those terms. But I, I am English, and I prefer the triumph of the wrong cause. I prefer that the other side wins, because Franco could be an upset or a threat to British interests, and the others no."[131]

The Germans were quite aware of British sentiment, naturally, and therefore were much concerned that the supervisory committee for the nonintervention agreement be located in London rather than Paris. The German Foreign Ministry official responsible for this matter expressed his view on

August 29, 1936, as follows: "Naturally, we have to count on complaints of all kinds being brought up in London regarding failure to observe the obligation not to intervene, but we cannot avoid such complaints in any case. It can, in fact, only be agreeable to us if the center of gravity, which after all has thus far been in Paris because of the French initiative, is transferred to London."[132] They were not disappointed. In November, Foreign Secretary Anthony Eden stated in the House of Commons: "So far as breaches [of the nonintervention agreement] are concerned, I wish to state categorically that I think there are other Governments more to blame than those of Germany and Italy."[133] There was no factual basis for this statement, but it did reflect British attitudes. It is interesting that according to German sources, England was at that time supplying Franco with munitions through Gibraltar and, at the same time, providing information to Germany about Russian arms deliveries to the Republic.[134]

The British left was for the most part in support of the liberal-Communist coalition, regarding Caballero as an "infantile leftist" and the anarchists as generally unspeakable.

The British policy of mild support for Franco was to be successful in preserving British interests in Spain, as the Germans soon discovered. A German Foreign Ministry note of October 1937 to the embassy in Nationalist Spain included the following observation: "That England cannot permanently be kept from the Spanish market as in the past is a fact with which we have to reckon. England's old relations with the Spanish mines and the Generalissimo's desire, based on political and economic considerations, to come to an understanding with England place certain limits on our chances of reserving Spanish raw materials to ourselves permanently."[135]

One can only speculate as to what might have been the effects of British support for the Republic. A discussion of this matter would take us far afield, into a consideration of British diplomacy during the late 1930s. It is perhaps worth mention, now that the "Munich analogy" is being bandied about in utter disregard for the historical facts by Secretary Rusk and a number of his academic supporters, that "containment of Communism" was not a policy invented by George Kennan in 1947. Specifically, it was a dominant theme in the diplomacy of the 1930s. In 1934, Lloyd George stated that "in a very short time, perhaps in a year, perhaps in two, the conservative elements in this country will be looking to Germany as the bulwark against Communism in Europe.... Do not let us be in a hurry to condemn Germany. We shall be welcoming Germany as our friend."[136] In September 1938, the Munich agreement was concluded; shortly after, both France and Britain did welcome Germany as "our friend." As noted earlier (see note 99), even Churchill's role at this time is subject to some question. Of course, the Munich agreement was the death knell for the Spanish Republic, exactly as the necessity to rely on the Soviet Union signaled the end of the Spanish revolution in 1937.

The United States, like France, exhibited less initiative in these events than Great Britain, which had far more substantial economic interests in Spain and was more of an independent force in European affairs. Nevertheless, the American record is hardly one to inspire pride. Technically, the United States adhered to a position of strict neutrality. However, a careful look raises some doubts. According to information obtained by Jackson, "the American colonel who headed the Telephone Company had placed private lines at the disposal of the Madrid plotters for their conversations with Generals Mola and Franco,"[137] just prior to the insurrection on July 17. In August, the American government urged the Martin Aircraft Company not to honor an agreement made prior to the insurrection to supply aircraft to the Republic, and it also pressured the Mexican government not to reship to Spain war materials purchased in the United States.[138] An American arms exporter, Robert Cuse, insisted on his legal right to ship airplanes and aircraft engines to the Republic in December 1936, and the State Department was forced to grant authorization. Cuse was denounced by Roosevelt as unpatriotic, though Roosevelt was forced to admit that the request was quite legal. Roosevelt contrasted the attitude of other businessmen to Cuse as follows:

> Well, these companies went along with the request of the Government. There is the 90 percent of business that is honest, I mean ethically honest. There is the 90 percent we are always pointing at with pride. And then one man does what amounts to a perfectly legal but thoroughly unpatriotic act. He represents the 10 percent of business that does not live up to the best standards. Excuse the homily, but I feel quite deeply about it.[139]

Among the businesses that remained "ethically honest" and therefore did not incur Roosevelt's wrath was the Texaco Oil Company, which violated its contracts with the Spanish Republic and shipped oil instead to Franco. (Five tankers that were on the high seas in July 1936 were diverted to Franco, who received six million dollars worth of oil on credit during the Civil War.) Apparently, neither the press nor the American government was able to discover this fact, though it was reported in left-wing journals at the time.[140] There is evidence that the American government shared the fears of Churchill and others about the dangerous forces on the Republican side. Secretary of State Cordell Hull, for example, informed Roosevelt on July 23, 1936, that "one of the most serious factors in this situation lies in the fact that the [Spanish] Government has distributed large quantities of arms and ammunition into the hands of irresponsible members of left-wing political organizations."[141]

Like Churchill, many responsible Americans began to rethink their attitude towards the Republic after the social revolution had been crushed.[142] However, relations with Franco continued cordial. In 1957, President Eisenhower congratulated Franco on the "happy anniversary" of his rebellion,[143] and Secretary Rusk added his tribute in 1961. Upon criticism, Rusk was defended by the American ambassador to Madrid, who observed that Spain is "a nation which understands the implacable nature of the communist threat,"[144] like Thailand, South Korea, Taiwan, and selected other countries of the Free World.[145]

In the light of such facts as these, it seems to me that Jackson is not treating the historical record seriously when he dismisses the proposals of the Spanish left as absurd. Quite possibly Berneri's strategy would have failed, as did that of the liberal-Communist coalition that took over the Republic. It was far from senseless, however. I think that the failure of historians to consider it more seriously follows, once again, from the elitist bias that dominates the writing of history—and, in this case, from a certain sentimentality about the Western democracies.

The study of collectivization published by the CNT in 1937[146] concludes with a description of the village of Membrilla. "In its miserable huts live the poor inhabitants of a poor province; eight thousand people, but the streets are not paved, the town has no newspaper, no cinema, neither a cafe nor a library. On the other hand, it has many churches that have been burned." Immediately after the Franco insurrection, the land was expropriated and village life collectivized. "Food, clothing, and tools were distributed equitably to the whole population. Money was abolished, work collectivized, all goods passed to the community, consumption was socialized. It was, however, not a socialization of wealth but of poverty." Work continued as before. An elected council appointed committees to organize the life of the commune and its relations to the outside world. The necessities of life were distributed freely, insofar as they were available. A large number of refugees were accommodated. A small library was established, and a small school of design.

The document closes with these words:

> The whole population lived as in a large family; functionaries, delegates, the secretary of the syndicates, the members of the municipal council, all elected, acted as heads of a family. But they were controlled, because special privilege or corruption would not be tolerated. Membrilla is perhaps the poorest village of Spain, but it is the most just.

An account such as this, with its concern for human relations and the ideal of a just society, must appear very strange to the consciousness of the sophisticated intellectual, and it is therefore treated with scorn, or taken to be naive or primitive or otherwise irrational. Only when such prejudice is abandoned will it be possible for historians to undertake a serious study of the popular movement that transformed Republican Spain in one of the most remarkable social revolutions that history records.

Franz Borkenau, in commenting on the demoralization caused by the authoritarian practices of the central government, observes (p. 295) that "newspapers are written by Europeanized editors, and the popular movement is inarticulate as to its deepest impulses...[which are shown only]...by acts." The objectivity of scholarship will remain a delusion as long as these inarticulate impulses remain beyond its grasp. As far as the Spanish revolution is concerned, its history is yet to be written.

I have concentrated on one theme—the interpretation of the social revolution in Spain—in one work of history, a work that is an excellent example of liberal scholarship. It seems to me that there is more than enough evidence to show that a deep bias against social revolution and a commitment to the values and social order of liberal bourgeois democracy has led the author to misrepresent crucial events and to overlook major historical currents. My intention has not been to bring into question the commitment to these values—that is another matter entirely. Rather, it has been to show how this commitment has led to a striking failure of objectivity, providing an example of "counterrevolutionary subordination" of a much more subtle and interesting sort—and ultimately, I believe, a far more important one—than those discussed in the first part of this essay.

III

74

In opening this discussion of the Spanish revolution I referred to the classical left-wing critique of the social role of intellectuals, Marxist or otherwise, in modern society, and to Luxemburg's reservations regarding Bolshevism. Western sociologists have repeatedly emphasized the relevance of this analysis to developments in the Soviet Union,[147] with much justice. The same sociologists formulate "the world revolution of the epoch" in the following terms: "The major transformation is the decline of business (and of earlier social formations) and the rise of intellectuals and semi-intellectuals to effective power."[148] The "ultra-left" critic foresaw in these developments a new attack on human freedom and a more efficient system of exploitation. The Western sociologist sees in the rise of intellectuals to effective power the hope for a more humane and smoothly functioning society, in which problems can be solved by "piecemeal technology." Who has the sharper eye? At least this much is plain: there are dangerous tendencies in the ideology of the welfare state intelligentsia who claim to possess the technique and understanding required to manage our "postindustrial society" and to organize an international society dominated by American superpower. Many of these dangers are revealed, at a purely ideological level, in the study of the counterrevolutionary subordination of scholarship. The dangers exist both insofar as the claim to knowledge is real and insofar as it is fraudulent. Insofar as the technique of management and control exists, it can be used to consolidate the authority of those who exercise it and to diminish spontaneous and free experimentation with new social forms, as it can limit the possibilities for reconstruction of society in the interests of those who are now, to a greater or lesser extent, dispossessed. Where the techniques fail, they will be supplemented by all of the methods of coercion that modern technology provides, to preserve order and stability.

For a glimpse of what may lie ahead, consider the Godkin lectures of McGeorge Bundy, recently delivered at Harvard.[149] Bundy urges that more power be concentrated in the executive branch of the government, now "dangerously weak in relation to its present tasks." That the powerful executive will act with justice and wisdom—this presumably needs no argument. As an example of the superior executive who should be attracted to government and given still greater power, Bundy cites Robert McNamara. Nothing could reveal more clearly the dangers inherent in the "new society" than the role that McNamara's Pentagon has played for the past half-dozen years. No doubt McNamara succeeded in doing with utmost efficiency that which should not be done at all. No doubt he has shown an unparalleled mastery of the logistics of coercion and repression, combined with the most astonishing inability to comprehend political and human factors. The efficiency of the Pentagon is no less remarkable than its pratfalls.[150] When understanding fails, there is always more force in reserve. As the "experiments in material and human resources control" collapse and "revolutionary development" grinds to a halt, we simply resort more openly to the Gestapo tactics that are barely concealed behind the facade of "pacification."[151] When American cities explode, we can expect the same. The technique of "limited warfare" translates neatly into a system of domestic repression—far more humane, as will quickly be explained, than massacring those who are unwilling to wait for the inevitable victory of the war on poverty.

Why should a liberal intellectual be so persuaded of the virtues of a political system of four-year dictatorship? The answer seems all too plain.

Source: Noam Chomsky, "Objectivity and Liberal Scholarship," in *American Power and the New Mandarins* (New York: New Press, 2002), pp. 23–158. First edition Pantheon, 1969.

NOTES

1 "Politics and the Morality of Scholarship," in Max Black, ed., *The Morality of Scholarship* (Ithaca, N.Y., Cornell University Press, 1967), pp. 59–88.

2 "The War and Its Effects—II," *Congressional Record*, December 13, 1967.

3 *Congressional Record*, July 27, 1967.

4 William A. Nighswonger, *Rural Pacification in Vietnam* (Praeger Special Studies; New York, Fredrick A. Praeger, Inc., 1967)—one of a series of "specialized research monographs in U.S. and international economics and politics."

5 Ithiel de Sola Pool, "The Necessity for Social Scientists Doing Research for Governments," *Background*, Vol. 10 (August 1966), p. 111.

6 Max Ways writes in *Fortune* that "McNamara, his systems analysts, and their computers are not only contributing to the practical effectiveness of U.S. action, but *raising the moral level of policy* by a more conscious and selective attention to the definition of its aims." [italics mine]. Cited by Andrew Kopkind, "The Future-Planners," *New Republic*, February 25, 1967, p. 23. Comment would be superfluous.

7 Daniel Bell, "Notes on the Post-Industrial Society: Part I," *The Public Interest*, No. 6, 1967, pp. 24–25.

8 Some of the dangers are noted by Richard Goodwin, in a review of Thomas Schelling's *Arms and Influence* in the *New Yorker*, February 17, 1968, pp. 127–34. He observes that "the most profound objection to this kind of strategic theory is not its limited usefulness but its danger, for it can lead us to believe we have an understanding of events and a control over their flow which we do not have" A still more profound objection, I think, is that the pretended objectivity of "strategic theory" can be used to justify the attempt to control the flow of events.

9 Seymour M. Lipset, *Political Man* (Garden City, N.W., Doubleday & Company, Inc., 1960), p. 406.

10 "Status Politics and new Anxieties," in *The End of Ideology* (New York, The Free Press, 1960), p. 119.

11 "The Necessity and Difficulty of Planning the Future Society," address given at the American Institute of Planners Conference, Washington, D.C., October 3, 1967. Citing this, Senator Fulbright (*op. cit.*) comments aptly that "poverty, which is a tragedy in a poor country, blights our affluent society with something more than tragedy; being unnecessary, it is deeply immoral as well" He also compares "the $904 billion we have spent on military power since World War II" with "the $96 billion we have spent, out of our regular national budget, on education, health, welfare housing, and community development" In his *Challenge to Affluence* (New York, Pantheon Books, 1963), Myrdal concludes that "In society at large there is more equality of opportunity today than there ever was. But for the bottom layer there is less or none" (p. 38). He questions the assumption that "American is still the free and

open society of its cherished image and well-established ideals" and remarks that "as less and less work is required of the type that people in the urban and rural slums can offer, they will be increasingly isolated and expose to unemployment and plain exploitation. There is an ugly smell rising from the basement of the stately American mansion" (p. 49).

[12] Adam Ulam, *The Unfinished Revoution* (New York, Vintage Books, 1964), p. 97.

[13] In 1965, 20 companies out of 420,000 made 38 percent of profits after taxes, and earnings on foreign investments were well over three times what they were 15 years earlier. The sales of GM exceeded the GNP of all but nine foreign countries. The 10 largest companies reported profits equal to the next 490. On thousand companies disappeared through merger.

[14] "American in the Technetronic Age," *Encounter*, Vol. 30 (January 1968), pp. 16–26.

[15] "Marxian Socialism in the United States," in Donald D. Egbert and S. Persons, eds., *Socialism and American Life* (Princeton, N.J., Princeton University Press, 1952), Vol.1, p. 329.

[16] *Op. cit.*, p. 5. Less typical, and more realistic, is his belief that these problems also "seem to defy the social scientist's expertise." For some general discussions of this "generosity," see, for example, David Horowitz, *Hemispheres North and South* (Baltimore, The Johns Hopkins Press, 1966), and many special studies. American public officials do not share this faith in our generosity, by and large. For example, the Assistant Secretary of State for Latin American affairs observed bluntly that "the State Department is not disposed to favor large loans of public funds to countries not welcoming our private capital" (*State Department Bulletin* No.22, 1950, cited in Fredrick Clairmonte, *Economic Liberalism and Underdevelopment* [Bombay and London, Asia Publishing House, 1960], p. 248). Eugene Black, testifying before Congress on the Asian Development Bank, pointed out that "when the Bank makes loans you have international bids, and I am sure that with our ability and ingenuity in this country, we will get our share of the business. We certainly ought to get more than the small amount we contribute" David Bell testified that "the Bank will play a major role in carrying forward another policy of our own assistance program— strengthening the role of the private sector...by identifying particular projects which can attract private capital to this region." Nothing here about "the generosity that characterizes our policy."

Equally revealing is the history of programs such as the Alliance for Progress. As Senator Gore commented, this program "has in large measure come to be subsidy for American business and American exporters" (*Congressional Record*, July 22, 1966)— a fairly accurate judgment, so it appears. For example, the AID lending program in Latin America, according to former Alliance for Press official William Rogers (*The Twilight Struggle* [New York, Random House, 1967], p. 205), is based on two elements: "a demonstrated balance of payments needed to increase the nation's ability to import U.S. goods and services, and the adoption of public policies and programs which would insure against capital flight on the international account side or the misuse of domestic resources through inefficient budgeting, reducing local savings or inflation." Commenting on this, Robert Smith notes that "the latter standard included increased tax revenues, reduction of budget deficit, elimination of 'distorting subsidies to public activities,' and the adoption of 'state incentives to private sector investment and growth.'" (*New Politics*, Vol. 6 [Spring 1967], pp. 49–57. For some remarks on the other side of our assistance program, military aid, see the articles of James Petras in this and the preceding issue.)

17 "To Intervene or Not to Intervene," *Foreign Affairs*, Vol. 45 (April 1967), pp. 425–36.

18 *New York Times*, December 20, 1967. The *Times* refers to what is printed as "excerpts," but it is not materially different from the full document. I understand that it has since been signed by many other scholars.

19 See the reviews by Coral Bell and B. R. O'G. Anderson in the *China Quarterly*, No. 28 (October-December 1966), pp. 140–143. It should be noted that opposition to social change, and support for the counterrevolutionary violence that is used to suppress it, are the longstanding features of American cultural history. Thus according to American historian Louis Hartz, "there is no doubt that the appearance of even a mild socialism in 1848, of Ledru Rollin and the national workshops, was enough to produce general American dismay. There was no outcry in America against the suppression of the June revolt of the workers in Paris, as there was none over the suppression of the Communards in 1871. Here was violence, and plenty of it, but it was being used for order and law, as one editorial writer put it [in the *New York Journal of Commerce*]." (*The Nature of Revolution*, Testimony before the Senate Committee on Foreign Relations, February 26, 1968 [Washington, Government Printing Office, 1968]).

20 "The Public and the Polity," Ithiel de Sola Pool, ed., *Contemporary Political Science: Toward Empirical Theory* (New York, McGraw-Hill Book Company, 1967), p. 26.

21 Clairmonte, *op. cit.*, p. 325.

22 Recent confirmatory evidence is given by George M. Kahin, in a memorandum of April 13, 1967, in the *Congressional Record*. He cites the marine Corps estimate that in this province, the principal area of marine strength, 18 out of 549 hamlets had been "secured."

23 Albert Shaw, editor of the *American Review of Reviews*, commenting, in 1893, on American's failure to acquire colonies. Cited in Ernest R. May, *Imperial Democracy* (New York, Harcourt, Brace & World, Inc., 1961), p. 23.

24 Quoted by Robert Guillain in *Le Monde*, May 25, 1966; reprinted, in English translation, as *Vietnam, the Dirty War* (London, Housmans, 1966).

25 According to Jonathan Randal (*New York Times*, June 11, 1967), "only one officer above the rank of lieutenant colonel did not serve in the French army against the Vietminh in the French Indochina war."

26 Douglas Pike, *Viet Cong*, (Cambridge, mass., The M.I.T. Press, 1966), pp. 361–62.

27 *Vietnam: A Dragon Embattled* (New York, Frederick A. Praeger, Inc., 1967), Vol. 2, p. 952. See also note 29.

28 *World Communism* (1939; reprinted Ann Arbor, University of Michigan Press, 1962), p. 24.

29 *Op. cit.*, Vol. 2, p. 856. As Buttinger explains, "Local elections would have given the Vietminh control of most of the rural communities. The Vietminh was not only popular and in effective political control of large regions, but it alone had people with the requisite organizational skills to exploit whatever opportunities for democratic self-expression the regime opened up." He adds that "the NLF was truly the Vietminh reborn," and speaks of "the similarity, or better, near identity, of the Vietminh and the NLF."

30 Roger Hilsman, "Internal War: The New Communist Tactic," in Franklin Mark Osanka, ed., *Modern Guerilla Warfare* (New York, The Free Press, 1962), p. 460.

31 Alastair Buchan, director of the Institute for Strategic Studies in London, describes the South Koreans as an "organization of Asian 'black and tans'" ("Questions about Vietnam," *Encounter*, Vol. 30 [January 1968], pp. 3–12).

On the reasons for the remarkable success of pacification success of pacification in Binh Dinh Province, see Bernard Fall, *Last Reflections on a War* (Garden City, N.Y., Doubleday & Company, Inc., 1967), p. 1967), p. 159. This was one of "the areas where American-Korean multidivision operations have literally smothered the opposition" with vast search-and-destroy operations" and continuing "tight military control"—or so it seemed, until late 1967, and finally February 1968, when the lid blew off. A report on Binh Dinh Province, the "showcase" province for pacification, in the *New York Times*, February 20, tells the story. "The enemy moves in December— which several military men called a 'softening up' for the offensive—resulted in a wave of allied air strikes on villages. Hundreds of homes were destroyed"—the standard American response. An American official reports: "What the Vietcong did was occupy the hamlets we pacified just for the purpose of having the allies move in and bomb them out. By their presence, the hamlets were destroyed." No doubt our psychological warfare specialists are now explaining to the Vietnamese, who seem to have some difficulty understanding these subtleties, that the destruction of the villages is the fault of the Vietcong. In any event, the report continues, "the entire 1968 program for the province has now been shelved" and "the program is now set back anywhere from 14 to 18 months"—that is, back to the time of the initial saturation with American and Korean troops. "It has all gone down the drain," said one gloomy American official.

32 *United States Policy and the Third World* (Boston, Little, Brown, and Company, 1967), Ch. 3.

33 Morton H. Halperin, *Contemporary Military Strategy* (Boston, Little, Brown, and Company, 1967), pp. 141–2. I am indebted to Herbert P. Bix for bringing this contribution to the social sciences to my attention.

34 Wolf, *op. cit.*, p. 69.

35 There is little point in a lengthy discussion of Wolf's concept of international affairs or his empirical studies. To take a few examples, he assumes without question that North Vietnam's willingness to "disrupt the regime" in the South was motivated in part by "the marked economic and social improvements accomplished by the Diem regime from 1955 to 1960—dramatic by comparison with the economic stagnation in North Vietnam" (for fact rather than fancy on relative development, see Buttinger, *op. cit.*, Vol. 2, pp. 928, 966 f.); and also that India's "moderately successful growth" was part of the motivation behind "China's aggressive actions in October 1962." See also note 36. As to the solidity of Wolf's empirical studies, it is perhaps enough to note that his most significant result, the correlation between higher GNP and higher level of political democracy in Latin America, arises principally from the conclusion (based on data from 1950 to 1960) that Brazil and Argentina (along with Mexico and Chile) rank high on the scale of political democracy (cf. p. 124). The general level of sophistication is illustrated, for example, by a solemn reference to a consultant for having explained that in determining the "total military value" of a set of alternatives, it is not enough to sum up the separate values; one must also weight responses by probability of occurrence.

36 "But in all cases, the primary consideration should be whether the proposed measure is likely to increase the cost and difficulties of insurgent operations and help to disrupt the insurgent organization, rather than whether it wins popular loyalty and support, or whether it contributes to a more productive, efficient, or equitable use of resources" (Wolf, *op. cit.*, p. 69). We must understand that "successful counterinsurgency programs can be conducted among a rural populate that is passive or even hostile, rather than loyal, to the government." As evidence, Wolf cites his belief that "The growth of the Viet Cong and of the Pathet Lao probably occurred despite the opposition of a large majority of the people in both Vietnam and Laos" (*ibid*, p. 48). If they can do it, so can we.

In contrast, Robert Scigliano (of the Michigan State University Vietnam Advisory Group) reported that "using the estimate of American officials in Saigon at the end of 1962, about one-half of the South Vietnamese support the NLP" (*South Vietnam: Nation Under Stress* [Boston, Houghton Mifflin Company, 1963], p. 145). Arthur Dommen reports (*Conflict in Laos: The Politics of Neutralization* [New York, Frederick A. Praeger, Inc., 1964]) that "the Pathet Lao needed no propaganda to turn the rural population against the townspeople" (p. 107). The American Mission took care of this, with its lavish aid (1/2 of 1 percent of which was spent on agriculture, the livelihood of 96 percent of the population) leading to immense corruption, the proliferation of luxurious villas and large automobiles alongside of grinding poverty; and with its constant subversion in support, first of the "pro-Western neutralist" Phoui Sannankone, and then of the military dictator Phoumi Nosavan. As Roger Hilsman puts it, the real Pathet Lao "threat" was "expansion of political control based on winning peasant support in the villages" (*To Move a Nation*, [Garden City, N.Y., Doubleday & Company, Inc., 1967], p. 112). The lack of support for the Pathet Lao was amply demonstrated in the 1958 elections, in which 9 of their 13 candidates won, and Souphanouvong, the leading Pathet Lao figure, received more votes than any other candidate in the country. It was this election victory that set off the American attempts at subversion. As Dommen says, "once again the United States threw its support to the most feudal elements of the society."

To Charles Wolf, all of this demonstrates that counterinsurgency, like insurgency, can succeed without concern for popular loyalty and participation.

37 Cited in Clairmonte, *op. cit.*, p. 92. The ancestors of whom Merivale speaks are those who crushed the Indian textile industry by embargoes and import duties, as was quite necessary. "Had this not been the case, the mills of Paisley and Manchester would have been stopped in their outset, and could scarcely have been against set in motion, even by the power of steam. They were created by the sacrifice of Indian manufacturers" (Horace Wilson, 1826, cited by Clairmonte, p. 87).

This is the classic example of the creation of underdevelopment through imperialism. For a detailed study of this process see Andre Gunder Frank, *Capitalism and Underdevelopment in Latin America*, (New York, Monthly Review Press, 1967).

38 See Robert E. Osgood, *Ideals and Self-Interest in America's Foreign Relations* (Chicago, University of Chicago Press, 1953), pp. 72–73.

39 "Some Reflections on U.S. Policy in Southeast Asia." In William Henderson, ed., *Southeast Asia: Problems of United States Policy* (Cambridge, Mass., The M.I.T. Press, 1963), pp. 249-63. This collection of papers was published with the encouragement of the Asia Society because of "the scholarly quality of the papers and their enlightening contribution to the formulation of United States policy in the area."

40 *Thailand and the United States* (Washington, Public Affairs Press, 1965).

41 The Bank of America placed a full-page ad in the Fourth of July edition, 1951, of the *Bangkok Post* saluting the kingdom of Thailand with these words: "In both Thailand and America democracy has gone hand in hand with national sovereignty. Today both nations stand in the forefront of world efforts to promote and defend the democratic way of life."

42 In an article on "U.S.-Thai links" in the *Christian Science Monitor*, October 14, 1967.

43 Just a few paragraphs earlier we read that in the postwar period "the Americans rapidly expanded the Thai armed forces from 50,000 to 100,000 men... the United States quickly increased the policy forces, and this helped suppress opponents of the government. The technical assistance program was largely converted to military objectives. The internal impact of this policy further strengthened the power and prestige of the Thai military leaders who had seized the government in 1947. The effort to move toward some form of constitutional rule was halted, and the democratic institutions inaugurated by civilian leaders just after the war were abolished. Political parties were suppressed. The press was censored. Power became increasingly centralized in the hands of a few military leaders." All of this, however, did no constitute "interference in the domestic affairs of other nations," and is not "contrary to American traditions."

44 *Western Interests in the Pacific Realm* (New York, Random House, 1967).

45 Of what importance, then, is the fact that the overwhelming majority of Okinawans, including 80 percent of those whose business would be impaired or destroyed by this move, want the island returned to Japan, according to the Asahi polls (see *Japan Quarterly*, Vol. 15 [January–March 1968], pp. 42–52)? As to the "strategic trust territories," Adam says, we must also not become overly sentimental: "A strategic trust is based on the assumption of the overriding importance of national defense and the preservation of world order as against the cultural and political freedom of the indigenous inhabitants."

46 H.S. Malaviya, quoted in Clairmonte (*op. cit.*, p. 114), who cites substantial evidence in support of the following evaluation of the consequences of Western dominance: "The systematic destruction of Indian manufacturers; the creation of the Zemindari [landed aristocracy] and its parasitical outgrowths; the changes in agrarian structure; the financial losses incurred by tribute; the sharp transition from a pre-monetised economy to one governed by the international price mechanism—these were some of the social and institutional forces that were to bring the apocalypse of death and famine to millions—with few or no compensatory benefits to the ryot [peasant]" (p. 107). See also note 37.

47 Cited in Paul Avrich, *The Russian Anarchists* (Princeton, N.J., Princeton University Press, 1967), pp. 93–94. A recent reformulation of this view is given by Anton Pannekoek, the Dutch scientist and spokesman for libertarian communism, in his *Workers Councils* (Melbourne, 1950), pp. 36–37:

> It is not for the first time that ruling class tries to explain, and so to perpetuate, its rule as the consequences of an inborn difference between two kinds of people, one destined by nature to ride, the other to be ridden. The landowning aristocracy of former centuries defended their privileged position by boasting their extraction from a nobler race of conquerors that had subdued the lower race of common people. Big capitalists explain their dominating place by the assertion that they have brains and other people have none. In the same way now especially the intellectuals, considered themselves the rightful rulers of to-morrow, claim their spiritual superiority. They form the rapidly increasing class of university-trained officials and free professions, specialized in mental work, in study of books and of science, and they consider themselves as the people most gifted with intellect. Hence they are destined to be leaders of the production, whereas the ungifted mass shall execute the manual work, for which no brains are needed. They are no defenders of capitalism; not capital, but intellect should direct labor. The more so, since now society is such a complicated structure, based on abstract and difficult science, that only the highest intellectual acumen is capable of embracing, grasping and handling it. Should the working masses, from lack of insight, fail to acknowledge this need of supe-

rior intellectual lead, should they stupidly try to take the direction into their own hands, chaos and ruin will be the inevitable consequence.

[48] See note 7. Albert Parry has suggested that there are important similarities between the emergence of a scientific elite in the Soviet Union and the United States, in their growing role in decision making, citing Bell's thesis in support. See the *New York Times*, March 27, 1966, reporting on the Midwest Slavic Conference.

[49] Letter to Herzen and Ogarett, 1866, cited in Daniel Guérin, *Jeunesse du socialisme libertaire* (Paris, Librarie Marcel Riviere, 1959), p. 119.

[50] Rosa Luxemburg, *The Russian Revolution*, trans. Bertram D. Wolfe (Ann Arbor, University of Michigan Press, 1961), p. 71.

[51] Luxemburg, cited by Guérin, *Jeunesse de socialisme libertaire*, pp. 106–7.

[52] *Leninism or Marxism*, in Luxemburg, *op. cit.*, p. 102.

[53] For a very enlightening study of this matter, emphasizing domestic issues, see Michael Paul Rogin, *The Intellectuals and McCarthy: The Radical Specter* (Cambridge, Mass., The M.I.T. Press, 1967).

[54] *The Spanish Republic and the Civil War: 1931–1939* (Princeton, N.J., Princeton University Press, 1965).

[55] Respectively, President of the Republic, Prime Minister from May until the Franco insurrection, and member of the conservative wing of the Popular Front selected by Azana to try to set up a compromise government after the insurrection.

[56] It is interesting that Douglas Pike's very hostile account of the National Liberation Front, cited earlier, emphasizes the popular and voluntary element in its striking organizational successes. What he describes, whether accurately or not one cannot tell, is a structure of interlocking self-help organizations, loosely coordinated and developed through persuasion rather than force—in certain respects, of a character that would have appealed to anarchist thinkers. Those who speak so freely of the "authoritarian Vietcong" may be correct, but they have presented little evidence to support their judgment. Of course, it must be understood that Pike regards the element of voluntary mass participation in self-help associations as the most dangerous and insidious feature of the NLF organizational structure.

Also relevant is the history of collectivization in China, which, as compared with the Soviet Union, shows a much higher reliance on persuasion and mutual aid than on force and terror, and appears to have been more successful. See Thomas P. Bernstein, "Leadership and Mass Mobilisation in the Soviet and Chinese Collectivization Campaigns of 1929–30 and 1955–56: A Comparison," *China Quarterly*, No. 31 (July–September 1967), pp. 1–47, for some interesting and suggestive comments and analysis.

The scale of the Chinese Revolution is so great and reports in depth are so fragmentary that it would no doubt be foolhardy to attempt a general evaluation. Still, all the reports that I have been able to study suggest that insofar as real successes were achieved in the several stages of land reform, mutual aid, collectivization, and formation of communes, they were traceable in large part to the complex interaction of the Communist party cadres and the gradually evolving peasant associations, a relation which seems to stray far from the Leninist model of organization. This is particularly evident in William Hinton's magnificent study *Fanshen* (New York, Monthly Review Press, 1966), which is unparalleled, to my knowledge, as an analysis of a moment of profound revolutionary change. What seems to me particularly striking in his account of the early stages of revolution in one Chinese village is not only the extent to which party cadres submitted themselves to popular control, but also, and more significant, the ways in which exercise of control over steps of the revolutionary process was a factor in developing the consciousness and insight of those who took part in the revolution, not only from a political and social point of view, but also with respect to the human relationships that were created. It is interesting, in this connection, to note the strong populist element in early Chinese Marxism. For some very illuminating observations about this general matter, see Maurice Meisner, *Li Ta-chao and the Origins of Chinese Marxism* (Cambridge, Mass., Harvard University Press, 1967).

I am not suggesting that the anarchist revolution in Spain—with its background of more than thirty years of education and struggle—is being relived in Asia, but rather that the spontaneous and voluntary elements in popular mass movements have probably been seriously misunderstood because of the instinctive antipathy towards such phenomena among intellectuals, and more recently, because of the insistence on interpreting them in terms of Cold War mythology.

57 "The Spanish Background," *New Left Review*, No. 40 (November–December 1966), pp. 85–90.

58 Jose Peirats, *La C.N.T. en la revolution española* (Toulouse, Ediciones C.N.T., 1951–52), 3 vols. Jackson makes one passing reference to it. Peirats has since published a general history of the period, *Los anarquistas en la crisis politica española* (Buenos Aires, Editorial Alfa-Argentina, 1964). This highly informative book should certainly be made available to an English-speaking audience.

59 An exception to the rather general failure to deal with the anarchist revolution is Hugh Thomas' "Anarchist Agrarian Collectives in the Spanish Civil War," in Martin Gilbert, ed., *A Century of Conflict, 1850–1950: Essays for A.J.P. Taylor* (New York, Atheneum Publishers, 1967), pp. 245–63. See note 106 below for some discussion. There is also much useful information in what to my mind is the best general history of the Civil War, *La Revolution et la guerre d'Espagne*, by Pierre Broué and Emile Temime (Paris, Les Editions de Minuit, 1961). A concise and informative recent account is contained in Daniel Guérin, *L'Anarchisme* (Paris, Gallimard, 1965). In his extensive study, *The Spanish Civil War* (New York, Harper & Row Publishers 1961; paperback ed., 1963), Hugh Thomas barely refers to the popular revolution, and some of the major events are not mentioned at all—see, for example, note 97, below.

60 *Collectivisations: l'oeuvre constructive de la Revolution espagnole*, 2nd ed. (Toulouse, Editions C.N.T., 1965). The first edition was published in Barcelona (Editions

C.N.T.-F.A.I., 1937). There is an excellent and sympathetic summary by the Marxist scholar Karl Korsch, "Collectivization in Spain," in *Living Marxism*, Vol. 4 (April 1939), pp. 179–82. In the same issue (pp. 170–171), the liberal Communist reaction to the Spanish Civil War is summarized succinctly, and I believe accurately, as follows: "With their empty chatter as to the wonders of Bolshevik discipline, the geniality of Caballero, and the passions of the Pasionaria, the 'modern liberals' merely covered up their real desire for the destruction of all revolutionary possibilities in the Civil War, and their preparation for the possible war over the Spanish issue in the interest of their diverse fatherlands…what was truly revolutionary in the Spanish Civil War resulted from the direct actions of the workers and pauperized peasants, and not because of a specific form of labor organization nor an especially gifted leadership." I think that the record bears out this analysis, and I also think that it is this fact that accounts for the distaste for the revolutionary phase of the Civil War and its neglect in historical scholarship.

[61] An illuminating eyewitness account of this period is that of Franz Borkenau, *The Spanish Cockpit* (1938; reprinted Ann Arbor, University of Michigan Press, 1963).

[62] Figures from Guérin, *L'Anarchisme*, p. 154.

[63] A useful account of this period is given by Felix Morrow, *Revolution and Counter-Revolution in Spain* (1938; reprinted London, New Park Publications, 1963)

[64] Cited by Camillo Berneri in his "Lettre ouverte a la camarade Frederica [sic] Montseny," *Guerre de classes en Espagne* (Paris, 1946), a collection of items translated from his journal *Guerra di Classe*. Berneri was the outstanding anarchist intellectual in Spain. He opposed the policy of joining the government and argued for an alternative, more typically anarchist strategy to which I will return below. His own view towards joining the government was stated succinctly by a Catalan worker whom he quotes, with reference to the Republic of 1931: "It is always the old dog with a new collar." Events were to prove the accuracy of this analysis.

Berneri has been a leading spokesman of Italian anarchism. He left Italy after Mussolini's rise to power, and came to Barcelona on July 19, 1936. He formed the first Italian units for the antifascist war, according to anarchist historian Rudolf Rocker (*The Tragedy of Spain* [New York, Freie Arbeiter Stimme, 1937], p. 44). He was murdered, along with his older comrade Barbieri, during the May Days of 1937. (Arrested on May 5 by the Communist-controlled police, he was shot during the following night.) Hugh Thomas, in *The Spanish Civil War*, p. 428, suggests that "the Thomas' book, which is largely devoted to military history, mentions Berneri's murder but makes no other reference to his ideas or role.

Berneri's name does not appear in Jackson's history.

[65] Burnett Bolloten, *The Grand Camouflage: The Communist Conspiracy in the Spanish Civil War* (New York, Frederick A. Praeger, Inc., 1961), p. 86. This book, by a UP correspondent in Spain during the Civil War, contains a great deal of important documentary evidence bearing on the questions considered here. The attitude of the wealthy farmers of this area, most of them former supporters of the right-wing organ-

izations that had now disappeared, is well described by the general secretary of the Peasant Federation, Julio Mateu: "Such is the sympathy for us [that is, the Communist party] in the Valencia countryside that hundreds and thousands of farmers would join our party if we were to let them. These farmers…love our party like a scared thing…they [say] 'The Communist Party is our party.' Comrades, what emotion the peasants display when they utter these words" (cited in Bolloten, p. 86). There is some interesting speculation about the backgrounds for the writing of this very important book in H.R. Southworth, *Le mythe de la croisade de Franco* (Ruedo Iberico, Paris, 1964; Spanish edition, same publisher, 1963).

The Communist headquarters in Valencia had on the wall two posters: "Respect the property of the small peasant" and "Respect the property of the small industrialist" (Borkenau, *The Spanish Cockpit*, p. 117). Actually, it was the rich farmer as well who sought protection from the Communists, whom Borkenau describes as constituting the extreme right wing of the Republican forces. By early 1937, according to Borkenau, the Communist party was "to a large extent…the party of the military and administrative personnel, in the second place the party of the petty bourgeoisie and certain well-to-do peasant groups, in the third place the party of the employees, and only in the fourth place the party of the industrial workers" (p. 192). The party also attracted many policy and army officers. The police chief in Madrid and chief of intelligence, for example, were party members. In general, the party, which had been insignificant before the revolution, "gave urban and rural middle classes a powerful access of life and vigour" as it defended them from the revolutionary forces (Bolloten, *op. cit.*, p. 86). Gerald Brenan describes the situation as follows, in *The Spanish Labyrinth* (1943; reprinted Cambridge, Cambridge University Press, 1960), p. 325:

> Unable to draw to themselves the manual workers, who remained firmly fixed in their unions, the Communists found themselves the refuge for all those who had suffered from the excesses of the Revolution of who feared where it might lead them. Well-to-do Catholic orange-growers in Valencia, peasants in Catalonia, shopkeepers and business men, Army officers and Government officials enrolled in their ranks….Thus [in Catalonia] one had a strange and novel situation: on the one side stood the huge compact proletariat of Barcelona with its long revolutionary tradition, and on the other the white-collar workers and *petite bourgeoisie* of the city, organized and armed by the Communist party against it.

Actually, the situation that Brenan describes is not as strange a one as he suggests. It is, rather, a natural consequence of Bolshevik elitism that the "Red bureaucracy" should act as a counterrevolutionary force except under the conditions where its present or future representatives are attempting to seize power for themselves, in the name of the masses whom they pretend to represent.

66 Bolloten, *op. cit.*, p. 189. The legalization of revolutionary actions already undertaken and completed recalls the behavior of the "revolutionary vanguard" in the Soviet Union in 1918. Cf. Arthur Rosenburg, *A History of Bolshevism* (1932; repub-

lished in translation from the original German, New York, Russell and Russell, Publishers, 1965), Ch. 6. He describes how the expropriations, "accomplished as the result of spontaneous action on the part of workers and against the will of the Bolsheviks," were reluctantly legalized by Lenin months later and then placed under central party control. On the relation of the Bolsheviks to the anarchists in postrevolutionary Russia, interpreted from a pro-anarchist point of view, see Guérin, *L'Anarchisme* pp. 96–125. See also Avrich, *op. cit.*, Part II, pp. 123–254.

[67] Bolloten, *op. cit.*, p. 191.

[68] *Ibid.*, p. 194.

[69] For some details, see Vernon Richards, *Lessons of the Spanish Revolution* (London, Freedom Press, 1953), pp. 83–88.

[70] For a moving eyewitness account, see George Orwell, *Homage to Catalonia* (1938; reprinted New York, Harcourt, Brace & World, 1952, and Boston, Beacon Press, 1955; quotations in this book from Beacon Press edition). This brilliant book received little notice at the time of its first publication, no doubt because the picture Orwell drew was in sharp conflict with established liberal dogma. The attention that it has received as a cold-war document since its republication in 1952 would, I suspect, have been of little comfort to the author.

[71] Cited by Rocker, *The Tragedy of Spain*, p. 28.

[72] See *ibid.* for brief review. It was a great annoyance to Hitler that these interests were, to a large extent, protected by Franco.

[73] *Ibid.*, p. 35.

[74] *Op. cit.*, pp. 324 f.

[75] Borkenau, *The Spanish Cockpit*, pp. 289–92. It is because of the essential accuracy of Borkenau's account that I think Hobsbawm (*op. cit.*) is quite mistaken in believing that the Communist policy "was undoubtedly the only one which could have won the Civil War." In fact, the assumption that the Western democracies would join the antifascist effort if only Spain could be preserved as, in effect, a Western colony. Once the Communist leaders saw the futility of this hope, they abandoned the struggle, which was not in their eyes an effort to win the Civil War, but only to serve the interests of Russian foreign policy. I also disagree with Hobsbawm's analysis of the anarchist revolution, cited earlier, for reasons that are implicit in this entire discussion.

[76] *Op. cit.*, pp. 143–44.

[77] Cited by Rosenberg, *op. cit.*, pp. 168–69.

[78] Bolloten, *op. cit.*, p. 84.

[79] *Ibid.*, p. n85. As noted earlier, the "small farmer" included the prosperous orange growers, etc. (see note 65).

[80] Brenan, *op. cit.*, p. 321.

[81] Correspondence from Companys to Prieto, 1939. While Companys, as a Catalonian with separatist impulses, would naturally be inclined to defend Catalonian achievements, he was surely not sympathetic to collectivization, despite his cooperative attitude during the period when the anarchists, with real power in their hands, permitted him to retain nominal authority. I know of no attempt to challenge the accuracy of his assessment. Morrow (*op. cit.*, p. 77) quotes the Catalonian Premier, the entrepreneur Juan Tarradellas, as defending the administration of the collectivized was industries against a Communist (PSUC) attack, which he termed the "most arbitrary falsehoods." There are many other reports commenting on the functioning of the collectivized industries by nonanarchist first hand observers, that tend to support Companys. For example, the Swiss socialist Andres Oltmares is quoted by Rocker (*The Tragedy of Spain*, p. 24) as saying that after the revolution the Catalonian workers' syndicates "in seven weeks accomplished fully as much as France did in fourteen months after the outbreak of the World War." Continuing, he says:

> In the midst of the civil war the Anarchists have proved themselves to be political organizers of the first rank. They kindled in everyone the required sense of responsibility, and knew how by eloquent appeals to keep alive the spirit of sacrifice for the general welfare of the people.
>
> As a Social Democrat I speak here with inner joy and sincere admiration of my experience in Catalonia. The anti-capitalist transformation took place here without their having to resort to a dictatorship. The members of the syndicates are their own masters, and carry on production and the distribution of products of labor under their own management with the advice of technical experts in whom they have confidence. The enthusiasm of the workers is great that they scorn any personal advantage and are concerned only for the welfare of all.

Even Borkenau concludes, rather grudgingly, that industry was functioning fairly well, as far as he could see. The matter deserves a serious study.

[82] Quoted in Richards, *op. cit.*, pp. 46–47.

[83] *Ibid.* Richards suggests that the refusal of the central government to support the Aragon front my have been motivated in part by the general policy of counterrevolution. "This front, largely manned by members of the C.N.T.-F.A.I., was considered of great strategic importance by the anarchists, having as its ultimate objective the linking of Catalonia with the Basque country and Asturias, i.e., a linking of the industrial region [of Catalonia] with an important source of raw materials." Again, it would be interesting to undertake a detailed investigation of this topic.

That the Communists withheld arms from the Aragon front seems established beyond question, and it can hardly be doubted that the motivation was political. See, for example, D.T. Cattell, *Communism and the Spanish Civil War* (1955; reprinted

New York, Russell and Russell, Publishers, 1965), p. 110. Cattell, who in general bends over backwards to try to justify the behavior of the central government, concludes that in this case there is little doubt that the refusal of aid was politically motivated. Brenan takes the same view, claiming that the Communists "kept the Aragon front without arms to spite the Anarchists." The Communists resorted to some of the most grotesque slanders to explain the lack of arms on the Aragon front; for example, the *Daily Worker* attributed the arms shortage to the fact that "the Trotskyist General Kopp has been carting enormous supplies of arms and ammunition across no-man's land to the fascists" (cited by Morrow, *op. cit.*, p. 145). As Morrow points out, George Kopp is a particularly bad choice as a target for such accusations. His record is well known, for example, from the account given by Orwell, who served under his command (see Orwell, *op. cit.*, pp. 209). Orwell was also able to refute, from firsthand observations, many of the other absurdities that were appearing in the liberal press about the Aragon front, for example, the statement by Ralph Bates in the New Republic that the POUM troops were "playing football with the Fascists in no man's land." At that moment, as Orwell observes, "The P.O.U.M. troops were suffering heavy casualties and a number of my personal friends were killed and wounded."

84 Cited in *Living Marxism*, p. 172.

85 Bolloten, *op. cit.*, p. 49, comments on the collectivization of the dairy trade in Barcelona, as follows: "The Anarchosyndicalists eliminated as unhygienic over forty pasteurizing plants, pasteurized all the milk in the remaining nine, and proceeded to displace all dealers by establishing their own dairies. Many of the retailers entered the collective, but some refused to do so: 'They asked for a much higher wage than that paid to the workers…, claiming that they could not manage on the one allotted to them' [*Tierra y Libertad*, August 21, 1937—the newspaper of the FAI, the anarchist activists]." His information is primarily from anarchist sources, which he uses much more extensively than any historian other than Peirats. He does not present any evaluation of these sources, which—like all others—must be used critically.

86 Morrow, *op. cit.*, p. 136.

87 Borkenau, *The Spanish Cockpit*, p. 182.

88 *Ibid.*, p. 183.

89 *Ibid.*, p. 184. According to Borkenau, "it is doubtful whether Comorera is personally responsible for this scarcity; it might have arisen anyway, in pace with the consumption of the harvest." This speculation may or may not be correct. Like Borenau, we can only speculate as to whether the village and workers' committees would have been able to continue to provision Barcelona, with or without central administration, had it not been for the policy of "abstract liberalism," which was of a piece with the general Communist-directed attempts to destroy the Revolutionary organizations and the structures developed in the Revolutionary period.

90 Orwell, *op. cit.*, pp. 109–11. Orwell's description of Barcelona in December (pp. 4–5), when he arrived for the first time, deserves more extensive quotation:

It was the first time I had ever been in a town where the working class was in the saddle. Practically every building of any size had been seized by the workers and was draped with red flats or with the red and black flag of the Anarchists; every wall was scrawled with the hammer and sickle and with the initials of the revolutionary parties; almost every church had been gutted and its images burnt. Churches here and there were being systematically demolished by gangs of workmen. Every shop and café had an inscription saying that it had been collectivized; even the bootblacks had been collectivized and their boxes painted red and black. Waiters and shop-walkers looked you in the face and treated you as an equal. Servile and even ceremonial forms of speech had temporarily disappeared. Nobody said "Senor" or "Don" or even "Usted"; everyone called everyone else "Comrade" and "Thou," and said "Salud!" instead of "Buenos dias." Tipping had been forbidden by law since the time of Primo de Rivera; almost my first experience was receiving a lecture from a hotel manager for trying to tip a lift-boy. There were no private motor cars, they had all been commandeered, and all the trams and taxis and much of the other transport were painted red and black. The revolutionary posters were everywhere, flaming from the walls in clean reds and blues that made the few remaining advertisements look like daubs of mud. Down the Ramblas, the wide central artery of the town where crowds of people streamed constantly to and fro, the loud-speakers were bellowing revolutionary songs all day and far into the night. And it was the aspect of the crowds that was the queerest thing of all. In outward appearance it was a town in which the wealthy classes had practically ceased to exist. Except for a small number of women and foreigners there were no "well-dressed" people at all. Practically everyone wore rough working-class clothes, or blue overalls or some variant of the militia uniform. All this was queer and moving. There was much in it that I did not understand, in some ways I did not even like it, but I recognized it immediately as a state of affairs worth fighting for. Also I believed that things were as they appeared, that this was really a workers' State and that the entire bourgeoisie had either fled, been killed, or voluntarily come over to the workers' side; I did not realize that great numbers of well-to-do bourgeois were simply lying low and disguising themselves as proletarians for the time being...

...waiting for that happy day when Communist power would reintroduce the old state society and destroy popular involvement in the war.

In December 1936, however, the situation was still as described in the following remarks (p. 6):

Yet so far as one can judge the people were contented and hopeful. There was no unemployment, and the price of living was still extremely low; you saw few conspicuously destitute people, and no beggars except the gypsies. Above all, there was a belief in the revolution and the future, a feeling of having suddenly emerged into an era of equality and freedom. Human beings were trying to behave as human beings and not as cogs in the capitalist machine. In the barbers' shops were Anarchist notices (the barbers were mostly Anarchists) solemnly explaining that barbers were no longer slaves. In the streets were coloured posters appealing to prostitutes to stop being prostitutes. To anyone from the hard-boiled, sneering civilization of the English-speaking races there was something rather pathetic in the literalness with which these idealistic Spaniards took the hackneyed phrases of revolution. At that time revolutionary ballads of the naivest kind, all about proletarian brotherhood and the wickedness of Mussolini, were being sold on the streets for a few centimes each. I have often seen an illiterate militiaman buy one of these ballads laboriously spell out the words, and then, when he had got the hang out of it, begin singing it to an appropriate tune.

Recall the dates. Orwell arrived in Barcelona in late December 1936. Comorera's decree abolishing the workers' supply committees and the bread committees was on January 7. Borkenau returned to Barcelona in mid-January; Orwell in April.

91 See Bolloten, *op. cit.*, p. 71, citing the anarchist spokesman Juan Peiro, in September 1936. Like other anarchists and left-wing Socialists, Peiro sharply condemns the use of force to introduce collectivization, taking the position such as Ricardo Zabalza, general secretary of the Federation of Land Workers, who stated, on January 8, 1937: "I prefer a small, enthusiastic collective, formed by a group of active and honest workers, to a large collective set up by force and compost of peasants without enthusiasm, who would sabotage it until it failed. Voluntary collectivization may seem the longer course, but the example of the small, well-managed collective will attract the entire peasantry, who are profoundly realistic and practical, whereas forced collectivization would end by discrediting socialized agriculture" (cited by Bolloten *op. cit.*, p. 59). However, there seems no doubt that the precepts of the anarchist and left-socialist spokesmen were often violated in practice.

92 Borkenau, *The Spanish Cockpit*, pp. 219–21. Of this officer, Jackson says only that he was "a dependable professional officer." After the fall of Málaga, Lieutenant Colonel Villalba was tried for treason, for having deserted the headquarters and abandoned his troops. Broué and Témime remark that it is difficult to determine what justice there was in the charge.

93 Jesus Hernandez and Juan Comorera, *Spain Organises for Victory: The Policy of the Communist Party of Spain Explained* (London, Communist Party of Great Britain, n.d.), cited by Richards, *op. cit.*, pp. 99–100. There was no accusation that the phone service was restricted, but only that the revolutionary workers could maintain "a close

check on the conversations that took place between the politicians." As Richards further observes, "It is, of course, a quite different matter when the 'indiscreet ear' is that of the O.G.P.U."

94 Broué and Témime, *op. cit.*, p. 266.

95 Jackson, *op. cit.*, p. 370. Thomas suggests that Sese was probably killed accidentally (*The Spanish Civil War*, p. 428).

96 The anarchist mayor of the border town of Puigcerdá had been assassinated in April, after Negrín's carabineros had taken over the border posts. That same day a prominent UGT member, Roldan Cortada, was murdered in Barcelona, it is presumed by CNT militants. This presumption is disputed by Peirats (*Los Anarquistas*: see note 58), who argues, with some evidence, that the murder may well have been a Stalinist provocation. In reprisal, a CNT man was killed. Orwell, whose eyewitness account of the May Days is unforgettable, points out the "One can gauge the attitude of the foreign capitalist Press toward the Communist-Anarchist feud by the fact that Roldan's murder was given wide publicity, while the answering murder was carefully unmentioned" (*op. cit.*, p. 119). Similarly, one can gauge Jackson's attitude towards this struggle by his citation of Sese's murder as a critical event, while the murder of Berneri goes unmentioned (cf. notes 64 and 95). Orwell remarks elsewhere that "In the English press, in particular, you would have to search for a long time before finding any favourable reference, at any period of the war, to the Spanish Anarchists. They have been systematically denigrated, and, as I know by my own experience, it is almost impossible to get anyone to print anything in their defence" (p. 159). Little has changed since.

97 According to Orwell (*op. cit.*, pp. 153–54), "A British cruiser and two British destroyers had closed in upon the harbour, and no doubt there were other warships not far away. The English newspapers gave it out that these ships were proceeding to Barcelona 'to protect British interests,' but in fact they made no move to do so; that is they did not land any men or take off any refuges. There can be no certainty about this, but it was at least inherently likely that the British Government, which had not raised a finger to save the Spanish Government from Franco, would interview quickly enough to save it from its won working class." This assumption may well have influenced the left-wing leadership to restrain the Barcelona workers from simply taking control of the whole city, as apparently they could easily have done in the initial stages of the May Days.

Hugh Thomas comments (*The Spanish Civil War*, p. 428) that there was "no reason" for Orwell's "apprehension" on this matter. In the light of the British record with regard to Spain, it seems to me that Thomas is simply unrealistic, as compared with Orwell, in this respect.

98 Orwell, *op. cit.*, pp. 143–44.

99 *Controversy*, August 1937, cited by Morrow, p. 173. The prediction was incorrect, though not unreasonable. Had the Western powers and the Soviet Union wished, compromise would have been possible, it appears, and Spain might have been saved

the terrible consequences of a Franco victory. See Brenan, *op. cit.*, p. 331. He attributes the British failure to support an armistice and possible reconciliation to the fact that Chamberlain "saw nothing disturbing in the prospect of an Italian and German victory." It would be interesting to explore more fully the attitude of Winston Churchill. In April 1937 he stated that a Franco victory would not harm British interests. Rather, the danger was "a success of the trotskyists and anarchists" (cited by Broué and Témime, *op. cit.*, p. 172). Of some interest, in this connection, is the recent discovery of an unpublished Churchill essay written in March 1939—six months after Munich—in which he said that England "would welcome and aid a genuine Hitler of peace and toleration" (see *New York Times*, December 12, 1965).

[100] I find no mention at all in Hugh Thomas, *The Spanish Civil War*. The account here is largely taken from Broué and Témime, pp. 279–80.

[101] *Op. cit.*, p. 405. A footnote comments on the "leniency" of the government to those arrested. Jackson has nothing to say about the charges against Ascaso and others, or the manner in which the old order was restored in Aragon.

To appreciate these events more fully, one should consider, by comparison, the concern for civil liberties shown by Negron on the second, antifascist front. In an interview after the war he explained to John Whitaker (*We Cannot Escape History* [New York, The Macmillan Company, 1943], pp. 116–18) why his government had been so ineffective in coping with the fifth column, even in the case of known fascist agents. Negron explained that "we couldn't arrest a man on suspicion; we couldn't break with the rules of evidence. You can't risk arresting an innocent man because you are positive in your own mind that he is guilty. You prosecute a war, yes; but you also live with your conscience." Evidently, these scruples did not pertain when it was the rights of anarchist and socialist workers, rather than fascist agents, that were at stake.

[102] Cf. Broué and Témime, p. 262. Ironically, the government forces included some anarchist troops, the only ones to enter Barcelona.

[103] See Bolloten, *op. cit.*, p. 55, n. 1, for an extensive list of sources.

[104] Broué and Témime cite the socialists Alardo Prats, Fenner Brockway, and Carlo Rosseli. Borkenau, on the other hand, suspected that the role of terror was great in collectivization. He cites very little to substantiate his feeling, though some evidence is available from anarchist sources. See note 91 above.

Some general remarks on collectivization by Rosselli and Brockway are cited by Rudolf Rocker in his essay "Anarchism and Anarcho-syndicalism," n. 1 in Paul Eltzbach, ed., *Anarchism* (London, Freedom Press, 1960), p. 266:

> Rosselli: In three months Catalonia has been able to set up a new social order on the ruins of an ancient system. This is chiefly due to the Anarchists, who have revealed a quite remarkable sense of proportion, realistic understanding, and organizing ability....All the revolutionary forces of Catalonia have united in a program of Sydicalist-Socialist character...Anarcho-Syndicalism, hitherto so despised, has revealed itself as a great constructive force. I am no

Anarchist, but I regard it as my duty to express here my opinion of the Anarchists of Catalonia, who have all too often been represented as a destructive if not a criminal element.

Brockway: I was impressed by the strength of the C.N.T. It was unnecessary to tell that it is the largest and most vital of the working class organizations in Spain. That was evident on all sides. The large industries were clearly in the main in the hands of the C.N.T.—railways, road transport, shipping, engineering, textiles, electricity, building, agriculture....I was immensely impressed by the constructive revolutionary work which is being done by the C.N.T. Their achievements of workers' control in industry is an inspiration... There are still some Britishers and Americans who regard the Anarchists of Spain as impossible, undisciplined uncontrollables. This is poles away from the truth. The Anarchists of Spain, through the C.N.T., are doing one of the biggest constructive jobs ever done by the working class. At the front they are fighting Fascism. Behind the front they are actually the new workers' society. They see that the war against Fascism and the carrying through the social revolution are inseparable. Those who have seen them and understood what they are doing must honor them and be grateful to them.... That is surely the biggest thing which has hitherto been done by the workers in any part of the world.

105 Cited by Richards, *op. cit.*, pp. 76–81, where long descriptive quotations are given.

106 See Hugh Thomas, "Anarchist Agrarian Collectives in the Spanish Civil War" (note 59). He cites figures showing that agricultural production went up in Aragon and Castille, where collectivization was extensive, and down in Catalonia and the Levant, where peasant proprietors were the dominant element.

Thomas' is, to my knowledge, the only attempt by a profssional historian to assess the data on agricultural collectivization in Spain in a systematic way. He concludes that the collectives were probably "a considerable social success" and must have had strong popular support, but he is more doubtful about their economic viability. His suggestion that "Communist pressure on the collectives may have given them the necessary urge to survive" seems quite unwarranted, as does his suggestion that "the very existence of the war...may have been responsible for some of the success the collectives had." On the contrary, their success and spontaneous creation throughout Republican Spain suggest that they answered to deeply felt popular sentiments, and both the war and Communist pressure appear to have been highly disruptive factors—ultimately, of course, destructive factors.

Other dubious conclusions are that "in respect of redistribution of wealth, anarchist collectives were hardly much improvement over capitalism" since "no effective way of limiting consumption in richer collectives was devised to help poorer ones," and that there was no possibility of developing large-scale planning. On the contrary, Bolloten (*op. cit.*, pp. 176–79) points out that "In order to remedy the defects of collectivization, as well as to iron out discrepancies in the living standards of the workers in flourishing and impoverished enterprises, the Anarchosyndicalists, although rootedly opposed to nationalization, advocated the centralization—or, socialization, as they called it—under trade union control, of entire branches of production." He mentions a number of examples of partial socialization that had some success, citing as the major difficulty that prevented still greater progress the insistence of the Communist party and the UFT leadership—though apparently not all of the rank-and-file members of the UFT—on government ownership and control. According to Richards (*op. cit.*, p. 82): "In June, 1937 ...a National Plenum of Regional Federations of Peasants was held in Valencia to discuss the formation of a National Federation of Peasants for the co-ordination and extension of the collectivist movement and also to ensure an equitable distribution of the produce of the land, not only between the collectives but for the whole country. Again in Castille in October 1937, a merging of the 100,000 members of the Regional Federation of Peasants and the 13,000 members in the food distributive trades took place. It represented a logical step in ensuring better co-ordination, and was accepted for the whole of Spain at the National congress of Collectives held in Valencia in November 1937." Still other plans were under consideration for regional and national coordination—see, for example, D.A. de Santillan, *After the Revolution* (New York, Greenberg Publisher, Inc., 1937), for some ideas.

Thomas feels that collectives could not have survived more than "a few years while primitive misery was being overcome." I see nothing in his data to support this conclusion. The Palestinian experience has shown that collectives can remain both a social and an economic success over a long period. The success of Spanish collectivization under war conditions, seems amazing. One can obviously not be certain whether these successes could have been secured and extended had it not been for the combined fascist, Communist, and liberal attack, but I can find no objective basis for the almost universal skepticism. Again, this seems to me merely a matter of irrational prejudice.

107 The following is a brief description by the anarchist writer Gaston Leval, *Ne Franco, Ne Stalin, le collecttivita anarchiche spagnole nella lotta contro Franco e la reazione staliniana* (Milan, Istituto Editoriale Italiano, 1952), pp. 303 f.; sections reprinted in *Collectivites anarchists en Espagne revolutionnaire, Noir et Rouge*, undated.

> In the middle of the month of June, the attack began in Aragon on a grand scale and with hitherto unknown methods. The harvest was approaching. Rifles in hand, treasury guards under Communist orders stopped trucks loaded with provisions on the highways and brought them to their offices. A little later, the same guards poured into the collectives and confiscated great quantities of wheat under the authority of the general staff with the headquarters in Barbastro....Later open attacks began, under the command of Lister with troops withdrawn from the front at Belchite more than 50 kilometers away, in the month of August....The final result was

that 30 percent of the collectives were completely destroyed. In Alcolea, the municipal council that governed the collective was arrested; the people who lived in the Home for the Aged…were thrown out on the street. In Mas de las Matas, in Monzon, in Barbastro, on all sides, there were arrests. Plundering took place everywhere. The stores of the cooperatives and their grain supplies were rifled; furnishings were destroyed. The governor of Aragon, who was appointed by the central government after the dissolution of the Council of Aragon—which appears to have been the signal for the armed attack against the collectives—protested. He was told to go to the devil.

On October 22, at the National Congress of Peasants, the delegation of the Regional Committee of Aragon presented a report of which the following is the summary:

"More than 600 organizers of collectives have been arrested. The government has appointed management committees that seized the warehousing and distrusted their contents at random. Land, draught animals, and tools were given to individual families or to the fascists who had been spared by the revolution. The harvest was distributed in the same way. The animal raised by the collectives suffered the same fate. A great number of collectivized pig farms, stables, and dairies were destroyed. In certain communes, such as Brodon and Calaceite, even seed was confiscated and the peasants are now unable to work the land."

The estimate that 30 percent of the collectives were destroyed is consistent with figures reported by Peirats (*Los anarquistas en la crisis politica española*, p. 300). He points out that only 200 delegates attended the congress of collectives of Aragon in September 1937 ("held under the shadow of the bayonets of the Eleventh Division" of Lister) as compared with 500 delegates at the congress of the preceding February. Peirats states that an army division of Catalan separatists and another division of the PSUC also occupied parts of Aragon during this operation, while three anarchist divisions remained at the front, under orders from the CNT-FAI leadership. Compare Jackson's explanation of the occupation of Aragon: "The peasants were known to hate the Consejo, *the anarchists had deserted the front during the Barcelona fighting,* and the very existence of the Consejo was a standing challenge to the authority of the central government" (italics mine).

[108] Regarding Bolloten's work, Jackson has this to say: "Throughout the present chapter, I have drawn heavily on this carefully documented study of the Communist Party in 1936–37. It is unrivaled in its coverage of the wartime press, of which Bolloten, himself a UP correspondent in Spain made a large collection" (p. 363 n.).

[109] See note 64. A number of citations from Berneri's writings are given by Broué and Témime. Morrow also presents several passages from his journal, *Guerra di Classe*. A

collection of his works would be a very useful contribution to our understanding of the Spanish Civil War and to the problems of revolutionary war in general.

110 Cattell, *op. cit.*, p. 208. See also the remarks by Borkenau, Brenan, and Bolloten cited earlier. Neither Cattell nor Borkenau regards this decline of fighting spirit as a major factor, however.

111 *op. cit.*, p. 195, n. 7.

112 To this extent, Trotsky took a similar position. See his *Lesson of Spain* (London, Workers' International Press, 1937).

113 Cited in Richards, *op. cit.*, p. 23.

114 H.E. Kaminsk, *Ceux de Barcelone* (Paris, Les Editions Denoel, 1937), p. 181. This book contains very interesting observations on anarchist Spain by a skeptical though sympathetic eyewitness.

115 May 15, 1937. Cited by Richards, *op. cit.*, p. 106.

116 Cited by Broué and Témime , *op. cit.*, p. 258, n. 34. The conquest of Saragossa was the goal, never realized, of the anarchist militia in Aragon.

117 *Ibid.*, p. 175.

118 *Ibid.*, p. 193.

119 The fact was not lost of foreign journalists. Morrow (*op. cit.*, p. 68) quotes James Minifie in the *New York Herald Tribune*, April 28, 1937: "A reliable police force is being built up quietly but surely. The Valencia government discovered an ideal instrument for this purpose in the Carabineros. These were formerly customs officers and guards, and always had a good reputation for loyalty. It is reported on good authority that 40,000 have been recruited for this force, and that 20,000 have already been armed and equipped....The anarchists have already noticed and complained about the increased strength of this force at a time when we all know there's little enough traffic coming over the frontiers, land or sea. They realize that it will be used against them." Consider what these soldiers, as well as Lister's division or the *asaltos* described by Orwell, might have accomplished on the Aragon front, for example. Consider also the effect on the militiamen, deprived of arms by the central government, of the knowledge that these well-armed, highly trained troops were liquidating the accomplishments of their revolution.

120 Cited in Rocker, *The Tragedy of Spain*, p. 37.

121 For references, see Bolloten, *op. cit.*, p. 192, no. 12.

122 Cited in Rocker, *The Tragedy of Spain*, p. 37.

123 Liston M. Oak, "Balance Sheet of the Spanish Revolution," *Socialist Review*, Vol. 6 (September 1937), pp. 7–9, 26. This reference was brought to my attention by William B. Watson. A striking example of the distortion introduced by propaganda efforts of the 1930s is the strange story of the influential film *The Spanish Earth*, filmed in 1937 by Joris Ivens with a text (Written afterwards) by Hemingway—a project that was apparently initiated by Dos Passos. A very revealing account of this

matter, and of the perception of the Civil War by Hemingway and Dos Passos, is given in W.B. Watson and Barton Whaley, "The Spanish Earth of Dos Passos and Hemingway," unpublished, 1967. The film dealt with the collectivized village of Fuentiduena in Valencia (a village collectivized by the UGT, incidentally). For the libertarian Dos Passos, the revolution was the dominant theme; it was the antifascist war, however, that was to preoccupy Hemingway. The role of Dos Passos was quickly forgotten, because of the fact (as Watson and Whaley point out) that Dos Passos had become anathema to the Left for his criticisms of communist policies in Spain.

[124] As far as the East is concerned, Rocker (*The Tragedy of Spain*, p. 25) claims that "the Russian press, for reasons that are easily understood" never uttered one least little word about the efforts of the Spanish workers and peasants at social reconstruction." I cannot check the accuracy of this claim, but it would hardly be surprising if it were correct.

[125] See Patricia A.M. Van der Esch, *Prelude to War: The International Repercussions of the Spanish Civil War (1935–1939)* (The Hague, Martinus Nijhoff, 1951), p. 47, and Brenan, *op. cit.*, p. 329, n. 1. The conservative character of the Basque government was also, apparently, largely a result of French pressure. See Broué and Témime , *op. cit.*, p. 172, n. 8.

[126] See Dante A. Puzzo, *Spain and the Great Powers: 1936–1941* (New York, Columbia University Press, 1962), pp. 86 f. This book gives a detailed and very insightful analysis of the international background of the Civil War.

[127] Jules Sauerwein, dispatch to the *New York Times* dated July 26. Cited by Puzzo, *op. cit.*, p. 84.

[128] Cf., for example, Jackson, *op. cit.*, pp. 248 f.

[129] As reported by Herschel V. Johnson of the American embassy in London; cited by Puzzo, *op. cit.*, p. 100.

[130] See Broué and Témime, *op. cit.*, pp. 288–289.

[131] Cited by Thomas, *The Spanish Civil War*, p. 531, n. 3. Rocker, *The Tragedy of Spain*, p. 14, quotes (without reference) a proposal by Churchill for a five-year "neutral dictatorship" to "tranquilize" the country, after which they could "perhaps look for a revival of parliamentary institutions."

[132] Puzzo, *op. cit.*, p. 116.

[133] *Ibid.*, p. 147. Eden is referring, of course, to the Soviet Union. For an analysis of Russian assistance to the Spanish Republic, see Cattell, *op. cit.*, Ch. 8.

[134] Cf. Puzzo, *op. cit.*, pp. 147–48.

[135] *Ibid.*, p. 212.

[136] *Ibid.*, p. 93.

[137] *Op. cit.*, p. 248.

[138] Puzzo, *op. cit.*, p. 151 f.

[139] *Ibid.*, pp. 154–55 and n. 27.

[140] For some references, see Allen Guttmann, *The Wound in the Heart: America and the Spanish Civil War* (New York, The Free Press, 1962), pp. 137–138. The earliest quasi-official reference that I know of is Herbert Feis, *The Spanish Story*, (New York, Alfred A Knopf, 1948), where data is given in an appendix. Jackson (*op. cit.*, p. 256) refers to this matter, without noting that Texaco was violating a prior agreement with the Republic. He states that the American government could do nothing about this, since "oil was not considered a war material under the Neutrality Act." He does not point out, however, that Robert Cuse, the Martin Company, and the Mexican government were put under heavy pressure to withhold supplies from the Republic, although this too was quite legal. As noted, the Texaco Company was never even branded "unethical" or "unpatriotic," these epithets of Roosevelt's being reserved for those who tried to assist the Republic. The cynic might ask just why oil was excluded from the Neutrality Act of January 1937, noting that while Germany and Italy were capable of supplying arms to Franco, they could not meet his demands for oil.

The Texaco Oil Company continued to act upon the pro-Nazi sympathies of its head, Captain Thorkild Rieber, until August 1940, when the publicity began to be a threat to business. See Feis, *op. cit.*, for further details. For more on these matters, see Richard P. Traina, *American Diplomacy and the Spanish Civil War* (Bloomington, Indiana University Press, 1968), pp. 166 f.

[141] Puzzo, *op. cit.*, p. 160. He remarks: "A government in Madrid in which Socialists, Communists, and anarchists sat was not without menace to American business interests both in Spain and Latin America" (p. 165). Hull, incidentally, was in error about the acts of the Spanish government. The irresponsible left-wing elements had not been given arms but had seized them, thus preventing an immediate Franco victory.

[142] See Jackson, *op. cit.*, p. 458.

[143] Cf. Buttmann, *op. cit.*, p. 197. Of course, American liberalism was always proloyalist, and opposed both to Franco and to the revolution. The attitude toward the latter is indicated with accuracy by this comparison, noted by Guttmann, p. 165: "300 people met in Union Square to hear Liston Oak [see note 123] expose the Stalinists' role in Spain; 20,000 met in Madison Square Garden to help Earl Browder and Norman Thomas celebrate the preservation of bourgeois democracy," in July 1937.

[144] *Ibid.*, p. 198.

[145] To conclude these observations about the international reaction, it should be noted that the Vatican recognized the Franco government *de facto* in August 1937 and *de jure* in May 1938. Immediately upon Franco's final victory, Pope Pius XII made the following statement: "Peace and victory have been willed by God to Spain...which has now given to proselytes of the materialistic atheism of our age the highest proof that above all things stands the eternal value of religion and of the Spirit." Of course, the position of the Catholic Church has since undergone important shifts—something that cannot be said of the American government.

[146] See note 60.

147 See, for example, the reference to Machajski in Harold D. Lasswell, *The World Revolution of Our Time: A Framework for Basic Policy Research* (Hoover Institute Studies; Stanford, Calif., Stanford University Press, 1951); reprinted with extensions, in Harold D. Lasswell and Daniel Lerner, eds., *World Revolutionary Elites: Studies in Coercive Ideological Movements* (Cambridge, Mass., The M.I.T. Press, 1965), pp. 29–96. Daniel Bell has a more extensive discussion of Machajski's critique of socialism as the ideology of a new system of exploitation in which the "intellectual workers" will dominate, in a very informative essay that bears directly on a number of the topics that have been mentioned here: "Two Roads from Marx: The Themes of Alienation and Exploitation, and Workers' Control in Socialist Thought," in *The End of Ideology*, pp. 335–68.

148 Lasswell, op. cit., p. 85. In this respect, Lasswell's prognosis resembles that of Bell in the essays cited earlier.

149 Summarized in the *Christian Science Monitor*, March 15, 1968. I have not seen the text and therefore cannot judge the accuracy of the report.

150 To mention just the most recent example: on January 22, 1968, McNamara testified before the Senate Armed Services Committee that "the evidence appears overwhelming that beginning in 1966 Communist local and guerrilla forces have sustained substantial attrition. As a result, there has been a drop in combat efficiency and *morale....*" The Tet offensive was launched within a week of this testimony. See *I.F. Stone's Weekly*, February 19, 1968, for some highly appropriate commentary.

151 The reality behind the rhetoric has been amply reported. A particularly revealing description is given by Katsuichi Honda, a reporter for *Asahi Shimbun*, in *Vietnam— A Voice from the Villages*, 1967, obtainable from the Committee for the English Publication of "Vietnam—a Voice from the Villages," c/o Mrs. Reiko Ishida, 2-13-7, Bunkyo-Ku, Tokyo.

TWO
LANGUAGE AND FREEDOM
(1970)

When I was invited to speak on the topic "language and freedom," I was puzzled and intrigued. Most of my professional life has been devoted to the study of language. There would be no great difficulty in finding a topic to discuss in that domain. And there is much to say about the problems of freedom and liberation as they pose themselves to us and to others in the mid-twentieth century. What is troublesome in the title of this lecture is the conjunction. In what way are language and freedom to be interconnected?

As a preliminary, let me say just a word about the contemporary study of language, as I see it. There are many aspects of language and language use that raise intriguing questions, but—in my judgment—only a few have so far led to productive theoretical work. In particular, our deepest insights are in the area of formal grammatical structure. A person who knows a language has acquired a system of rules and principles—a "generative grammar," in technical terms—that associates sound and meaning in some specific fashion. There are many reasonably well-founded and, I think, rather enlightening hypotheses as to the character of such grammars, for quite a number of languages. Furthermore, there has been a renewal of interest in "universal grammar," interpreted now as the theory that tries to specify the general properties of these languages that can be learned in the normal way by humans. Here too, significant progress has been achieved. The subject is of particular importance. It is appropriate to regard universal grammar as the study of one of the essential faculties of mind. It is, therefore, extremely interesting to discover, as I believe we do, that the principles of universal grammar are rich, abstract, and restrictive, and can be used to construct principled explanations for a variety of phenomena. At the present stage of our understanding, if language is to provide a springboard for the investigation of other problems of man, it is these aspects of language to which we will have to turn our attention, for the simple reason that it is only these aspects that are reasonably well understood. In another sense, the study of formal properties of language reveals something of the nature of man in a negative way: it underscores, with great clarity, the limits of our understanding of those qualities of mind that are apparently unique to man and that must enter into his cultural achievements in an intimate, if still quite obscure manner.

In searching for a point of departure, one turns naturally to a period in the history of Western thought when it was possible to believe that "the thought of making freedom the sum and substance of philosophy has emancipated the human spirit in all its relationships, and…has given to science in all its parts a more powerful reorientation than any earlier revolution."[1] The word "revolution" bears multiple associations in this passage, for Schelling also proclaims that "man is born to act and not to speculate"; and when he writes that "the time has come to proclaim to a nobler humanity the freedom of the spirit, and no longer to have patience with men's tearful regrets for their lost chains," we hear the echoes of the libertarian thought and revolutionary acts of the late eighteenth century. Schelling writes that "the beginning and end of all philosophy is—Freedom." These words are invested with meaning and urgency at a time when men are struggling to cast off their chains, to resist authority that has lost its claim to legitimacy, to construct more humane and more democratic social institutions. It is at such a time that the philosopher may be driven to inquire into the nature of human freedom and its limits, and perhaps to conclude, with Schelling, that with respect to the human ego, "its essence is freedom"; and with respect to philosophy, "the highest dignity of Philosophy consists precisely therein, that it stakes all on human freedom."

We are living, once again, at such a time. A revolutionary ferment is sweeping the so-called Third World, awakening enormous masses from torpor and acquiescence in traditional authority. There are those who feel that the industrial societies as well are ripe for revolutionary change—and I do not refer only to representatives of the New Left. See for example, the remarks of Paul Ricoeur cited in chapter 6 [of Chomsky's *For Reasons of State*], pages 308–9.

The threat of revolutionary change brings forth repression and reaction. Its signs are evident in varying forms, in France, in the Soviet Union, in the United States—not least, in the city where we are meeting. It is natural, then, that we should consider, abstractly, the problems of human freedom, and turn with interest and serious attention to the thinking of an earlier period when archaic social institutions were subjected to critical analysis and sustained attack. It is natural and appropriate, so long as we bear in mind Schelling's admonition, that man is born not merely to speculate but also to act.

One of the earliest and most remarkable of the eighteenth-century investigations of freedom and servitude is Rousseau's *Discourse on Inequality* (1775), in many ways a revolutionary tract. In it, he seeks to "set forth the origin and progress of inequality, the establishment and abuse of political societies, insofar as these things can be deduced from the nature of man by the light of reason alone." His conclusions were sufficiently shocking that the judges of the prize competition of the Academy of Dijon, to whom the work was originally submitted, refused to hear the manuscript through.[2] In it, Rousseau challenges the legitimacy of virtually every social institution, as well as individual control of property and wealth. These are "usurpations…established only on a precarious and abusive right…. Having been acquired only by force, force could take them away without [the rich] having grounds for complaint." Not even property acquired by personal industry is held "upon better titles." Against such a claim, one might object: "Do you not know that a multitude of your brethren die or suffer from need of what you have in excess, and that you needed express and unanimous consent of the human race to appropriate for yourself anything from common subsistence that exceeded your own?" It is contrary to the law of nature that "a handful of men be glutted with superfluities while the starving multitude lacks necessities."

Rousseau argues that civil society is hardly more than a conspiracy by the rich to guarantee their plunder. Hypocritically, the rich call upon their neighbors to "institute regulations of justice and peace to which all are obliged to conform, which make an exception of no one, and which compensate in some way for the caprices of fortune by equally subjecting the powerful and the weak to mutual duties"—those laws which, as Anatole France was to say, in their majesty deny to the rich and the poor equally the right to sleep under the bridge at night. By such arguments, the poor and weak were seduced: "All ran to meet their chains thinking they secured their freedom...." Thus society and laws "gave new fetters to the weak and new forces to the rich, destroyed natural freedom for all time, established forever the law of property and inequality, changed a clever usurpation into an irrevocable right, and for the profit of a few ambitious men henceforth subjected the whole human race to work, servitude and misery." Governments inevitably tend towards arbitrary power, as "their corruption and extreme limit." This power is "by its nature illegitimate," and new revolutions must

> dissolve the government altogether or bring it closer to its legitimate institution.... The uprising that ends by strangling or dethroning a sultan is as lawful an act as those by which he disposed, the day before, of the lives and goods of his subjects. Force alone maintained him, force alone overthrows him.

What is interesting, in the present connection, is the path that Rousseau follows to reach these conclusions "by the light of reason alone," beginning with his ideas about the nature of man. He wants to see man "as nature formed him." It is from the nature of man that the principles of natural right and the foundations of social existence must be deduced.

> This same study of original man, of his true needs, and of the principles underlying his duties, is also the only good means one could use to remove those crowds of difficulties which present themselves concerning the origin of moral inequality, the true foundation of the body politic, the reciprocal rights of its members, and thousand similar questions as important as they are ill explained.

To determine the nature of man, Rousseau proceeds to compare man and animal. Man is "intelligent, free...the sole animal endowed with reason." Animals are "devoid of intellect and freedom."

In every animal I see only an ingenious machine to which nature has given senses in order to revitalize itself and guarantee itself, to a certain point, from all that tends to destroy or upset it. I perceive precisely the same things in the human machine, with the difference that nature alone does everything in the operations of a beast, whereas man contributes to his operations by being a free agent. The former chooses or rejects by instinct and the latter by an act of freedom, so that a beast cannot deviate from the rule that is prescribed to it even when it would be advantageous for it to do so, and a man deviates from it often to his detriment....it is not so much understanding which constitutes the distinction of man among the animals as it is his being a free agent. Nature commands every animal, and the beast obeys. Man feels the same impetus, but he realizes that he is free to acquiesce or resist; and it is above all in the consciousness of this freedom that the spirituality of his soul is shown. For physics explains in some way the mechanism of the senses and the formation of ideas; but in the power of willing, or rather of choosing, and in the sentiment of this power are found only purely spiritual acts about which the laws of mechanics explain nothing.

104   Thus the essence of human nature is man's freedom and his consciousness of his freedom. So Rousseau can say that "the jurists, who have gravely pronounced that the child of a slave would be born a slave, have decided in other terms that a man would not be born a man."[3]

Sophistic politicians and intellectuals search for ways to obscure the fact that the essential and defining property of man is his freedom: "they attribute to men a natural inclination to servitude, without thinking that it is the same for freedom as for innocence and virtue—their value is felt only as long as one enjoys them oneself and the taste for them is lost as soon as one has lost them." In contrast, Rousseau asks rhetorically "whether, freedom being the most noble of man's faculties, it is not degrading one's nature, putting oneself on the level of beasts enslaved by instinct, even offending the author of one's being, to renounce without reservation the most precious of all his gifts and subject ourselves to committing all the crimes he forbids us in order to please a ferocious or insane master"—a question that has been asked, in similar terms, by many an American draft resister in the last few years, and by many other who are beginning to recover from the catastrophe of twentieth-century Western civilization, which has so tragically confirmed Rousseau's judgment:

Hence arose the national wars, battles, murders, and reprisals which make nature tremble and shock reason, and all those horrible prejudices which rank the honor of shedding human blood among the virtues. The most decent men learned to consider it one of their duties to murder their fellowmen; at length men were seen to massacre each other by the thousands without knowing why; more murders were committed on a single day of fighting and more horrors in the capture of a single city than were committed in the state of nature during whole centuries over the entire face of the earth.

The proof of his doctrine that the struggle for freedom is an essential human attribute, that the value of freedom is felt only as long as one enjoys it, Rousseau sees in "the marvels done by all free peoples to guard themselves from oppression." True, those who have abandoned the life of a free man

do nothing but boast incessantly of the peace and repose they enjoy in their chains.... But when I see the others sacrifice pleasures, repose, wealth, power, and life itself for the preservation of this sole good which is so disdained by those who have lost it; when I see animals born free and despising captivity break their heads against the bars of their prison; when I see multitudes of entirely naked savages scorn European voluptuousness and endure hunger, fire, the sword, and death to preserve only their independence, I feel that it does not behoove slaves to reason about freedom.

Rather similar thoughts were expressed by Kant, forty years later. He cannot, he says, accept the proposition that certain people "are not ripe for freedom," for example, the serfs of some landlord. **105**

If one accepts this assumption, freedom will never be achieved; for one can not arrive at the maturity for freedom without having already acquired it; one must be free to learn how to make use of one's powers freely and usefully. The first attempts will surely be brutal and will lead to a state of affairs more painful and dangerous than the former condition under the dominance but also the protection of an external authority. However, one can achieve reason only through one's own experiences and one must be free to be able to undertake them.... To accept the principle that freedom is worthless for those under one's control and that one has the right to refuse it to them forever, is an infringement on the rights of God himself, who has created man to be free.[4]

The remark is particularly interesting because of its context. Kant was defending the French Revolution, during the Terror, against those who claimed that it showed the masses to be unready for the privilege of freedom. Kant's remarks have contemporary relevance. No rational person will approve of violence and terror. In particular, the terror of the postrevolutionary state, fallen into the hands of a grim autocracy, has more than once reached indescribable levels of savagery. Yet no person of understanding or humanity will too quickly condemn the violence that often occurs when long-subdued masses rise against their oppressors, or take their first steps towards liberty and social reconstruction.

Let me return now to Rousseau's argument against the legitimacy of established authority, whether that of political power or of wealth. It is striking that his argument, up to this point, follows a familiar Cartesian model. Man is uniquely beyond the bounds of physical explanation; the beast, on the other hand, is merely an ingenious machine, commanded by natural law. Man's freedom and his consciousness of this freedom distinguish him from the beast-machine. The principles of mechanical explanation are incapable of accounting for these human properties, though they can account for sensation and even the combination of ideas, in which regard "man differs from a beast only in degree."

To Descartes and his followers, such as Cordemoy, the only sure sign that another organism has a mind, and hence also lies beyond the bounds of mechanical explanation, is its use of language in the normal, creative human fashion, free from control by identifiable stimuli, novel and innovative, appropriate to situations, coherent, and engendering in our minds new thoughts and ideas.[5] To the Cartesians, it is obvious by introspection that each man possesses a mind, a substance whose essence is thought; his creative use of language reflects this freedom of thought and conception. When we have evidence that another organism too uses language in this free and creative fashion, we are led to attribute to it as well a mind like ours. From similar assumptions regarding the intrinsic limits of mechanical explanation, its inability to account for man's freedom and consciousness of his freedom, Rousseau proceeds to develop his critique of authoritarian institutions, which deny to man his essential attribute of freedom, in varying degree.

Were we to combine these speculations, we might develop an interesting connection between language and freedom. Language, in its essential properties and the manner of its use provides the basic criterion for determining that another organism is a being with a human mind and the human capacity for free thought and self-expression, and with the essential human need for freedom from the external constraints of repressive authority. Furthermore, we might try to proceed from the detailed investigation of language and its use to a deeper and more specific understanding of the human mind. Proceeding on this model, we might further attempt to study other aspects of that human nature which, as Rousseau rightly observes, must be correctly conceived if we are to be able to develop, in theory, the foundations for a rational social order.

I will return to this problem, but first I would like to trace further Rousseau's thinking about the matter. Rousseau diverges from the Cartesian tradition in several respects. He defines the "specific characteristic of the human species" as man's "faculty of self-perfection," which, "with the aid of circumstances, successively develops all the others, and resides among us as much in the species as in the individual." The faculty of self-perfection and of perfection of the human species through cultural transmission is not, to my knowledge, discussed in any similar terms by the Cartesians. However, I think that Rousseau's remarks might be interpreted as a development of the Cartesian tradition in an unexplored direction, rather than as a denial and rejection of it. There is no inconsistency in the notion that the restrictive attributes of mind underlie a historically evolving human nature that develops within the limits that they set; or that these attributes of mind provide the possibility for self-perfection; or that, by providing that consciousness of freedom, these essential attributes of human nature give man the opportunity to create social conditions and social forms to maximize the possibilities for freedom, diversity, and individual self-realization. To use an arithmetical analogy, the integers do no fail to be an infinite set merely because they do not exhaust the rational numbers. Analogously, it is no denial of man's capacity for infinite "self-perfection" to hold that there are intrinsic properties of mind that constrain his development. I would like to argue that in a sense the opposite is true, that without a system of formal constraints there are no creative acts; specifically, in the absence of intrinsic and restrictive properties of mind, there can be only "shaping of behavior" but no creative acts of self-perfection. Furthermore, Rousseau's concern for the evolutionary character of self-perfection brings us back, from another point of view, to a concern for human language, which would appear to be a prerequisite for such evolution of society and culture, for Rousseau's perfection of the species, beyond the most rudimentary forms.

Rousseau holds that "although the organ of speech is natural to man, speech itself is nonetheless not natural to him." Again, I see no inconsistency between this observation and the typical Cartesian view that innate abilities are "dispositional," faculties that lead us to produce ideas (specifically, innate ideas) in a particular manner under given conditions of external stimulation, but that also provide us with the ability to proceed in our thinking without such external factors. Language too, then, is natural to man only in a specific way. This is an important and, I believe, quite fundamental insight of the rationalist linguists that was disregarded, very largely, under the impact of empiricist psychology in the eighteenth century and since.[6]

Rousseau discusses the origin of language at some length, though he confesses himself to be unable to come to grips with the problem in a satisfactory way. Thus

> if men needed speech in order to learn to think, they had even
> greater need of knowing how to think in order to discover the
> art of speech.... So that one can hardly form tenable conjectures
> about this art of communicating thoughts and establishing

intercourse between minds; a sublime art which is now very far from its origin....

He holds that "general ideas can come into the mind only with the aid of words, and the understanding grasps them only through propositions"—a fact which prevents animals, devoid of reason, from formulating such ideas or ever acquiring "the perfectibility which depends upon them." Thus he cannot conceive of the means by which "our new grammarians began to extend their ideas and to generalize their words," or to develop the means "to express all the thoughts of men": "numbers, abstract words, aorists, and all the tenses of verbs, particles, syntax, the linking of propositions, reasoning, and the forming of all the logic of discourse." He does speculate about later stages of the perfection of the species, "when the ideas of men began to spread and multiply, and when closer communication was established among them, [and] they sought more numerous signs and a more extensive language." But he must, unhappily, abandon "the following difficult problem: which was most necessary, previously formed society for the institution of languages, or previously invented languages for the establishment of society?"

The Cartesians cut the Gordian knot by postulating the existence of a species-specific characteristic, a second substance that serves what we might call a "creative principle" alongside the "mechanical principle" that determines totally the behavior of animals. There was, for them, no need to explain the origin of language in the course of historical evolution. Rather, man's nature is qualitatively distinct: there is no passage from body to mind. We might reinterpret this idea in more current terms by speculating that rather sudden and dramatic mutations might have led to qualities of intelligence that are, so far as we know, unique to man, possession of language in the human sense being the most distinctive index of these qualities.[7] If this is correct, as at least a first approximation to the facts, the study of language might be expected to offer an entering wedge, or perhaps a model, for an investigation of human nature that would provide the grounding for a much broader theory of human nature.

To conclude these historical remarks, I would like to turn, as I have elsewhere,[8] to Wilhelm von Humboldt, one of the most stimulating and intriguing thinkers of the period. Humboldt was, on the one hand, one of the most profound theorists of general linguistics, and on the other, an early and forceful advocate of libertarian values. The basic concept of his philosophy is *Bildung*, by which, as J.W. Burrow expresses it, "he meant the fullest, richest and most harmonious development of the potentialities of the individual, the community or the human race."[9] His own thought might serve as an exemplary case. Though he does not, to my knowledge, explicitly relate his ideas about language to his libertarian social thought, there is quite clearly a common ground from which they develop, a concept of human nature that inspires each. Mill's essay *On Liberty* takes as its epigraph Humboldt's formulation of the "leading principle" of his thought: "the absolute and essential importance of human development in its richest diversity." Humboldt concludes his critique of the authoritarian state by saying: "I have felt myself animated throughout with a sense of the deepest respect for the inherent dignity of human nature, and for freedom, which alone befits that dignity." Briefly put, his concept of human nature is this:

> The true end of Man, or that which is prescribed by the eternal and immutable dictates of reason, and not suggested by vague and transient desires, is the highest and most harmonious development of his powers to a complete and consistent whole. Freedom is the first and indispensable condition which the possibility of such a development presupposes; but there is besides another essential—intimately connected with freedom, it is true—a variety of situations.[10]

Like Rousseau and Kant, he holds that

> nothing promotes this ripeness for freedom so much as freedom itself. This truth, perhaps, may not be acknowledged by those who have so often used this unripeness as an excuse for continuing repression. But it seems to me to follow unquestionably from the very nature of man. The incapacity for freedom can only arise from a want of moral and intellectual power; to heighten this power is the only way to supply this want; but to do this presupposes the exercise of the power, and this exercise presupposes the freedom which awakens spontaneous activity. Only it is clear we cannot call it giving freedom, when bonds are relaxed which are not felt as such by him who wears them. But of no man on earth—however neglected by nature, and however degraded by circumstances—is this true of all the bonds which oppress him. Let us undo them one by one, as the feeling of freedom awakens in men's hearts, and we shall hasten progress at every step.

Those who do not comprehend this "may justly be suspected of misunderstanding human nature, and of wishing to make men into machines."

Man is fundamentally a creative, searching, self-perfecting being: "to inquire and to create—these are the centers around which all human pursuits more or less directly revolve." But freedom of thought and enlightenment are not only for the elite. Once again echoing Rousseau, Humboldt states: "There is something degrading to human nature in the idea of refusing to any man the right to be a man." He is, then, optimistic about the effects on all of "the diffusion of scientific knowledge by freedom and enlightenment." But "all moral culture springs solely and immediately from the inner life of the soul, and can only be stimulated in human nature, and never produced by external and artificial contrivances." "The cultivation of the understanding, as of any of man's other faculties, is generally achieved by his own activity, his own ingenuity, or his own methods of using the discoveries of others...." Education, then, must provide the opportunities for self-fulfillment; it can at best provide a rich and challenging environment for the individual to explore, in his own way. Even a language cannot, strictly speaking, be taught, but only "awakened in the mind: one can only provide the thread along which it will develop of itself." I think that Humboldt would have found congenial much of Dewey's thinking about education. And he might also have appreciated the recent revolutionary extension of such ideas, for example, by the radical Catholics of Latin America who are concerned with the "awakening of consciousness," referring to "the transformation of the passive exploited lower classes into conscious and critical masters of their own destinies"[11] much in the manner of Third World revolutionaries elsewhere. He would, I am sure, have approved of their criticism of schools that are

> more preoccupied with the transmission of knowledge than with the creation, among other values, of a critical spirit. From the social point of view, the educational systems are oriented to maintaining the existing social and economic structures instead of transforming them.[12]

But Humboldt's concern for spontaneity goes well beyond educational practice in the narrow sense. It touches also the question of labor and exploitation. The remarks, just quoted, about the cultivation of understanding through spontaneous action continue as follows:

> ...man never regards what he possesses as so much his own, as what he does; and the labourer who tends a garden is perhaps in a truer sense its owner, than the listless voluptuary who enjoys its fruits.... In view of this consideration,[13] it seems as if all peasants and craftsmen might be elevated into artists; that is, men who love their labour for its own sake, improve it by their own plastic genius and inventive skill, and thereby cultivate their intellect, ennoble their character, and exalt and refine their pleasures. And so humanity would be ennobled by the very things which now, though beautiful in themselves, so often serve to degrade it.... But, still, freedom is undoubtedly the indispensable condition, without which even the pursuits most congenial to individual human nature, can never succeed in producing such salutary influences. Whatever does not spring from a man's free choice, or is only the result of instruction and guidance, does not enter into his very being, but remains alien to his true nature; he does not perform it with truly human energies, but merely with mechanical exactness.

If a man acts in a purely mechanical way, reacting to external demands or instruction rather than in ways determined by his own interests and energies and power, "we may admire what he does, but we despise what he is."[14]

On such conceptions Humboldt grounds his ideas concerning the role of the state, which tends to "make man an instrument to serve its arbitrary ends, overlooking his individual purposes." His doctrine is classical liberal, strongly opposed to all but the most minimal forms of state intervention in personal or social life.

Writing in the 1790s, Humboldt had no conception of the forms that industrial capitalism would take. Hence he is not overly concerned with the dangers of private power.

> But when we reflect (still keeping theory distinct from practice) that the influence of a private person is liable to diminution and decay, from competition, dissipation of fortune, even death; and that clearly none of these contingencies can be applied to the State; we are still left with the principle that the latter is not to meddle in anything which does not refer exclusively to security....

He speaks of the essential equality of the condition of private citizens, and of course has no idea of the ways in which the notion "private person" would come to be reinterpreted in the era of corporate capitalism. He did not foresee that "Democracy with its motto of *equality of all citizens before the law* and Liberalism with its *right of man over his own person* both [would be] wrecked on realities of capitalist economy."[15] He did not foresee that in a predatory capitalist economy, state intervention would be an absolute necessity to preserve human existence and to prevent the destruction of the physical environment—I speak optimistically. As Karl Polanyi, for one, has pointed out, the self-adjusting market "could not exist for any length of time without annihilating the human and natural substance of society; it would have physically destroyed man and transformed his surroundings into a wilderness."[16] Humboldt did not foresee the consequences of the commodity character of labor, the doctrine (in Polanyi's words) that "it is not for the commodity to decide where it should be offered for sale, to what purpose it should be used, at what price it should be allowed to change hands, and in what manner it should be consumed or destroyed." But the commodity, in this case, is a human life, and social protection was therefore a minimal necessity to constrain the irrational and destructive workings of the classical free market. Nor did Humboldt understand that capitalist economic relations perpetuated a form of bondage which, as early as 1767, Simon Linguet had declared to be even worse than slavery.

> It is the impossibility of living by any other means that compels our farm laborers to till the soil whose fruits they will not eat, and our masons to construct buildings in which they will not

live. It is want that drags them to those markets where they await masters who will do them the kindness of buying them. It is want that compels them to go down on their knees to the rich man in order to get from him permission to enrich him.... What effective gain has the suppression of slavery brought him?... He is free, you say. Ah! That is his misfortune. The slave was precious to his master because of the money he had cost him. But the handicraftsman costs nothing to the rich voluptuary who employs him.... These men, it is said, have no master—they have one, and the most terrible, the most imperious of masters, that is *need*. It is this that reduces them to the most cruel dependence.[17]

If there is something degrading to human nature in the idea of bondage, then a new emancipation must be awaited, Fourier's "third and last emancipatory phase of history," which will transform the proletariat to free men by eliminating the commodity character of labor, ending wage slavery, and bringing the commercial, industrial, and financial institutions under democratic control.[18]

Perhaps Humboldt might have accepted these conclusions. He does agree that state intervention in social life is legitimate if "freedom would destroy the very conditions without which not only freedom but even existence itself would be inconceivable"—precisely the circumstances that arise in an unconstrained capitalist economy. In any event, his criticism of bureaucracy and the autocratic state stands as an eloquent forewarning of some of the most dismal aspects of modern history, and the basis of his critique is applicable to a broader range of coercive institutions than he imagined.

Though expressing a classical liberal doctrine, Humboldt is no primitive individualist in the style of Rousseau. Rousseau extols the savage who "lives within himself"; he has little use for "the sociable man, always outside of himself, [who] knows how to live only in the opinion of others...from [whose] judgement alone...he draws the sentiment of his own existence."[19] Humboldt's vision is quite different:

> ...the whole tenor of the ideas and arguments unfolded in this essay might fairly be reduced to this, that while they would break all fetters in human society, they would attempt to find as many new social bonds as possible. The isolated man is no more able to develop than the one who is fettered.

Thus he looks forward to a community of free association without coercion by the state or other authoritarian institutions, in which fee men can create and inquire, and achieve the highest development of their power—far ahead of his time, he presents an anarchist vision that is appropriate, perhaps, to the next state of industrial society. We can perhaps look forward to a day when these various strands will be brought together within the framework of libertarian socialism, a social form that barely exists today though its elements can be perceived: in the guarantee of individual rights that has achieved its highest form—though still tragically flawed—in the Western democracies; in the Israeli *kibbutzim*; in the experiments with workers' councils in Yugoslavia; in the effort to awaken popular consciousness and create a new involvement in the social process which is a fundamental element in the Third World revolutions, coexisting uneasily with indefensible authoritarian practice.

A similar concept of human nature underlies Humboldt's work on language. Language is a process of free creation; its laws and principles are fixed, but the manner in which the principles of generation are used is free and infinitely varied. Even the interpretation and use of words involves a process of free creation. The normal use of language and the acquisition of language depend on what Humboldt calls the fixed form of language, a system of generative processes that is rooted in the nature of the human mind and constrains but does not determine the free creations of normal intelligence or, at a higher and more original level, of the great writer or thinker. Humboldt is, on the one hand, a Platonist who insists that learning is a kind of reminiscence, in which the mind, stimulated by experience, draws from its own internal resources and follows a path that it itself determines; and he is also a romantic attuned to cultural variety, and the endless possibilities for the spiritual contributions of the creative genius. There is no contradiction in this, any more than there is a contradiction in the insistence of aesthetic theory that individual works of genius are constrained by principle and rule. The normal, creative use of language, which to the Cartesian rationalist is the best index of the existence of another mind, presupposes a system of rules and generative principles of a sort that the rationalist grammarians attempted, with some success, to determine and make explicit.

113

The many modern critics who sense an inconsistency in the belief that free creation takes place within—presupposes, in fact—a system of constraints and governing principles are quite mistaken; unless, of course, they speak of "contradiction" in the loose and metaphoric sense of Schelling, when he writes that "without the contradiction of necessity and freedom not only philosophy but every nobler ambition of the spirit would sink to that death which is peculiar to those sciences in which that contradiction serves no function." Without this tension between necessity and freedom, rule and choice, there can be no creativity, no communication, no meaningful acts at all.

I have discussed these traditional ideas at some length, not out of antiquarian interest, but because I think that they are valuable and essentially correct, and that they project a course we can follow with profit. Social action must be animated by a vision of a future society, and by explicit judgments of value concerning the character of this future society. These judgments must derive from some concept of the nature of man, and one may seek empirical foundations by investigating man's nature as it is revealed by his behavior and his creations, material, intellectual, and social. We have, perhaps, reached a point in history when it is possible to think seriously about a society in which freely constituted social bonds replace the fetters of autocratic institutions, rather in the sense conveyed by the remarks of Humboldt that I quoted, and elaborated more fully in the tradition of libertarian socialism in the years that followed.[20]

Predatory capitalism created a complex industrial system and an advanced technology; it permitted a considerable extension of democratic practice and fostered certain liberal values, but within limits that are now being pressed and must be overcome. It is not a fit system for the mid-twentieth century. It is incapable of meeting human needs that can be expressed only in collective terms, and its concept of competitive man who seeks only to maximize wealth and power, who subjects himself to market relationships, to exploitation and external authority, is antihuman and intolerable in the deepest sense. An autocratic state is no acceptable substitute; nor can the militarized state capitalism evolving in the United States or the bureaucratized, centralized welfare state be accepted as the goal of human existence. The only justification for repressive institutions is material and cultural deficit. But such institutions, at certain stages of history, perpetuate and produce such a deficit, and even threaten human survival. Modern science and technology can relieve men of the necessity for specialized, imbecile labor. They may, in principle, provide the basis for a rational social order based on free association and democratic control, if we have the will to create it.

A vision of a future social order is in turn based on a concept of human nature. If in fact man is an indefinitely malleable, completely plastic being, with no innate structures of mind and no intrinsic needs of a cultural or social character, then he is a fit subject for the "shaping of behavior" by the state authority, the corporate manager, the technocrat, or the central committee. Those with some confidence in the human species will hope this is not so and will try to determine the intrinsic human characteristics that provide the framework for intellectual development, the growth of moral consciousness, cultural achievement, and participation in a free community. In a partly analogous way, a classical tradition spoke of artistic genius acting within and in some ways challenging a framework of rule. Here we touch on matters that are little understood. It seems to me that we must break away, sharply and radically, from much of modern social and behavioral science if we are to move towards a deeper understanding of these matters.[21]

Here too, I think that the tradition I have briefly reviewed has a contribution to offer. As I have already observed, those who were concerned with human distinctiveness and potential repeatedly were led to a consideration of the properties of language. I think that the study of language can provide some glimmerings of understanding of rule-governed behavior and the possibilities for free and creative action within the framework of a system of rules that in part, at least, reflect intrinsic properties of human mental organization. It seems to me fair to regard the contemporary study of language as in some ways a return to the Humboldtian concept of the form of language: a system of generative processes rooted in innate properties of mind but permitting, in Humboldt's phrase, an infinite use of finite means. Language cannot be described as a system of organization of behavior. Rather, to understand how language is used, we must discover the abstract Humboldtian form of language—its generative grammar, in modern terms. To learn a language is to construct for oneself this abstract system, of course unconsciously. The linguist and psychologist can proceed to study the use and acquisition of language only insofar as he has some grasp of the properties of the system that has been mastered by the person who knows the language. Furthermore, it seems to me that a good case can be made in support of the empirical claim that such a system can be acquired, under the given conditions of time and access, only by a mind that is endowed with certain specific properties that we can now tentatively describe in some detail. As long as we restrict ourselves, conceptually, to the investigation of behavior, its organization, its development through interaction with the environment, we are bound to miss these characteristics of language and mind. Other aspects of human psychology and culture might, in principle, be studied in a similar way.

Conceivably, we might in this way develop a social science based on empirically well-founded propositions concerning human nature. Just as we study the range of humanly attainable languages, with some success, we might also try to study the forms of artistic expression or, for that matter, scientific knowledge that humans can conceive, and perhaps even the range of ethical systems and social structures in which humans can live and function, given their intrinsic capacities and needs. Perhaps one might go on to project a concept of social organization that would—under given conditions of material and spiritual culture—best encourage and accommodate the fundamental human need—if such it is—for spontaneous initiative, creative work, solidarity, pursuit of social justice.

I do not want to exaggerate, as I no doubt have, the role of investigation of language. Language is the product of human intelligence that is, for the moment, most accessible to study. A rich tradition held language to be a mirror of mind. To some extent, there is surely truth and useful insight in this idea.

I am no less puzzled by the topic "language and freedom" than when I began—and no less intrigued. In these speculative and sketchy remarks there are gaps so vast that one might question what would remain, when metaphor and unsubstantiated guess are removed. It is sobering to realize—as I believe we must—how little we have progressed in our knowledge of man and society, or even in formulating clearly the problems that might be seriously studied. But there are, I think, a few footholds that seem fairly firm. I like to believe that the intensive study of one aspect of human psychology—human language—may contribute to a humanistic social science that will serve, as well, as an instrument for social action. It must, needless to say, be stressed that social action cannot await a firmly established theory of man and society, nor can the validity of the latter be determined by our hopes and moral judgments. The two—speculation and action—must progress as best they can, looking forward to the day when theoretical inquiry will provide a firm guide to the unending, often grim, but never hopeless struggle for freedom and social justice.

NOTES

This essay was presented as a lecture at the University Freedom and the Human Sciences Symposium, Loyola University, Chicago, January 8–9, 1970, and published in Noam Chomsky, *For Reasons of State* (New York: New Press, 2003), pp. 387–408. First edition Pantheon, 1970.

1 F. W. J. Schelling, *Philosophical Inquires into the Nature of Human Freedom*.

2 R. D. Masters, introduction to his edition of *First and Second Discourses*, by Jean-Jacques Rousseau.

3 Compare Proudhon, a century later: "No long discussion is necessary to demonstrate that the power of denying a man his thought, his will, his personality, is a power of life and death, and that to make a man a slave is to assassinate him."

4 Cited in Lehning, ed., Bakunin, *Etatisme et anarchie*, editor's note 50, from P. Schrecker, "Kant et la révolution française," *Revue philosophique*, September–December 1939.

5 I have discussed this matter in *Cartesian Linguistics* and *Language and Mind*.

6 See the references of note 5, and also my *Aspects of the Theory of Syntax*, chapter 1, sec. 8.

7 I need hardly add that this is not the prevailing view. For discussion, see E. H. Lenneberg, *Biological Foundations of Language*; my *Language and Mind*; E. A. Drewe, G. Ettlinger, A. D. Milner, and R. E. Passingham, "A Comparative Review of the Results of Behavioral Research on Man and Monkey," Institute of Psychiatry, London, unpublished draft, 1969; P. H. Lieberman, D. H. Klatt, and W. H. Wilson, "Vocal Tract Limitations on the Vowel Repertoires of Rhesus Monkey and other Nonhuman Primates," *Science*, June 6, 1969 and P. H. Lieberman, "Primate Vocalizations and Human Linguistic Ability," *Journal of the Acoustical Society of America*, vol. 44, no. 6 (1968).

8 In the books cited above, and in *Current Issues in Linguistic Theory*.

9 J. W. Burrow, introduction to his edition of *The Limits of State Action*, by Wilhelm von Humboldt, from which most of the following quotes are taken.

10 Compare the remarks of Kant, quoted above. Kant's essay appeared in 1793; Humboldt's ideas were written in 1791–1792. Parts appeared but it did not appear in full during his lifetime. See Burrow, introduction to Humboldt, *Limits of State Action*.

11 Thomas G. Sanders, "The Church in Latin America," *Foreign Affairs*, vol. 48, no. 2 (1970).

12 *Ibid.* The source is said to be the ideas of Paulo Freire. Similar criticism is widespread in the student movement in the West. See, for example, Mitchell Cohen and Dennis Hale, eds., *The New Student Left*, chapter 3.

13 Namely, that man "only attains the most matured and graceful consummation of his activity, when his way of life is harmoniously in keeping with his character"—that is, when his actions flow from inner impulse.

14 The latter quote is from Humboldt's comments on the French constitution, 1791—parts translated in Marianne Cowan, ed., *Humanist Without Portfolio*.

15 Rudolf Rocker, "Anarchism and Anarcho-syndicalism," in Paul Eltzbacher, *Anarchism*. In his book *Nationalism and Culture*, Rocker describes Humboldt as "the most prominent representative in Germany" of the doctrine of natural rights and of the opposition to the authoritarian state. Rousseau he regards as a precursor of authoritarian doctrine, but he considers only the *Social Contract*, not the far more libertarian *Discourse on Inequality*. Burrow observes that Humboldt's essay anticipates "much nineteenth century political theory of a populist, anarchist and syndicalist kind" and notes the hints of the early Marx. See also my *Cartesian Linguistics*, n. 51, for some comments.

16 Karl Polanyi, *The Great Transformation*.

17 Cited by Paul Mattick, "Workers' control," in Priscilla Long, ed., *The New Left*, p. 377. See also chapter 4, p. 143.

18 Cited in Martin Buber, *Paths in Utopia*, p. 19.

19 Yet Rousseau dedicates himself, as a man who has lost his "original simplicity" and can no longer "do without laws and chiefs," to "respect the sacred bonds" of his society and "scrupulously obey the laws, and the men who are their authors and ministers," while scorning "a constitution that can be maintained only with the help of so many respectable people...and from which, despite all their care, always arise more real calamities than apparent advantages."

20 See chapter 4.

21 See chapter 7 [of Chomsky's *For Reasons of State*, (New Press, 2003)] for a discussion of the fraudulent claims in this regard of certain varieties of behavioral science.

THREE
NOTES ON ANARCHISM
(1970)

A French writer, sympathetic to anarchism, wrote in the 1890s that "anarchism has a broad back, like paper it endures anything"—including, he noted, those whose acts are such that "a mortal enemy of anarchism could not have done better."[1] There have been many styles of thought and action that have been referred to as "anarchist." It would be hopeless to try to encompass all of these conflicting tendencies in some general theory or ideology. And even if we proceed to extract from the history of libertarian thought a living, evolving tradition, as Daniel Guérin does in *Anarchism*, it remains difficult to formulate its doctrines as a specific and determinate theory of society and social change. The anarchist historian Rudolf Rocker, who presents a systematic conception of the development of anarchist thought towards anarchosyndicalism, along lines that bear comparison to Guérin's work, puts the matter well when he writes that anarchism is not

> a fixed, self-enclosed social system but rather a definite trend in the historic development of mankind, which, in contrast with the intellectual guardianship of all clerical and governmental institutions, strives for the free unhindered unfolding of all the individual and social forces in life. Even freedom is only a relative, not an absolute concept, since it tends constantly to become broader and to affect wider circles in more manifold ways. For the anarchist, freedom is not an abstract philosophical concept, but the vital concrete possibility for every human being to bring to full development all the powers, capacities, and talents with which nature has endowed him, and turn them to social account. The less this natural development of man is influenced by ecclesiastical or political guardianship, the more efficient and harmonious will human personality become, the more will it become the measure of the intellectual culture of the society in which it has grown.[2]

One might ask what value there is in studying a "definite trend in the historic development of mankind" that does not articulate a specific and detailed social theory. Indeed, many commentators dismiss anarchism as utopian, formless, primitive, or otherwise incompatible with the realities of a complex society. One might, however, argue rather differently: that at every stage of history our concern must be to dismantle those forms of authority and oppression that survive from an era when they might have been justified in terms of the need for security or survival or economic development, but that now contribute to—rather than alleviate—material and cultural deficit. If so, there will be no doctrine of social change fixed for the present and future, nor even, necessarily, a specific and unchanging concept of the goals towards which social change should tend. Surely our understanding of the nature of man or of the range of viable social forms is so rudimentary that any far-reaching doctrine must be treated with great skepticism, just as skepticism is in order when we hear that "human nature" or "the demands of efficiency" or "the complexity of modern life" requires this or that form of oppression and autocratic rule.

Nevertheless, at a particular time there is every reason to develop, insofar as our understanding permits, a specific realization of this definite trend in the historic development of mankind, appropriate to the tasks of the moment. For Rocker, "the problem that is set for our time is that of freeing man from the curse of economic exploitation and political and social enslavement"; and the method is not the conquest and exercise of state power, nor stultifying parliamentarianism, but rather "to reconstruct the economic life of the peoples from the ground up and build it up in the spirit of Socialism."

> But only the producers themselves are fitted for this task, since they are the only value-creating element in society out of which a new future can arise. Theirs must be the task of freeing labor from all the fetters which economic exploitation has fastened on it, of freeing society from all the institutions and procedure of political power, and of opening the way to an alliance of free groups of men and women based on co-operative labor and a planned administration of things in the interest of the community. To prepare the toiling masses in city and country for this great goal and to bind them together as a militant force is the objective of modern Anarcho-syndicalism, and in this its whole purpose is exhausted. [p. 108]

119

As a socialist, Rocker would take for granted "that the serious, final, complete liberation of the workers is possible only upon one condition: that of the appropriation of capital, that is, of raw material and all the tools of labor, including land, by the whole body of the workers."[3] As an anarcho-syndicalist, he insists, further, that the workers' organizations create "not only the ideas, but also the facts of the future itself" in the prerevolutionary period, that they embody in themselves the structure of the future society—and he looks forward to a social revolution that will dismantle the state apparatus as well as expropriate the expropriators. "What we put in place of the government is industrial organization."

> Anarcho-syndicalists are convinced that a Socialist economic order cannot be created by the decrees and statutes of a government, but only by the solidaric collaboration of the workers with hand and brain in each special branch of production; that is,

through the taking over of the management of all plants by the producers themselves under such form that the separate groups, plants, and branches of industry are independent members of the general economic organism and systematically carry on production and the distribution of the products in the interest of the community on the basis of free mutual agreements. [p. 94]

Rocker was writing at a moment when such ideas had been put into practice in a dramatic way in the Spanish Revolution. Just prior to the outbreak of the revolution, the anarchosyndicalist economist Diego Abad de Santillan had written:

...in facing the problem of social transformation, the Revolution cannot consider the state as a medium, but must depend on the organization of producers.

We have followed this norm and we find no need for the hypothesis of a superior power to organized labor, in order to establish a new order of things. We would thank anyone to point out to us what function, if any, the State can have in an economic organization, where private property has been abolished and in which parasitism and special privilege have no place. The suppression of the State cannot be a languid affair; it must be the task of the Revolution to finish with the State. Either the Revolution gives social wealth to the producers in which case the producers organize themselves for due collective distribution and the State has nothing to do; or the Revolution does not give social wealth to the producers, in which case the Revolution has been a lie and the State would continue.

Our federal council of economy is not a political power but an economic and administrative regulating power. It receives its orientation from below and operates in accordance with the resolutions of the regional and national assemblies. It is a liaison corps and nothing else.[4]

Engels, in a letter of 1883, expressed his disagreement with this conception as follows:

The anarchists put the thing upside down. They declare that the proletarian revolution must *begin* by doing away with the political organization of the state.... But to destroy it at such a moment would be to destroy the only organism by means of which the victorious proletariat can assert its newly-conquered power, hold down its capitalist adversaries, and carry out that economic revolution of society without which the whole victory must end in a new defeat and in a mass slaughter of the workers similar to those after the Paris commune.[5]

In contrast, the anarchists—most eloquently Bakunin—warned of the dangers of the "red bureaucracy," which would prove to be "the most vile and terrible lie that our century has created."[6] The anarchosyndicalist Fernand Pelloutier asked: "must even the transitory state to which we have to submit necessarily and fatally be the collectivist jail? Can't it consist in a free organization limited exclusively by the needs of production and consumption, all political institutions having disappeared?"[7]

I do not pretend to know the answer to this question. But it seems clear that unless there is, in some form, a positive answer, the chances for a truly democratic revolution that will achieve the humanistic ideals of the left are not great. Martin Buber put the problem succinctly when he wrote: "One cannot in the nature of things expect a little tree that has been turned into a club to put forth leaves."[8] The question of conquest or destruction of state power is what Bakunin regarded as the primary issue dividing him from Marx.[9] In one form or another, the problem has arisen repeatedly in the century since, dividing "libertarian" from "authoritarian" socialists.

Despite Bakunin's warnings about the red bureaucracy, and their fulfillment under Stalin's dictatorship, it would obviously be a gross error in interpreting the debates of a century ago to rely on the claims of contemporary social movements as to their historical origins. In particular, it is perverse to regard Bolshevism as "Marxism in practice." Rather, the left-wing critique of Bolshevism, taking account of the historical circumstances of the Russian Revolution, is far more to the point.[10]

> The anti-Bolshevik, left-wing labor movement opposed the Leninists because they did not go far enough in exploiting the Russian upheavals for strictly proletarian ends. They became prisoners of their environment and used the international radical movement to satisfy specifically Russian needs, which soon became synonymous with the needs of the Bolshevik Party-State. The "bourgeois" aspects of the Russian Revolution were now discovered in Bolshevism itself: Leninism was adjudged a part of international social-democracy, differing from the latter only on tactical issues.[11]

If one were to seek a single leading idea within the anarchist tradition, it should, I believe, be that expressed by Bakunin when, in writing on the Paris Commune, he identified himself as follows:

> I am a fanatic lover of liberty, considering it as the unique condition under which intelligence, dignity and human happiness can develop and grow; not the purely formal liberty conceded, measured out and regulated by the State, an eternal lie which in reality represents nothing more that the privilege of some founded on the slavery of the rest; not the individualistic, egoistic,

shabby, and fictitious liberty extolled by the School of J.-J. Rousseau and the other schools of bourgeois liberalism, which considers the would-be rights of all men, represented by the State which limits the rights of each—an idea that leads inevitably to the reduction of the rights of each to zero. No, I mean the only kind of liberty that is worthy of the name, liberty that consists in the full development of all of the material, intellectual and moral powers that are latent in each person; liberty that recognizes no restrictions other than those determined by the laws of our own individual nature, which cannot properly be regarded as restrictions since these laws are not imposed by any outside legislator beside or above us, but are immanent and inherent, forming the very basis of our material, intellectual and moral being—they do not limit us but are the real and immediate conditions of our freedom.[12]

These ideas grow out of the Enlightenment; their roots are in Rousseau's *Discourse on Inequality*, Humboldt's *The Limits of State Action*, Kant's insistence, in his defense of the French Revolution, that freedom is the precondition for acquiring the maturity for freedom, not a gift to be granted when such maturity is achieved (see chapter 2, p. 105). With the development of industrial capitalism, a new and unanticipated system of injustice, it is libertarian socialism that has preserved and extended the radical humanist message of the Enlightenment and the classical liberal ideals that were perverted into an ideology to sustain the emerging social order. In fact, on the very same assumptions that led classical liberalism to oppose the intervention of the state in social life, capitalist social relations are also intolerable. This is clear, for example, from the classic work of Humboldt, *The Limits of State Action*, which anticipated and perhaps inspired Mill (see chapter 2, pp. 108–109). This classic of liberal thought, completed in 1792, is in its essence profoundly, though prematurely, anticapitalist. Its ideas must be attenuated beyond recognition to be transmuted into an ideology of industrial capitalism.

Humboldt's vision of a society in which social fetters are replaced by social bonds and labor is freely undertaken suggests the early Marx (see chapter 2, note 15), with his discussion of the "alienation of labor when work is external to the worker ... note part of his nature...[so that] he does not fulfill himself in his work but denies himself...[and is] physically exhausted and mentally debased," alienated labor that "casts some of the workers back into a barbarous kind of work and turns others into machines," thus depriving man of his "species character" of "free conscious activity" and "productive life." Similarly, Marx conceives of "a new type of human being who *needs* his fellow-men.... [The workers' association becomes] the real constructive effort to create the social texture of future human relations."[13] It is true that classical libertarian thought is opposed to state intervention in social life, as a consequence of deeper assumptions about the human need for liberty, diversity, and free association. On the same assumptions, capitalist relations of production, wage labor, competitiveness, the ideology of "possessive individualism"—all must be regarded as fundamentally antihuman. Libertarian socialism is properly to be regarded as the inheritor of the liberal ideals of the Enlightenment.

Rudolf Rocker describes modern anarchism as "the confluence of the two great currents which during and since the French revolution have found such characteristic expression in the intellectual life of Europe: Socialism and Liberalism." The classical liberal ideals, he argues, were wrecked on the realities of capitalist economic forms. Anarchism is necessarily anticapitalist in that it "opposes the exploitation of man by man." But anarchism also opposes "the dominion of man over man." It insists that *socialism will be free or it will not be at all. In its recognition of this lies the genuine and profound justification for the existence of anarchism.*[14] From this point of view, anarchism may be regarded as the libertarian wing of socialism. It is in this spirit that Daniel Guérin has approached the study of anarchism in *Anarchism* and other works.[15]

Guérin quotes Adolph Fischer, who said that "every anarchist is a socialist but not every socialist is necessarily an anarchist." Similarly Bakunin, in his "anarchist manifesto" of 1865, the program of his projected international revolutionary fraternity, laid down the principle that each member must be, to begin with, a socialist.

A consistent anarchist must oppose private ownership of the means of production and the wage slavery which is a component of this system, as incompatible with the principle that labor must be freely undertaken and under the control of the producer. As Marx put it, socialists look forward to a society in which labor will "become not only a means of life, but also the highest want in life,"[16] an impossibility when the worker is driven by external authority or need rather than inner impulse: "no form of wage-labor, even though one may be less obnoxious than another, can do away with the misery of wage-labor itself."[17] A consistent anarchist must oppose not only alienated labor but also the stupefying specialization of labor that takes place when the means for developing production

> mutilate the worker into a fragment of a human being, degrade him to become a mere appurtenance of the machine, make his work such a torment that its essential meaning is destroyed; estrange from him the intellectual potentialities of the labor process in very proportion to the extent to which science is incorporated into it as an independent power....[18]

Marx saw this not as an inevitable concomitant of industrialization, but rather as a feature of capitalist relations of production. The society of the future must be concerned to "replace the detail-worker of today...reduced to a mere fragment of a man, by the fully developed individual, fit for a variety of labours…to whom the different social function…are but so many modes of giving free scope to his own natural powers."[19] The prerequisite is the abolition of capital and wage labor as social categories (not to speak of the industrial armies of the "labor state" or the various modern forms of totalitarianism or state capitalism). The reduction of man to an appurtenance of the machine, a specialized tool of production, might in principle be overcome, rather than enhanced, with the proper development and use of technology, but not under the conditions of autocratic control of production by those who make man an instrument to sever their ends, overlooking his individual purposes, in Humboldt's phrase.

Anarchosyndicalists sought, even under capitalism, to create "free associations of free producers" that would engage in militant struggle and prepare to take over the organization of production on a democratic basis. These associations would serve as "a practical school of anarchism."[20] If private ownership of the means of production is, in Proudhon's often quoted phrase, merely a form of "theft"—"the exploitation of the weak by the strong"[21]—control of production by a state bureaucracy, no matter how benevolent its intentions, also does not create the conditions under which labor, manual and intellectual, can become the highest want in life. Both, then, must be overcome.

124

In his attack on the right of private or bureaucratic control over the means of production, the anarchist takes his stand with those who struggle to bring about "the third and last emancipatory phase of history," the first having made serfs out of slaves, the second having made wage earners out of serfs, and the third which abolishes the proletariat in a final act of liberation that places control over the economy in the hands of free and voluntary associations of producers (Fourier, 1848).[22] The imminent danger to "civilization" was noted by de Tocqueville, also in 1848:

> As long as the right of property was the origin and groundwork
> of many other rights, it was easily defended—or rather it was not
> attacked; it was then the citadel of society while all the other
> rights were its outworks; it did not bear the brunt of attack and,
> indeed, there was no serious attempt to assail it. But today, when
> the right of property is regarded as the last undestroyed remnant
> of the aristocratic world, when it alone is left standing, the sole
> privilege is an equalized society, it is a different matter. Consider
> what is happening in the hearts of the working-classes, although
> I admit they are quiet as yet. It is true that they are less inflamed
> than formerly by political passions properly speaking; but do
> you not see that their passions, far from being political, have
> become social? Do you not see that, little by little, ideas and
> opinions are spreading amongst them which aim not merely at

removing such and such laws, such a ministry or such a government, but at breaking up the very foundations of society itself?[23]

The workers of Paris, in 1871, broke the silence, and proceeded

> to abolish property, the basis of all civilization! Yes, gentlemen, the Commune intended to abolish that class property which makes the labor of the many the wealth of the few. It aimed at the expropriation of the expropriators. It wanted to make individual property a truth by transforming the means of production, land and capital, now chiefly the means of enslaving and exploiting labor, into mere instruments of free and associated labor.[24]

The Commune, of course, was drowned in blood. The nature of the "civilization" that the workers of Paris sought to overcome in their attack on "the very foundations of society itself" was revealed, once again, when the troops of the Versailles government reconquered Paris from its population. As Marx wrote, bitterly but accurately:

> The civilization and justice of bourgeois order comes out in its lurid light whenever the slaves and drudges of that order rise against their masters. Then this civilization and justice stand forth as undisguised savagery and lawless revenge...the infernal deeds of the soldiery reflect the innate spirit of that civilization of which they are the mercenary vindicators.... The bourgeoisie of the whole world, which looks complacently upon the wholesale massacre after the battle, is convulsed by horror at the desecration of brick and mortar... [Ibid., pp. 74, 77]

Despite the violent destruction of the Commune, Bakunin wrote that Paris opens a new era, "that of the definitive and complete emancipation of the popular masses and their future true solidarity, across and despite state boundaries...the next revolution of man, international and in solidarity, will be the resurrection of Paris"—a revolution that the world still awaits.

The consistent anarchist, then, should be a socialist, but a socialist of a particular sort. He will not only oppose alienated and specialized labor and look forward to the appropriation of capital by the whole body of workers, but he will also insist that this appropriation be direct, not exercised by some elite force acting in the name of the proletariat. He will, in short, oppose

> the organization of production by the Government. It means State-socialism, the command of the State officials over production and the command of managers, scientists, shop-officials in the shop.... The goal of the working class is liberation from exploitation. This goal is not reached and cannot be reached by a new directing and governing class substituting itself for the

bourgeoisie. It is only realized by the workers themselves being master over production.

These remarks are taken from "Five Theses on the Class Struggle" by the left-wing Marxist Anton Pannekoek, one of the outstanding theorists of the council communist movement. And in fact, radical Marxism merges with anarchist currents.

As a further illustration, consider the following characterization of "revolutionary Socialism":

> The revolutionary Socialist denies that State ownership can end in anything other than a bureaucratic despotism. We have seen why the State cannot democratically control industry. Industry can only be democratically owned and controlled by the workers electing directly from their own ranks industrial administrative committees. Socialism will be fundamentally an industrial system; its constituencies will be of an industrial character. Thus those carrying on the social activities and industries of society will be directly represented in the local and central councils of social administration. In this way the power of such delegates will flow upwards from those carrying on the work and conversant with the needs of the community. When the central administrative industrial committee meets it will represent every phase of social activity. Hence the capitalist political or geographical state will be replaced by the industrial administrative committee of Socialism. The transition from the one social system to the other will be the social revolution. The political State throughout history has meant the government of men by ruling classes; the Republic of Socialism will be the government of industry administered on behalf of the whole community. The former meant the economic and political subjection of the many; the latter will mean the economic freedom of all—it will be, therefore, a true democracy.

This programmatic statement appears in William Paul's *The State: its Origins and Function*, written in early 1917—shortly before Lenin's *State and Revolution*, perhaps his most libertarian work (see note 9). Paul was a member of the Marxist-De Leonist Socialist Labor Party and later one of the founders of the British Communist Party.[25] His critique of state socialism resembles the libertarian doctrine of the anarchists in its principle that since state ownership and management will lead to bureaucratic despotism, the social revolution must replace it by the industrial organization of society with direct workers' control. Many similar statements can be cited.

What is far more important is that these ideas have been realized in spontaneous revolutionary action, for example in Germany and Italy after World

War I and in Spain (not only in the agricultural countryside, but also in industrial Barcelona) in 1936. One might argue that some form of council communism is the natural form of revolutionary socialism in an industrial society. It reflects the intuitive understanding that democracy is severely limited when the industrial system is controlled by any form of autocratic elite, whether of owners, managers and technocrats, a "vanguard" party, or a state bureaucracy. Under these conditions of authoritarian domination the classical libertarian ideals developed further by Marx and Bakunin and all true revolutionaries cannot be realized; man will not be free to develop his own potentialities to their fullest, and the producer will remain "a fragment of a human being," degraded, a tool in the productive process directed from above.

The phrase "spontaneous revolutionary action" can be misleading. The anarchosyndicalists, at least, took very seriously Bakunin's remark that the workers' organizations must create "not only the ideas but also the facts of the future itself" in the prerevolutionary period. The accomplishments of the popular revolution in Spain, in particular, were based on the patient work of many years of organization and education, one component of a long tradition of commitment and militancy. The resolutions of the Madrid Congress of June 1931 and the Saragossa Congress in May 1936 foreshadowed in may ways the acts of the revolution, as did the somewhat different ideas sketched by Santillan (see note 4) in his fairly specific account of the social and economic organization to be instituted by the revolution. Guérin writes: "The Spanish revolution was relatively mature in the minds of the libertarian thinkers, as in the popular consciousness." And workers' organizations existed with the structure, the experience, and the understanding to undertake the task of social reconstruction when, with the Franco coup, the turmoil of early 1936 exploded into social revolution. In his introduction to a collection of documents on collectivization in Spain, the anarchist Augustin Souchy writes:

> For many years, the anarchists and syndicalists of Spain considered their supreme task to be the social transformation of the society. In their assemblies of Syndicates and groups, in their journals, their brochures and books, the problem of the social revolution was discussed incessantly and in a systematic fashion.[26]

All of this lies behind the spontaneous achievements, the constructive work of the Spanish Revolution.

The ideas of libertarian socialism, in the sense described, have been submerged in the industrial societies of the past half-century. The dominant ideologies have been those of state socialism or state capitalism (of an increasingly militarized character in the United States, for reasons that are not obscure).[27] But there has been a rekindling of interest in the past few years. These theses I quoted by Anton Pannekoek were taken from a recent pamphlet of a radical French workers' group (*Informations Correspondance Ouvrière*). The remarks by William Paul on revolutionary socialism are cited in a paper by Walter Kendall given at the National Conference on Workers' Control in Sheffield, England, in March 1969. The workers' control movement has become a significant force in England in the past few years. It has organized several conferences and has produced a substantial pamphlet literature, and counts among its active adherents representatives of some of the most important trade unions. The Amalgamated Engineering and Foundryworkers' Union, for example, has adopted, as official policy, the program of nationalization of basic industries under "workers' control at all levels."[28] On the Continent, there are similar developments. May 1968 of course accelerated the growing interest in council communism and related ideas in France and Germany, as it did in England.

Given the general conservative cast of our highly ideological society, it is not too surprising that the United States has been relatively untouched by these developments. But that too may change. The erosion of the cold-war mythology at least makes it possible to raise these questions in fairly broad circles. If the present wave of repression can be beaten back, if the left can overcome its more suicidal tendencies and build upon what has been accomplished in the past decade, then the problem of how to organize industrial society on truly democratic lines, with democratic control in the workplace and in the community, should become a dominant intellectual issue for those who are alive to the problems of contemporary society, and, as a mass movement for libertarian socialism develops, speculation would proceed to action.

In his manifesto of 1865, Bakunin predicted that one element in the social revolution will be "that intelligent and truly noble part of the youth which, though belonging by birth to the privileged classes, in its generous convictions and ardent aspirations, adopts the cause of the people." Perhaps in the rise of the student movement of the 1960s one sees steps towards a fulfillment of this prophecy.

Daniel Guérin has undertaken what he has described as a "process of rehabilitation" of anarchism. He argues, convincingly I believe, that "the constructive ideas of anarchism retain their vitality, that they may, when re-examined and sifted, assist contemporary socialist thought to undertake a new departure…[and] contribute to enriching Marxism."[29] From the "broad back" of anarchism he has selected for more intensive scrutiny those ideas and actions that can be described as libertarian socialist. This is natural and proper. This framework accommodates the major anarchist spokesmen as well as the mass actions that have been animated by anarchist sentiments and ideals. Guérin is concerned not only with anarchist thought but also with the spontaneous actions of popular forces that actually create new social forms in the course of revolutionary struggle. He is concerned with social as well as intellectual creativity. Furthermore, he attempts to draw from the constructive achievements of the past lessons that will enrich the theory of social liberation. For those who wish not only to understand the world, but also to change it, this is the proper way to study the history of anarchism.

Guérin describes the anarchism of the nineteenth century as essentially doctrinal, while the twentieth century, for the anarchists, has been a time of "revolutionary practice."[30] *Anarchism* reflects that judgment. His interpretation of anarchism consciously points towards the future. Arthur Rosenberg once pointed out that popular revolutions characteristically seek to replace "a feudal or centralized authority ruling by force" with some form of communal system which "implies the destruction and disappearance of the old form of State." Such a system will be either socialist or an "extreme form of democracy...[which is] the preliminary condition for Socialism inasmuch as Socialism can only be realized in a world enjoying the highest possible measure of individual freedom." This ideal, he notes, was common to Marx and the anarchists.[31] This natural struggle for liberation runs counter to the prevailing tendency towards centralization in economic and political life.

A century ago Marx wrote that the workers of Paris "felt there was but one alternative—the Commune, or the empire—under whatever name it might reappear."

> The empire had ruined them economically by the havoc it made of public wealth, by the wholesale swindling it fostered, by the props it lent to the artificially accelerated centralization of capital, and the concomitant expropriation of their own ranks. It had suppressed them politically, it had shocked them morally by its orgies, it had insulted their Voltairianism by handing over the education of their children to the *frères Ignorantins*, it had revolted their national feeling as Frenchmen by precipitating them headlong into a war which left only one equivalent for the ruins it made—the disappearance of the empire.[32]

The miserable Second Empire "was the only form of government possible at a time when the bourgeoisie had already lost, and the working class had not yet acquired, the faculty of ruling the nation."

It is not very difficult to rephrase these remarks so that they become appropriate to the imperial systems of 1970. The problem of "freeing man from the curse of economic exploitation and political and social enslavement" remains the problem of our time. As long as this is so, the doctrines and the revolutionary practice of libertarian socialism will serve as an inspiration and a guide.

NOTES

This essay is a revised version of the introduction to Daniel Guérin's *Anarchism: From Theory to Practice*. In a slightly different version, it appeared in the *New York Review of Books*, May 21, 1970. It was first published in book for by Pantheon in 1970 in *For Reasons of State*, and then republished in a 2003 New Press edition of the same book.

1 Octave Mirbeau, quoted in James Joll, *The Anarchists*, pp. 145–6.

2 Rudolf Rocker, *Anarchosyndicalism*, p. 31. [Republished in 2004 by AK Press as *Anarcho-Syndicalism: Theory and Practice*]

3 Cited by Rocker, *ibid.*, p. 77. This quotation and that in the next sentence are from Michael Bakunin, "The Program of the Alliance," in Sam Dolgoff, ed. and trans., *Bakunin on Anarchy*, p. 255.

4 Diego Abad de Santillan, *After the Revolution*, p. 86. In the last chapter, written several months after the revolution has begun, he expresses his dissatisfaction with what had so far been achieved along these lines. On the accomplishment of the social revolution in Spain, see my *American Power and the New Mandarins*, chapter 1, and references cited there; the important study by Broué and Témime has since been translated into English. Several other important studies have appeared since, in particular: Frank Mintz, *L'Autogestion dans l'Espagne révolutionnaire* (Paris: Editions Bélibaste, 1971); César M. Lorenzo, *Les Anarchistes espagnols et le pouvoir*, 1868–1969 (Paris: Editions du Seuil, 1969); Gaston Leval, *Espagne libertaire*, 1936–1939: *L'Oeuvre constructive de la Révolution espagnole* (Paris: Editions du Cercle, 1971). See also Vernon Richards, *Lessons of the Spanish Revolution*, enlarged 1972 edition.

5 Cited by Robert C. Tucker, *The Marxian Revolutionary Idea*, in his discussion of Marxism and anarchism.

6 Bakunin, in a letter to Herzen and Ogareff, 1866. Cited by Daniel Guérin, *Jeunesse du socialisme libertaire*, p. 119.

7 Fernand Pelloutier, cited in Joll, *Anarchists*. The source is "L'Anarchisme et les syndicats ouvriers," *Les Temps nouveaux*, 1895. The full text appears in Daniel Guérin, ed., *Ni Dieu, ni Maître*, an excellent historical anthology of anarchism. [AK Press, 1998]

8 Martin Buber, *Paths in Utopia*, p. 127.

9 "No state, however democratic," Bakunin wrote, "not even the reddest republic—can ever give the people what they really want, i.e. the free self-organization and administration of their own affairs from the bottom upward, without any interference or violence from above, because every state, even the pseudo-People's State concocted by Mr. Marx, is in essence only a machine ruling the masses from above, through a privileged minority of conceited intellectuals, who imagine that they know what the people need and want better than do the people themselves...." "But the people will feel not better if the stick with which they are being beaten is labeled 'the people's stick'" (*Statism and Anarchy* [1873], in Dolgoff, *Bakunin on Anarchy*, p. 338)—"the people's stick" being the democratic Republic.

Marx, of course, saw the matter differently.

For discussion of the impact of the Paris Commune on this dispute, see Daniel Guérin's comments in *Ni Dieu, ni Maître*; these also appear, slightly extended, in his *Pour un marxisme libertaire*. See also note 24.

10 On Lenin's "intellectual deviation" to the left during 1917, see Robert Vincent Daniels, "The State and Revolution: a Case Study in the Genesis and Transformation of Communist Ideology," *American Slavic and East European Review*, vol. 12, no. 1 (1953).

11 Paul Mattick, *Marx and Keynes*, p. 295.

12 Michael Bakunin, "La Commune de Paris et la notion de l'état," reprinted in Guérin, *Ni Dieu, ni Maître*. Bakunin's final remark on the laws of individual nature as the condition of freedom can be compared with the approach to creative thought developed in the rationalist and romantic traditions, discussed in chapter 9. See my *Cartesian Linguistics* and *Language and Mind*.

13 Shlomo Avineri, *The Social and Political Thought of Karl Marx*, p. 142, referring to comments in *The Holy Family*. Avineri states that within the socialist movement only the Israeli *kibbutzim* "have perceived that the modes and forms of present social organization will determine the structure of future society." This, however, was a characteristic position of anarchosyndicalism, as noted earlier.

14 Rocker, *Anarchosyndicalism*, p. 28.

15 See Guérin's works cited earlier.

16 Karl Marx, *Critique of the Gotha Programme*.

17 Karl Marx, *Grundrisse der Kritik der Politischen Ökonomie*, cited by Mattick, *Marx and Keynes*, p. 306. In this connection, see also Mattick's essay "Workers' Control," in Priscilla Long, ed., *The New Left*; and Avineri, *Social and Political Thought of Marx*.

18 Karl Marx, *Capital*, quoted by Robert Tucker, who rightly emphasizes that Marx sees the revolutionary more as a "frustrated producer" than a "dissatisfied consumer" (*The Marxian Revolutionary Idea*). This more radical critique of capitalist relations of production is a direct outgrowth of the libertarian thought of the Enlightenment.

19 Marx, *Capital*, cited by Avineri, *Social and Political Thought of Marx*, p. 83.

20 Pelloutier, "L'anarchisme."

21 "Qu'est-ce que la propriété?" The phrase "property is theft" displeased Marx, who saw in its use a logical problem, theft presupposing the legitimate existence of property. See Avineri, *Social and Political Thought of Marx*.

22 Cited in Buber's *Paths in Utopia*, p. 19.

23 Cited in J. Hampden Jackson, *Marx, Proudhon and European Socialism*, p. 60.

24 Karl Marx, *The Civil War in France*, p. 24. Avineri observes that this and other comments of Marx about the Commune refer pointedly to intentions and plans. As Marx made plain elsewhere, his considered assessment was more critical than in this address.

25 For some background, see Walter Kendall, *The Revolutionary Movement in Britain*.

26 *Collectivisations: L'Oeuvre constructive de la Révolution espagnole*, p. 8.

27 For discussion, see Mattick, *Marx and Keynes*, and Michael Kidron, *Western Capitalism Since the War*. See also discussion and references cited in my *At War with Asia*, chapter 1, pp. 23–6. [Republished by AK Press in 2004]

28 See Hugh Scanlon, *The Way Forward for Workers' Control*. Scanlon is president of the AEF, one of Britain's largest trade unions. The institute was established as a result of the sixth Conference on Workers' Control, March 1968, and serves as a center for disseminating information and encouraging research.

29 Guérin, *Ni Dieu, ni Maître*, introduction. [AK Press, 1998]

30 *Ibid.*

31 Arthur Rosenberg, *A History of Bolshevism*, p. 88.

32 Marx, *Civil War in France*, pp. 62–3.

FOUR
THE RELEVANCE
OF ANARCHO-SYNDICALISM
(1976)

Professor Chomsky, perhaps we should start by trying to define what is not meant by anarchism—the word anarchy is derived, after all, from the Greek, literally meaning "no government." Now presumably people who talk about anarchy or anarchism as a system of political philosophy don't just mean that, as it were, as of January 1st next year, government as we now understand it will suddenly cease; there would be no police, no rule of the road, no laws, no tax collectors, no Post Office, and so forth. Presumably it means something more complicated than that.

Well, yes to some of those questions, no to others. They may very well mean no policemen, but I don't think they would mean no rules of the road. In fact, I should say to begin with that the term anarchism is used to cover quite a range of political ideas, but I would prefer to think of it as the libertarian left, and from that point of view anarchism can be conceived as a kind of voluntary socialism, that is, as libertarian socialist or anarcho-syndicalist or communist anarchist, in the tradition of say Bakunin and Kropotkin and others. They had in mind a highly organized form of society, but a society that was organized on the basis of organic units, organic communities. And generally they meant by that the workplace and the neighborhood, and from those two basic units there could derive through federal arrangements a highly integrated kind of social organization, which might be national or even international in scope. And the decisions could be made over a substantial range, but by delegates who are always part of the organic community from which they come, to which they return and in which, in fact, they live.

So it doesn't mean a society in which there is literally speaking no government so much as a society in which the primary source of authority comes as it were from the bottom up, and not from the top down. Whereas representative democracy, as we have it in the United States and in Britain, would be regarded as a form of from-the-top down authority, even though ultimately the voters decide.

Representative democracy, as in, say, the United States or Great Britain, would be criticized by an anarchist of this school on two grounds. First of all because there is a monopoly of power centralized in the State, and secondly—and critically—because representative democracy is limited to the political sphere and in no serious way encroaches on the economic sphere. Anarchists of this tradition have always held that democratic control of one's productive life is at the core of any serious human liberation, or, for that matter, of any significant democratic practice. That is, as long as individuals are compelled to rent themselves on the market to those who are willing to hire them, as long as their role in production is simply that of ancillary tools, then there are striking elements of coercion and oppression that make talk of democracy very limited, if even meaningful.

Historically speaking, have there been any sustained examples on any substantial scale of societies which approximated to the anarchist ideal?

There are small societies, small in number, that I think have done so quite well, and there are a few examples of large-scale libertarian revolutions which were largely anarchist in their structure. As to the first, small societies extending over a long period, I myself think the most dramatic example is perhaps the Israeli Kibbutzim, which for a long period really were constructed on anarchist principles: that is, self-management, direct worker control, integration of agriculture, industry, service, personal participation in self-management. And they were, I should think, extraordinarily successful by almost any measure that one can impose.

But they were presumably, and still are, in the frame work of a conventional State which guarantees certain basic stabilities.

Well, they weren't always. Actually their history is rather interesting. Since 1948 they've been in the framework of the conventional State. Prior to that they were within the framework of the colonial enclave and in fact there was a subterranean, largely cooperative society which was not really part of the system of the British mandate, but was functioning outside of it. And to some extent that's survived the establishment of the State, though of course it became integrated into the State and in my view lost a fair amount of its libertarian socialist character through this process, and through other processes which are unique to the history of that region, which we need not go into.

However, as functioning libertarian socialist institutions, I think they are an interesting model that is highly relevant to advanced industrial societies in a way in which some of the other examples that have existed in the past are not. A good example of a really large-scale anarchist revolution—in fact the best example to my knowledge—is the Spanish revolution in 1936, in which over most of Republican Spain there was a quite inspiring anarchist revolution that involved both industry and agriculture over substantial areas, developed in a way which to the outside looks spontaneous. Though in fact if you look at the roots of it, you discover that it was based on some three generations of experiment and thought and work which extended anarchist ideas to very large parts of the population in this largely pre-industrial—though not totally pre-industrial—society. And that again was, by both human measures and indeed anyone's economic measures, quite successful. That is, production continued effectively; workers in farms and factories proved quite capable of managing their affairs without coercion from above, contrary to what lots of socialists, communists, liberals and others wanted to believe, and in fact you can't tell what would have happened. That anarchist revolution was simply destroyed by force, but during the period in which it was alive I think it was a highly successful and, as I say, in many ways a very inspiring testimony to the ability of poor working people to organize and manage their own affairs, extremely successfully, without coercion and control. How relevant the Spanish experience is to an advanced industrial society, one might question in detail.

It's clear that the fundamental idea of anarchism is the primacy of the individual—not necessarily in isolation, but with other individuals—and the fulfillment of his freedom. This in a sense looks awfully like the founding ideas of the United States of America. What is it about the American experience which has made freedom as used in that tradition become a suspect and indeed a tainted phrase in the minds of anarchists and libertarian socialist thinkers like yourself?

135

Let me just say I don't really regard myself as an anarchist thinker. I'm a derivative fellow traveler, let's say. Anarchist thinkers have constantly referred to the American experience and to the ideal of Jeffersonian democracy very very favorably. You know, Jefferson's concept that the best government is the government which governs least or Thoreau's addition to that, that the best government is the one that doesn't govern at all, is one that's often repeated by anarchist thinkers through modern times.

However, the ideal of Jeffersonian democracy, putting aside the fact that it was a slave society, developed in an essentially pre-capitalist system, that is in a society in which there was no monopolistic control, there were no significant centers of private power. In fact it's striking to go back and read today some of the classic libertarian texts. If one reads, say, Wilhelm von Humboldt's critique of the State of 1792, a significant classic libertarian text that certainly inspired Mill, one finds that he doesn't speak at all of the need to resist private concentration of power: rather he speaks of the need to resist the encroachment of coercive State power. And that is what one finds also in the early American tradition. But the reason is that that was the only kind of power there was. I mean, Humboldt takes for granted that individuals are roughly equivalent in their private power, and that the only real imbalance of power lies in the centralized authoritarian state, and individual freedom must be sustained against its intrusion—the State or the Church. That's what he feels one must resist.

Now when he speaks, for example, of the need for control of one's creative life, when he decries the alienation of labor that arises from coercion or even instruction or guidance in one's work, rather than self-management in one's work, he's giving an anti-statist or anti-theocratic ideology. But the same principles apply very well to the capitalist industrial society that emerged later. And I would think that Humboldt, had he been consistent, would have ended up being a libertarian socialist.

Don't these precedents suggest that there is something inherently pre-industrial about the applicability of libertarian ideas—that they necessarily presuppose a rather rural society in which technology and production are fairly simple, and in which the economic organization tends to be small-scale and localized?

Well, let me separate that into two questions: one, how anarchists have felt about it, and two, what I think is the case. As far as anarchist reactions are concerned, there are two. There has been one anarchist tradition—and one might think, say, of Kropotkin as a representative—which had much of the character you describe. On the other hand there's another anarchist tradition that develops into anarcho-syndicalism which simply regarded anarchist ideas as the proper mode of organization for a highly complex advanced industrial society. And that tendency in anarchism merges, or at least inter-relates very closely with a variety of left-wing Marxism, the kind that one finds in, say, the Council Communists that grew up in the Luxemburgian tradition, and that is later represented by Marxist theorists like Anton Pannekoek, who developed a whole theory of workers' councils in industry and who is himself a scientist and astronomer, very much part of the industrial world.

So which of these two views is correct? I mean, is it necessary that anarchist concepts belong to the pre-industrial phase of human society, or is anarchism the rational mode of organization for a highly advanced industrial society? Well, I myself believe the latter, that is, I think that industrialization and the advance of technology raise possibilities for self-management over a broad scale that simply didn't exist in an earlier period. And that in fact this is precisely the rational mode for an advanced and complex industrial society, one in which workers can very well become masters of their own immediate affairs, that is, in direction and control of the shop, but also can be in a position to make the major substantive decisions concerning the structure of the economy, concerning social institutions, concerning planning regionally and beyond. At present, institutions do not permit them to have control over the requisite information, and the relevant training to understand these matters. A good deal could be automated. Much of the necessary work that is required to keep a decent level of social life going can be consigned to machines—at least in principle—which means humans can be free to undertake the kind of creative work which may not have been possible, objectively, in the early stages of the industrial revolution.

I'd like to pursue in a moment the question of the economics of an anarchist society, but could you sketch in a little more detail the political constitution of an anarchist society, as you would see it, in modern conditions? Would there be political parties, for example? What residual forms of government would in fact remain?

Let me sketch what I think would be perhaps a rough consensus, and one that I think is essentially correct. Beginning with the two modes of immediate organization and control, namely organization and control in the workplace and in the community, one can imagine a network of workers' councils, and at a higher level, representation across the factories, or across branches of industry, or across crafts, and on to general assemblies of workers' councils that can be regional and national and international in character. And from another point of view one can project a system of governance that involves local assemblies—again federated regionally, dealing with regional issues, crossing crafts, industries, trades and so on, and again at the level of the nation or beyond, through federation and so on.

Now exactly how these would develop and how they would inter-relate and whether you need both of them or only one, well these are matters over which anarchist theoreticians have debated and many proposals exist, and I don't feel confident to take a stand. These are questions which will have to be worked out.

But there would not, for example, be direct national elections and political parties organized from coast to coast, as it were. Because if there were that would presumably create a kind of central authority which would be inimical to the idea of anarchism.

No, the idea of anarchism is that delegation of authority is rather minimal and that its participants at any one of these levels of government should be directly responsive to the organic community in which they live. In fact the optimal situation would be that participation in one of these levels of government should be temporary, and even during the period when it's taking place should be only partial; that is, the members of a workers' council who are for some period actually functioning to make decisions that other people don't have the time to make, should also continue to do their work as part of the workplace or neighborhood community in which they belong.

As for political parties, my feeling is that an anarchist society would not forcefully prevent political parties from arising. In fact, anarchism has always been based on the idea that any sort of Procrustean bed, any system of norms

137

that is imposed on social life will constrain and very much underestimate its energy and vitality and that all sorts of new possibilities of voluntary organization may develop at that higher level of material and intellectual culture. But I think it is fair to say that insofar as political parties are felt to be necessary, anarchist organization of society will have failed. That is, it should be the case, I would think, that where there is direct participation in self-management, in economic and social affairs, then factions, conflicts, differences of interest and ideas and opinion, which should be welcomed and cultivated, will be expressed at every one of these levels. Why they should fall into two, three or political parties, I don't quite see. I think that the complexity of human interest and life does not fall in that fashion. Parties represent basically class interests, and classes would have been eliminated or transcended in such a society.

One last question on the political organization: is there not a danger with this sort of hierarchical tier of assemblies and quasi-governmental structure, without direct elections, that the central body, or the body that is in some sense at the top of this pyramid, would get very remote from the people on the ground; and since it will have to have some powers if it's going to deal with international affairs, for example, and may even have to have control over armed forces and things like that, that it would be less democratically responsive than the existing regime?

138

It's a very important property of any libertarian society, to prevent an evolution in the direction that you've described, which is a possible evolution, and one that institutions should be designed to prevent. And I think that that's entirely possible. I myself am totally unpersuaded that participation in governance is a full-time job. It may be in an irrational society, where all sorts of problems arise because of the irrational nature of institutions. But in a properly functioning advanced industrial society organized along libertarian lines, I would think that executing decisions taken by representative bodies is a part-time job which should be rotated throughout the community and, furthermore, should be undertaken by people who at all times continue to be participants in their own direct activity.

It may be that governance is itself a function on a par with, say, steel production. If that turns out to be true—and I think that is a question of empirical fact that has to be determined, it can't be projected out of the mind—but if it turns out to be true then it seems to me the natural suggestion is that governance should be organized industrially, as simply one of the branches of industry, with their own workers' councils and their own self-governance and their own participation in broader assemblies.

I might say that in the workers' councils that have spontaneously developed here and there—for example, in the Hungarian revolution of 1956—that's pretty much what happened. There was, as I recall, a workers' council of State employees who were simply organized along industrial lines as another branch of industry. That's perfectly possible, and it should be or could be a barrier against the creation of the kind of remote coercive bureaucracy that anarchists of course fear.

If you suppose that there would continue to be a need for self-defense, on quite a sophisticated level, I don't see from your description how you would achieve effective control of this system of part-time representative councils at various levels from the bottom up, over an organization as powerful and as necessarily technically sophisticated as, for example, the Pentagon.

Well, first we should be a little clearer about terminology. You refer to the Pentagon, as is usually done, as a defense organization. In 1947, when the National Defense Act was passed, the former War Department—the American department concerned with war which up to that time was called honestly the War Department—had its name changed to the Defense Department. I was a student then and didn't think I was very sophisticated, but I knew and everyone knew that this meant that to whatever extent the American military had been involved in defense in the past—and partially it had been so—this was now over: since it was being called the Defense Department, that meant it was going to be a department of aggression, nothing else.

On the principle of never believe anything until it's officially denied.

Right. Sort of on the assumption that Orwell essentially had captured the nature of the modern state. And that's exactly the case. I mean the Pentagon is in no sense a defense department. It has never defended the United States from anyone: it has only served to conduct aggression, and I think that the American people would be much better off without a Pentagon. They certainly don't need it for defense. Its intervention in international affairs has never been—well, you know, never is a strong word, but I think you would be hard put to find a case—certainly it has not been its characteristic pose to support freedom or liberty or to defend people and so on. That's not the role of the massive military organization that is controlled by the Defense Department. Rather its tasks are two—both quite antisocial.

The first is to preserve an international system in which what are called American interests, which primarily means business interests, can flourish. And secondly, it has an internal economic task. I mean the Pentagon has been the primary Keynesian mechanism whereby the government intervenes to maintain what is ludicrously called the health of the economy by inducing production—that means production of waste.

Now both these functions serve certain interests, in fact dominant interests, dominant class interests in American society. But I don't think in any sense they serve the public interest, and I think that this system of production of waste and of destruction would essentially be dismantled in a libertarian society. Now one shouldn't be too glib about this. If one can imagine, let's say, a social revolution in the United States—that's rather distant, I would assume—but if that took place, it's hard to imagine that there would be any credible enemy from the outside that could threaten that social revolution—we wouldn't be attacked by Mexico or Cuba, let's say. An American revolution would not require, I think, defense against aggression. On the other hand, if a libertarian social revolution were to take place, say, in Western Europe, then I think the problem of defense would be very critical.

I was going to say, it can't surely be inherent in the anarchist idea that there should be no self-defense, because such anarchist experiments as there have been have, on the record, actually been destroyed from without.

Ah, but I think that these questions cannot be given a general answer, they have to be answered specifically, relative to specific historical and objective conditions.

It's just that I found a little difficulty in following your description of the proper democratic control of this kind of organization, because I find it a little hard to see the generals controlling themselves in the manner you would approve of.

That's why I do want to point out the complexity of the issue. It depends on the country and the society that you're talking about. In the United States one kind of problem arises. If there were a libertarian social revolution in Europe, then I think the problems you raise would be very serious, because there would be a serious problem of defense. That is, I would assume that if libertarian socialism were achieved at some level in Western Europe, there would be a direct military threat both from the Soviet Union and from the United States. And the problem would be how that should be countered. That's the problem that was faced by the Spanish revolution. There was direct military intervention by Fascists, by Communists and by liberal democracies in the background, and the question how one can defend oneself against attack at this level is a very serious one.

However, I think we have to raise the question whether centralized standing armies, with high technology deterrents, are the most effective way to do that. And that's by no means obvious. For example, I don't think that a Western European centralized army would itself deter a Russian or American attack to prevent libertarian socialism—the kind of attack that I would quite frankly expect at some level: maybe not military, at least economic.

But nor on the other hand would a lot of peasants with pitchforks and spades...

We're not talking about peasants; we're talking about a highly sophisticated, highly urban industrial society. And it seems to me its best method of defense would be its political appeal to the working class in the countries that were part of the attack. But again, I don't want to be glib; it might need tanks, it might need armies. And if it did, I think we can be fairly sure that that would contribute to the possible failure or at least decline of the revolutionary force— for exactly the reasons that you mentioned. That is, I think it's extremely hard to imagine how an effective centralized army, deploying tanks, planes, strategic weapons and so on, could function. If that's what's required to preserve the revolutionary structures, then I think they may well not be preserved.

If the basic defense is the political appeal, or the appeal of the political and economic organization, perhaps we could look in a little more detail at that. You wrote, in one of your essays, that "in a decent society, everyone would have the opportunity to find interesting work, and each person would be permitted the fullest possible scope for his talents." And then you went on to ask: "What more would be required in particular, extrinsic reward in the form of wealth and power? Only if we assume that applying one's talents in interesting and socially useful work is not rewarding in itself." I think that that line of reasoning is certainly one of the things that appeals to a lot of people. But it still needs to be explained, I think, why the kind of work which people would find interesting and appealing and fulfilling to do would coincide at all closely with the kind which actually needs to be done, if we're to sustain anything like the standard of living which people demand and are used to.

141

Well, there's a certain amount of work that just has to be done if we're to maintain that standard of living. It's an open question how onerous that work has to be. Let's recall that science and technology and intellect have not been devoted to examining that question or to overcoming the onerous and self-destructive character of the necessary work of society. The reason is that it has always been assumed that there is a substantial body of wage-slaves who will do it simply because otherwise they'll starve. However, if human intelligence is turned to the question of how to make the necessary work of society itself meaningful, we don't know what the answer will be. My guess is that a fair amount of it can be made entirely tolerable. It's a mistake to think that even back-breaking physical labor is necessarily onerous. Many people— myself included—do it for relaxation. Well recently, for example, I got it into my head to plant thirty-four trees in a meadow behind the house, on the State Conservation Commission, which means I had to dig thirty-four holes in the sand. You know, for me, and what I do with my time mostly, that's pretty hard work, but I have to admit I enjoyed it. I wouldn't have enjoyed it if I'd had work norms, if I'd had an overseer, and if I'd been ordered to do it at a certain moment, and so on. On the other hand, if it's a task taken on just out of interest, fine, that can be done. And that's without any technology, without any thought given to how to design the work, and so on.

I put it to you that there may be a danger that this view of things is a rather romantic delusion, entertained only by a small elite of people who happen, like professors, perhaps journalists and so on, to be in the very privileged situation of being paid to do what anyway they like to do.

That's why I began with a big "If." I said we first have to ask to what extent the necessary work of society—namely, that work which is required to maintain the standard of living that we want—needs to be onerous and undesirable. I think the answer is, much less than it is today; but let's assume there is some extent to which it remains onerous. Well, in that case, the answer's quite simple: that work has to be equally shared among people capable of doing it.

And everyone spends a certain number of months a year working on an automobile production line and a certain number of months collecting the garbage and...

142

If it turns out that these are really tasks which people will find no self-fulfillment in. Incidentally I don't quite believe that. As I watch people work, craftsmen, let's say, automobile mechanics for example, I think one often finds a good deal of pride in work. I think that that kind of pride in work well done, in complicated work well done, because it takes thought and intelligence to do it, especially when one is also involved in management of the enterprise, determination of how the work will be organized, what it is for, what the purposes of the work are, what'll happen to it and so on—I think all of this can be satisfying and rewarding activity which in fact requires skills, the kind of skills people will enjoy exercising. However, I'm thinking hypothetically now. Suppose it turns out that there is some residue of work which really no one wants to do, whatever that may be—okay, then I say that the residue of work must be equally shared, and beyond that people will be free to exercise their talents as they see fit.

I put it to you, Professor, that if that residue were very large, as some people would say it was, if it accounted for the work involved in producing ninety per cent of what we all want to consume—then the organization of sharing this, on the basis that everybody did a little bit of all the nasty jobs, would become wildly inefficient. Because after all, you have to be trained and equipped to do even the nasty jobs, and the efficiency of the whole economy would suffer and therefore the standard of living which it sustained would be reduced.

Well, for one thing, this is really quite hypothetical, because I don't believe that the figures are anything like that. As I say, it seems to me that if human intelligence were devoted to asking how technology can be designed to fit the needs of the human producer, instead of conversely—that is, now we ask how the human being with his special properties can be fitted into a technological system designed for other ends, namely production for profit—my feeling is that if that were done, we would find that the really unwanted work is far smaller than you suggest. But whatever it is, notice that we have two alternatives. One alternative is to have it equally shared, the other is to design social institutions so that some group of people will be simply compelled to do the work, on pain of starvation. Those are the two alternatives.

Not compelled to do it, but they might agree to do it voluntarily because they were paid an amount which they felt made it worthwhile.

Well, but you see I'm assuming that everyone essentially gets equal remuneration. Don't forget that we're not talking about a society now where the people who do the onerous work are paid substantially more than the people who do the work that they do on choice—quite the opposite. The way our society works, the way any class society works, the people who do the unwanted work are the ones who are paid least. That work is done and we sort of put it out of our minds, because it's assumed that there will be a massive class of people who control only one factor of production, namely their labor, and have to sell it, and they'll have to do that work because they have nothing else to do, and they'll be paid very little for it. I accept the correction. Let's imagine three kinds of society: one, the current one, in which the undesired work is given to wage-slaves. Let's imagine a second system in which the undesired work, after the best efforts to make it meaningful, is shared; and let's imagine a third system where the undesired work receives high extra pay, so that individuals voluntarily choose to do it. Well, it seems to me that either of the two latter systems is consistent with—vaguely speaking—anarchist principles. I would argue myself for the second rather than the third, but either of the two is quite remote from any present social organization or any tendency in contemporary social organization.

143

Let me put that to you in another way. It seems to me that there is a fundamental choice, however one disguises it, between whether you organize work for the satisfaction it gives to the people who do it, or whether you organize it on the basis of the value of what is produced for the people who are going to use or consume what is produced. And that a society which is organized on the basis of giving everybody the maximum opportunity to ful-

fill their hobbies, which is essentially the work for work's sake view, finds its logical culmination in a monastery, where the kind of work which is done, namely prayer, is work, for the self-enrichment of the worker and where nothing is produced which is of any use to anybody and you live either at a low standard of living, or you actually starve.

Well, there are some factual assumptions here, and I disagree with you about the factual assumptions. My feeling is that part of what makes work meaningful is that it does have use, that its products do have use. The work of the craftsman is in part meaningful to that craftsman because of the intelligence and skill that he puts into it, but also in part because the work is useful, and I might say the same is true of scientists. I mean, the fact that the kind of work you do may lead to something else—that's what it means in science, you know—may contribute to something else, that's very important, quite apart from the elegance and beauty of what you may achieve. And I think that covers every field of human endeavor. Furthermore, I think that if we look at a good part of human history, we'll find that people to a substantial extent did get some degree of satisfaction—often a lot of satisfaction—from the productive and creative work that they were doing. And I think that the chances for that are enormously enhanced by industrialization. Why? Precisely because much of the most meaningless drudgery can be taken over by machines, which means that the scope for really creative human work is substantially enlarged.

Now, you speak of work freely undertaken as a hobby. But I don't believe that. I think work freely undertaken can be useful, meaningful work done well. Also you pose a dilemma which many people pose, between desire for satisfaction in work and a desire to create things of value to the community. But it's not so obvious that there is any dilemma, any contradiction. So it's by no means clear—in fact I think it's false—that contributing to the enhancement of pleasure and satisfaction in work is inversely proportional to contributing to the value of the output.

Not inversely proportional, but it might be unrelated. I mean, take some very simple thing, like selling ice-creams on the beach on a public holiday. Its a service to society; undoubtedly people want ice-creams, they feel hot. On the other hand, it's hard to see in what sense there is either a craftsman's joy or a great sense of social virtue or nobility, in performing that task. Why would anyone preform that task if they were not rewarded for it?

I must say I've seen some very cheery-looking ice-cream vendors...

Sure, they're making a lot of money.

...who happen to like the idea that they're giving children ice-creams, which seems to me a perfectly reasonable way to spend one's time, as compared with thousands of other occupations that I can imagine.

Recall that a person has an occupation, and it seems to me that most of the occupations that exist—especially the ones that involve what are called services, that is, relations to human beings—have an intrinsic satisfaction and rewards associated with them, namely in the dealings with the human beings that are involved. That's true of teaching, and it's true of ice-cream vending. I agree that ice-cream vending doesn't require the commitment or intelligence that teaching does, and maybe for that reason it will be a less desired occupation. But if so, it will have to be shared.

However, what I'm saying is that our characteristic assumption that pleasure in work, pride in work, is either unrelated to or negatively related to the value of the output is related to a particular stage of social history, namely capitalism, in which human beings are tools of production. It is by no means necessarily true. For example, if you look at the many interviews with workers on assembly lines, for example, that have been done by industrial psychologists, you find that one of the things they complain about over and over again is the fact that their work simply can't be well done, the fact that the assembly line goes through so fast that they can't do their work properly. I just happened to look recently at a study of longevity in some journal of gerontology which tried to trace the factors that you could use to predict longevity—you know, cigarette-smoking and drinking, genetic factors—everything was looked at. It turned out in fact that the highest predictor, the most successful predictor, was job satisfaction.

145

People who have nice jobs live longer.

People who are *satisfied* with their jobs. And I think that makes a good deal of sense, you know, because that's where you spend your life, that's where your creative activities are. Now what leads to job satisfaction? Well, I think many things lead to it, and the knowledge that you are doing something useful for the community is an important part of it. Many people who are satisfied with their work are people who feel that what they're doing is important to do. They can be teachers, they can be doctors; they can be scientists, they can be craftsmen, they can be farmers. I mean, I think the feeling that what one is doing is important, is worth doing, contributes to those with whom one has social bonds, is a very significant factor in one's personal satisfaction.

And over and above that there is the pride and the self-fulfillment that comes from a job well done—from simply taking your skills and putting them to use. Now I don't see why that should in any way harm, in fact I should think it would enhance, the value of what's produced.

But let's imagine still that at some level it does harm. Well okay, at that point the society, the community, has to decide how to make compromises. Each individual is both a producer and a consumer, after all, and that means that each individual has to join in those socially determined compromises—if in fact there are compromises. And again I feel the nature of the compromise is much exaggerated because of the distorting prism of the really coercive and personally destructive system in which we live.

All right, you say the community has to make decisions about compromises, and of course Communist theory provides for this in its whole thinking about national planning, decisions about investment, direction of investment, and so forth. In an anarchist society it would seem that you're not willing to provide for that amount of governmental superstructure that would be necessary to make the plans, make the investment decisions, to decide whether you give priority to what people want to consume, or whether you give priority to the work people want to do.

I don't agree with that. It seems to me that anarchist, or, for that matter, left-Marxist structures, based on systems of workers' councils and federations, provide exactly the set of levels of decision-making at which decisions can be made about a national plan. Similarly, State socialist societies also provide a level of decision making—let's say the nation—in which national plans can be produced. There's no difference in that respect. The difference has to do with participation in those decisions and control over those decisions. In the view of anarchists and left-Marxists—like the workers' councils or the Council Communists, who were left-Marxists—those decisions are made by the informed working class through their assemblies and their direct representatives, who live among them and work among them. In the State socialist systems, the national plan is made by a national bureaucracy, which accumulates to itself all relevant information, makes decisions, offers them to the public, and occasionally every few years comes before the public and says, "You can pick me or you can pick him, but we're all part of this remote bureaucracy." These are the poles, these are the polar opposites within the socialist tradition.

So in fact there's a very considerable role for the State and possibly, even for civil servants, for bureaucracy, but it's the control over it that is different.

Well, you see, I don't really believe that we need a separate bureaucracy to carry out governmental decisions.

You need various forms of expertise.

Oh yes, but let's take expertise with regard to economic planning, because certainly in any complex industrial society there should be a group of technicians whose task is to produce plans, and to lay out the consequences of decisions, to explain to the people who have to make the decisions that if you decide this, you're going to likely get this consequence, because that's what your programming model shows, and so on. But the point is that those planning systems are themselves industries, and they will have their workers' councils and they will be part of the whole council system, and the distinction is that these planning systems do not make decisions. They produce plans in exactly the same way that automakers produce autos. The plans are then available for the workers' councils and council assemblies, in the same way that autos are available to ride in. Now of course what this does require is an informed and educated working class. But that's precisely what we are capable of achieving in advanced industrial societies.

How far does the success of libertarian socialism or anarchism really depend on a fundamental change in the nature of man, both in his motivation, his altruism, and also in his knowledge and sophistication?

I think it not only depends on it but in fact the whole purpose of libertarian socialism is that it will contribute to it. It will contribute to a spiritual transformation—precisely that kind of great transformation in the way humans conceive of themselves and their ability to act, to decide, to create, to produce, to enquire—precisely that spiritual transformation that social thinkers from the left-Marxist traditions, from Luxemburg say, through anarcho-syndicalists, have always emphasized. So on the one hand it requires that spiritual transformation. On the other hand, its purpose is to create institutions which will contribute to that transformation in the nature of work, the nature of creative activity, simply in social bonds among people, and through this interaction of creating institutions which permit new aspects of human nature to flourish. And then the building of still further libertarian institutions to which these liberated human beings can contribute: this is the evolution of socialism as I understand it.

And finally, Professor Chomsky, what do you think of the chances of societies along these lines coming into being in the major industrial countries in the West in the next quarter of a century or so?

I don't think I'm wise enough, or informed enough, to make predictions and I think predictions about such poorly-understood matters probably generally reflect personality more than judgment. But I think this much at least we can say: there are obvious tendencies in industrial capitalism towards concentration of power in narrow economic empires and in what is increasingly becoming a totalitarian state. These are tendencies that have been going on for a long time, and I don't see anything stopping them really. I think those tendencies will continue; they're part of the stagnation and decline of capitalist institutions.

147

Now it seems to me that the development towards state totalitarianism and towards economic concentration—and of course they are linked—will continually lead to revulsion, to efforts of personal liberation and to organizational efforts at social liberation. And that'll take all sorts of forms. Throughout all Europe, in one form or another, there is a call for what is sometimes called worker participation or co-determination, or even sometimes worker control. Now most of these efforts are minimal. I think that they're misleading, in fact may even undermine efforts for the working class to liberate itself. But in part they're responsive to a strong intuition and understanding that coercion and oppression, whether by private economic power or by the State bureaucracy, is by no means a necessary feature of human life. And the more those concentrations of power and authority continue, the more we will see revulsion against them and efforts to organize and overthrow them. Sooner or later they'll succeed, I hope.

This interview was conducted by Peter Jay on July 25, 1976, for a broadcast by BBC's *London Weekend TV*, and published in Noam Chomsky, *Radical Priorities*, expanded ed., edited by C. P. Otero (Oakland: AK Press, 2003), pp. 211–24.

FIVE
PREFACE TO
ANTOLOGIJA ANARHIZMA
(1986)

The anarchosyndicalist thinker Rudolf Rocker described modern anarchism as "the confluence of the two great currents, which during and since the French revolution have found such characteristic expression in the intellectual life of Europe: Socialism and Liberalism." Correspondingly, the most constructive elements of modern anarchism, both in theory and in practice, developed from a critique of liberal capitalism and of tendencies that depict themselves as socialist.

The liberal ideals of the Enlightenment could be realized only in very partial and limited ways in the emerging capitalist order: "Democracy with its motto of equality of all citizens before the law and Liberalism with its right of man over his own person both were wrecked on the realities of capitalist economy," Rocker correctly observed. Those who are compelled to rent themselves to owners of capital in order to survive are deprived of one of the most fundamental rights: the right to productive, creative and fulfilling work under one's own control, in solidarity with others. And under the ideological constraints of capitalist democracy, the prime necessity is to satisfy the needs of those in a position to make investment decisions; if their demands are not satisfied, there will be no production, no work, no social services, no means for survival. All necessarily subordinate themselves and their interests to the overriding need to serve the interests of the owners and managers of the society, who, furthermore, with their control over resources, are easily able to shape the ideological system (the media, schools, universities and so on) in their interests, to determine the basic conditions within which the political process will function, its parameters and basic agenda, and to call upon the resources of state violence, when need be, to suppress any challenge to entrenched power. The point was formulated succinctly in the early days of the liberal democratic revolutions by John Jay, the President of the Continental Congress and the first Chief Justice of the United States Supreme Court: "The people who own the country ought to govern it." And, of course, they do, whatever political faction may be in power. Matters could hardly be otherwise when economic power is narrowly concentrated and the basic decisions over the nature and character of life, the investment decisions, are in principle removed from democratic control,

Similarly, the principle of equality before the law can only be partially realized in capitalist democracy. The rule of law exists in varying degrees, but all too often, in operative reality, freedom in a capitalist society, like everything else, becomes a kind of commodity: one can have as much as one can purchase. In a wealthy society, much of the population can purchase quite a substantial amount, but the formal guarantees mean little to those who lack resources to avail themselves of them.

In general, the Enlightenment ideals can be realized only in ways that are pale reflection of their human significance. The phrase "capitalist democracy" is virtually a contradiction in terms, if by "democracy" we mean a system in which ordinary people have effective means to participate in the decisions that affect their lives and that engage their communities.

As for socialism, the anarchist insists, again in Rocker's words, that "socialism will be free or it will not be at all. In its recognition of this lies the genuine and profound justification for the existence of anarchism." In taking this proper stand, anarchists set themselves in opposition to the currents called "socialist" in the modern world. The world's two great propaganda systems are united in the doctrine that the society created by Lenin and Trotsky and molded further by Stalin and his successors, and others that draw from that experience, are "socialist." The reason for this unusual convergence in the Agitprop of the superpowers and colonized intellectuals elsewhere are plain enough. For leadership of the so-called "socialist states," the pretense serves to legitimate their rule, allowing them to exploit the aura of socialist ideals and the respect that is rightly accorded them to conceal their own often brutal practice as they destroy every vestige of genuine socialism. For the world's second major propaganda system, association of socialism with the Soviet Union and others who adopted the Leninist model serves as a powerful ideological weapon to enforce conformity and obedience to the state capitalist institutions, the only perceived alternative to the "socialist" dungeon.

In reality, the Bolsheviks set out at once, on achieving the state power, to destroy the rich potential of the instruments of the popular struggle and liberation created in revolutionary Russia, the Soviets and factory councils in particular, establishing the rule of the Party, in practice its Central Committee and its Maximal Leaders—exactly as Trotsky had predicted years earlier, as Rosa Luxemburg and other left Marxists warned at the time, and as the anarchists had always understood. Lenin called for "unquestioning submission to a single will" and demanded that "in the interests of socialism" the leadership must assume "dictatorial powers" over the workers who must "unquestioningly obey the single will of the leaders of the process," proceeding to transform the society into a labor army, eliminating any vestige of workers control and the "factionalism" that could permit free expression, independent thought and meaningful organization. None of this would have surprised Bakunin, who, long before, had warned that the "red bureaucracy" would prove to be "the most vile and terrible lie that our century created."

Bakunin's insights were developed in the context of a perceptive critique of the intelligentsia of the modern era, a "new class, a new hierarchy of real and counterfeit scientists and scholars," who will seek to create "the reign of scientific intelligence, the most aristocratic, despotic, arrogant and elitist of all regimes." They will seek to assume the reins of state power, he warned, exploiting popular struggles for their own ends, and in the name of "science" and their alleged superior understanding will drive the "ignorant masses" to a form of "socialism" that will "serve to conceal the domination of the masses by a handful of privileged elite." And where popular struggle fails, they will become the managers of the increasingly centralized state capitalist systems—the managers of the corporate economy, of state power, of the ideological institutions—while "the people will feel no better if the stick with which they are being beaten is labeled 'the people's stick.'"

Anarchists, and left Marxist elements that became increasingly marginalized as a result of the triumph of state socialism, have sought to explain and oppose these tendencies, but to date without notable success. Bakunin's observations foreshadow crucial features of the modern age. It is not difficult to comprehend the enormous appeal to the modern intelligentsia of Leninist doctrine, and the state capitalist doctrines that are in essence rather similar: these doctrines grant them the right to share in the exercise of power, to benefit from the skewed distribution of privilege, and sometimes, to concentrate power in their own hands. Revolutionary struggles have repeatedly led to the creation of popular forms that could serve as instruments of democratic participation and control over social and economic life, but these have been unable to withstand the onslaught to authoritarian elements within and powerful enemies without. It is a striking fact that so-called "socialist" and capitalist states often act in tacit cooperation to crush such tendencies, a notable example being the worker and peasant revolution in Spain in 1936–37, crushed by a combined assault led by the Soviet-controlled Communist Party, the liberal democracies, and the fascist forces, who fought one another, but joined to overcome the heresy of a socialism that would be free.

One great achievement of the 18th century was to create the ideas and in part even the basic forms of political democracy, including the protection of the rights of the person against authoritarian power. But it remains an unfulfilled goal to expand democracy beyond the narrow arena in which it partially functions, to all of social and economic life, with true control by producers over production and investment, and the elimination of structures of hierarchy and domination in the state system, the private economy, and much of social life. In most of the world, 18th century revolutions have yet to be achieved, let alone the task of overcoming penury, starvation, servitude to the domestic or foreign master, and achieving the bare minimum of a decent existence. Constructive efforts to overcome misery and oppression will naturally be blocked by those who benefit from their persistence, the great ongoing tragedy of the modern era. The rudiments of true socialism remain a vision and a great goal for future struggles. To undertake them or even to understand the problems that must be addressed, one must be able to free oneself from a network of deceit and distortion, of which the use of the term "socialism" to designate a system that forcefully rejects its basic principles is only one crucial element.

The record of anarchist ideas, and even more, of the inspiring struggles of people who have sought to liberate themselves from oppression and domination, must be treasured and preserved, not as means of freezing thought and conception in some new mold but as a basis for understanding of the social reality and committed work to change it. There is no reason to suppose that history is at an end, that the current structures of authority and domination are graven in stone. It would also be a great error to underestimate the power of social forces that will fight to maintain power and privilege.

Today's science is far from being able to establish the fact, but we can only hope that Bakunin's "instinct for freedom" is truly a central constituent element of human nature, one that will not long be submerged and controlled by authoritarian doctrine and the hopelessness it induces, by power and the ravages it perpetrates.

This essay originally appeared as the preface to: Rudolf Rizman (ed.), *Antologija anarhizma: Knjiznica revolucionarne teorije*, (Ljubljana 1986).

SIX
CONTAINING THE THREAT OF DEMOCRACY
(1990)

In his illuminating study of the Scottish intellectual tradition, George Davie identifies its central theme as a recognition of the fundamental role of "*natural beliefs* or principles of common sense, such as the belief in an independent external world, the belief in causality, the belief in ideal standards, and the belief in the self of conscience as separate from the rest of one." These principles are sometimes considered to have a regulative character; though never fully justified, they provide the foundations for thought and conception. Some held that they contain "an irreducible element of mystery," Davie points out, while others hoped to provide a rational foundation for them. On that issue, the jury is still out.[1]

We can trace such ideas to 17th century thinkers who reacted to the skeptical crisis of the times by recognizing that there are no absolutely certain grounds for knowledge, but that we do, nevertheless, have ways to gain a reliable understanding of the world and to improve that understanding and apply it—essentially the standpoint of the working scientist today. Similarly, in normal life a reasonable person relies on the natural beliefs of common sense while recognizing that they may be too parochial or misguided, and hoping to refine or alter them as understanding progresses.

Davie credits David Hume with providing this particular cast to Scottish philosophy, and more generally, with having taught philosophy the proper questions to ask. One puzzle that Hume raised is particularly pertinent to the questions we are hoping to address in these two days of discussion. In considering the First Principles of Government, Hume found "nothing more surprising" than

> to see the easiness with which the many are governed by the few; and to observe the implicit submission with which men resign their own sentiments and passions to those of their rulers. When we enquire by what means this wonder is brought about, we shall find, that as Force is always on the side of the governed, the governors have nothing to support them but opinion. 'Tis therefore, on opinion only that government is founded; and this maxim extends to the most despotic and most military governments, as well as to the most free and most popular.

One questionable feature of this analysis is the idea that force is on the side of the governed. Reality is more grim. A good part of human history supports the contrary thesis put forth a century earlier by advocates of the rule of Parliament against the King, but more crucially against the people: that "the power of the Sword is, and ever hath been, the Foundation of all Titles to Government."[2] Nevertheless, Hume's paradox is real. Even despotic rule is commonly founded on a measure of consent, and the abdication of rights is the hallmark of more free societies—a fact that calls for analysis.

The harsher side of the truth is clarified by the successes, and the tragedies, of the popular movements of the past decade. In the Soviet satellites, the governors had ruled by force, not opinion. When force was withdrawn, the fragile tyrannies quickly collapsed, for the most part with little bloodshed. These remarkable successes are a sharp departure from the historical norm. Throughout modern history, popular forces motivated by radical democratic ideals have sought to combat autocratic rule. Sometimes they have been able to expand the realms of freedom and justice before being brought to heel. Often they are simply crushed. But it is hard to think of another case when established power simply withdrew in the face of a popular uprising. No less remarkable is the behavior of the reigning superpower, which not only did not bar these developments as it regularly had done in the past, but even encouraged them, alongside of significant internal changes.

The historical norm is illustrated by the dramatically contrasting case of Central America, where any popular effort to overthrow the brutal tyrannies of the oligarchy and the military is met with murderous force, supported or directly organized by the ruler of the hemisphere. Ten years ago, there were signs of hope for an end to the dark ages of terror and misery, with the rise of self-help groups, unions, peasant associations, and other popular organizations that might have led the way to democracy and social reform. This prospect elicited a stern response by the United States and its client regimes, supported by Britain and other western allies, with slaughter, torture, and general barbarism on a scale reminiscent of Pol Pot. This violent western response to the threat of democracy left societies "affected by terror and panic," "collective intimidation and generalized fear" and "internalized acceptance of the terror," in the words of the Salvadoran Church, well after the shameful elections held to satisfy the consciences and propaganda needs of the masters. Early efforts in Nicaragua to direct resources to the poor majority led Washington to initiate economic and ideological warfare, and outright terrorism, to punish these transgressions by reducing life to the zero grade.

Western opinion regards such consequences as a success insofar as the challenge to power and privilege is rebuffed and the targets are properly chosen: killing priests is not clever, but union leaders and human rights activists are fair game—and of course peasants, Indians, students, and other low-life generally.

The pattern is uniform. U.S. occupying forces in Panama were quickly ordered to arrest most political activists and union leaders, because they are "bad guys of some sort," the U.S. Embassy told reporters.[3] The "good guys" to be restored to power are the bankers who were happily laundering drug money in the early 1980s. Then Noriega was also a "good guy," running drugs, killing and torturing and stealing elections—and, crucially, following American orders. He had not yet shown the dangerous streak of independence that transferred him to the category of demon. Apart from tactics, nothing changes over the years, including the inability of educated opinion to perceive that 2 and 2 is 4.

Central America represents the historical norm, not Eastern Europe. Hume's observation requires this correction. Recognizing that, it remains true, and important, that government is founded on opinion, which brings willing submission.

In the contemporary period, Hume's conception has been revived and elaborated, but with a crucial innovation: the theory is that control of thought is more important for governments that are free and popular than for despotic and military states. The logic is straightforward: a despotic state can control its domestic enemy by force, but as the state loses this weapon, other devices are required to prevent the ignorant masses from interfering with public affairs, which are none of their business.

The point is, in fact, far more general. The public must be reduced to passivity in the political realm, but for submissiveness to become a reliable trait, it must be entrenched in the realm of belief as well. The public are to be observers, not participants, consumers of ideology as well as products. Eduardo Galeano writes that "the majority must resign itself to the consumption of fantasy. Illusions of wealth are sold to the poor, illusions of freedom to the oppressed, dreams of victory to the defeated and of power to the weak."[4] That is the essential point.

I will come back to these central themes of modern political and intellectual culture. But let us first have a look at some of the "natural beliefs" that guide our conduct and our thought. One such belief is that a crucial element of essential human nature is what Bakunin called "an instinct for freedom." Hume's paradox arises only if we make this assumption. It is the failure to act upon this instinct that Hume found so surprising. The same failure inspired Rousseau's classic lament that people are born free but are everywhere in chains, seduced by the illusions of the civil society that is created by the rich to guarantee their plunder. There have been efforts to ground the instinct for freedom in a substantive theory of human nature. They are not without interest, but they surely come nowhere near establishing the case. Like other tenets of common sense, this belief remains a regulative principle that we adopt, or reject, on faith. Which choice we make can have large-scale effects for ourselves and others.

Those who adopt the common sense principle that freedom is our natural right and essential need will agree with Bertrand Russell that anarchism is "the ultimate ideal to which society should approximate." Structures of hierarchy and domination are fundamentally illegitimate. They can be defended only on grounds of contingent need, an argument that rarely stands up to analysis. As Russell went on to observe 70 years ago, "the old bonds of authority" have little intrinsic merit. Reasons are needed for people to abandon their rights, "and the reasons offered are counterfeit reasons, convincing only to those who have a selfish interest in being convinced." "The condition of revolt," he went on, "exists in women towards men, in oppressed nations toward their oppressors, and above all in labour towards capital. It is a state full of danger, as all past history shows, yet also full of hope."[5]

Russell traced the habit of submission in part to coercive educational practices. His views are reminiscent of the 17th and 18th century thinkers who held that the mind is not to be filled with knowledge "from without, like a vessel," but "to be kindled and awaked." "The growth of knowledge [resembles] the growth of Fruit; however external causes may in some degree cooperate, it is the internal vigour, and virtue of the tree, that must ripen the juices to their just maturity." Similar conceptions underlie Enlightenment thought on political and intellectual freedom, and on alienated labor, which turns the worker into instrument for other ends instead of a human being fulfilling inner needs—a fundamental principle of classical liberal thought, though long forgotten, because of its revolutionary implications. These ideas and values retain their power and their pertinence, and are very remote from realization, anywhere. As long as this is so, the libertarian revolutions of the 18th century remain far from consummated, a vision for the future.[6]

Hume posed his paradox for both despotic and more free societies. The latter case is by far the more important. As society becomes more free and diverse, the task of inducing submission becomes more complex and the problem of unraveling the mechanisms of indoctrination becomes more challenging. But intellectual interest aside, the case of free societies has greater human significance, because in this case we are talking about ourselves and can act upon what we learn. It is for just this reason that the dominant culture will always seek to externalize human concerns, directing them to the abuses of others. Fame, fortune, and respect await those who reveal the crimes of official enemies; those who undertake the vastly more important task of raising a mirror to ourselves can expect quite different treatment, in any society. George Orwell is famous for *Animal Farm* and *1984*, which focus on the official enemy, or could at least be interpreted in this light. Had he kept to the more interesting and significant question of thought control in relatively free and democratic societies, it would not have been appreciated, and instead of wide acclaim, he would have faced silent dismissal or obloquy. Let us nevertheless turn to the more important and unacceptable questions.

Keeping to governments that are more free and popular, why do the governed submit when force is on their side? First, we have to look at a prior question: to what extent *is* force on the side of the governed? Here some care is necessary. Societies are considered free and democratic insofar as the power of the state to coerce is limited. The United States is unusual in this respect: perhaps more than anywhere else in the world, the citizen is free from state coercion, at least, the citizen who is relatively privileged and of the right color, a substantial part of the population.

But it is a mere truism that the state represents only one segment of the nexus of power. Control over investment, production, commerce, finance, conditions of work, and other crucial aspects of social policy lies in private hands, and the same is true of articulate expression, largely dominated by major corporations that sell audiences to advertisers and naturally reflect the interests of the owners and their market.

Furthermore, through familiar mechanisms, private power sets narrow limits on the actions of government. The United States is again unusual in this respect among the industrial democracies. It is near the limit in its safeguards for freedom from state coercion, and also in the poverty of its political life. There is essentially one political party, the business party, with two factions. Shifting coalitions of investors account for a large part of political history. Unions or other popular organizations might offer a way for the general public to play some role in influencing programs and policy choices, but these scarcely exist. The ideological system is bounded by the narrow consensus of the privileged. Even elections are largely a ritual form. In congressional elections, virtually all incumbents are returned to office, a reflection of the vacuity of the political system and the choices it offers. There is scarcely a pretense that substantive issues are at stake in the presidential campaigns. Political commentators ponder such questions as whether Reagan will remember his lines, or whether Mondale looks too gloomy, or whether Dukakis can duck the slime tossed at him by Republican public relations strategists. Half the population does not even bother to push the buttons, and those who take the trouble often consciously vote against their interest.

These tendencies were accelerated during the Reagan years. The population overwhelmingly opposed the policies of his administration, and even the Reagan voters, by about 3 to 2, hoped that his legislative program would not be enacted. In the 1980 elections, 4 percent of the electorate voted for Reagan because they regarded him as a "real conservative." In 1984, the percentage dropped to 1 percent. That is what is called "a landslide victory for conservatism" in American political rhetoric. Furthermore, contrary to much pretense, Reagan's popularity was never particularly high, and much of the population seemed to understand that he was a media creation, who had only the foggiest idea of what government policy might be.[7] It is noteworthy that the fact is now tacitly conceded; the instant that the "great communicator" was no longer needed to read the lines written for him by the rich folk as he had been doing most of his life, he disappeared into total oblivion. After eight years of pretense about the "revolution" Reagan wrought, no one would dream of asking its standard bearer for his thoughts about any topic, because it is understood, as it always was, that he has none. When Reagan was invited to Japan as an elder statesman, his hosts were surprised—and given the fat fee, rather annoyed—to discover that he could not hold press conferences or talk on any subject. Their discomfiture aroused some amusement in the American press: the Japanese believed what they had read about this remarkable figure, failing to comprehend the workings of the mysterious occidental mind.

The hoax perpetrated by the media and the intellectual community is of some interest for Hume's paradox about submission and authority. State capitalist democracy has a certain tension with regard to the locus of power: in principle, the people rule, but effective power resides largely in private hands, with large-scale effects throughout the social order. One way to reduce the tension is to remove the public from the scene, except in form. The Reagan phenomenon offered a new way to achieve this fundamental goal of capitalist democracy. The United States functioned through the 1980s without a chief executive. This is a major advance in the marginalization of the public. It is as if there were an election every few years to choose a Queen to perform certain ritual tasks: to appear on ceremonial occasions, to read aloud the government's programs, and so on. As the most advanced and sophisticated of the state capitalist democracies, the United States has often led the way in devising means to control the domestic enemy, and the latest inspiration will doubtless be mimicked elsewhere, with the usual lag.

Even when issues arise in the political system, the concentration of effective power limits the threat. The question rarely arises in the United States because of the subordination of the political and ideological system to business interests, but in more democratic societies to the south, where conflicting ideas and approaches reach the political arena, the situation is different. As is again familiar, government policies that private power finds unwelcome will lead to capital flight, disinvestment, and social decline until "business confidence" is restored with the abandonment of a threat to privilege; these facts of life exert a decisive influence on the political system (with military force, supported by the ruler of the hemisphere, in reserve if matters get out of hand). To put the basic point crassly, unless the rich and powerful are satisfied, everyone will suffer, because they control the basic social levers, determining what will be produced and consumed, and what crumbs will filter down to their subjects. For the homeless in the streets, then, the primary objective is to ensure that the rich live happily in their mansions. This crucial factor, along with simple control over resources, severely limits the force available to the governed and diminishes Hume's paradox in a well-functioning capitalist democracy in which the general public is scattered and marginalized.

Still the problem remains. Hume is right to stress that control over thought is a major factor in suppressing the natural beliefs of common sense and thereby ensuring submission to power. The general public is not supposed to understand this; that would undermine the goals. But elites have long been well aware that when obedience cannot be secured by the bludgeon, democracy must be subverted by other means. It is revealing to see how these concerns have been articulated, over the years.

During the 17th century English revolution, libertarian groups "represented the first great outburst of democratic thought in history," one historian comments.[8] This expression of the instinct for freedom at once raised the problem of how to contain the threat. The libertarian ideas of the radical democrats were considered outrageous by respectable people. They favored universal education, guaranteed health care, and democratization of the law, which one described as a fox, with poor men the geese: "he pulls off their feathers and feeds upon them." They developed a kind of "liberation theology" which, as one critic ominously observed, preached "seditious doctrine to the people" and aimed "to raise the rascal multitude...against all men of best quality in the kingdom, to draw them into associations and combinations with one another...against all lords, gentry, ministers, lawyers, rich and peaceable men" (historian Clement Walker). The rabble did not want to be ruled by King or Parliament, but "by countrymen like ourselves, that know our wants." Their pamphlets explained further that "It will never be a good world while knights and gentlemen make us laws, that are chosen for fear and do but oppress us, and do not know the people's sores."

These ideas naturally appalled the men of best quality. They were willing to grant the people rights, but within reason, and on the principle that "when we mention the people, we do not mean the confused promiscuous body of the people." Particularly frightening were the itinerant preachers and mechanics preaching freedom and democracy, the agitators stirring up the rascal multitude, and the printers putting out pamphlets questioning authority and its mysteries. "There can be no form of government without its proper mysteries," one commentator warned, and these mysteries must be "concealed" from the common folk. In words echoed by Dostoevsky's Grand Inquisitor, the same observer went on to stress that "Ignorance, and admiration arising from ignorance, are the parents of civil devotion and obedience." The radical democrats had "cast all the mysteries and secrets of government...before the vulgar (like pearls before swine)," he continued, "and have...made the people so curious and so arrogant that they will never find humility enough to submit to a civil rule." It is dangerous, another commentator observed, to "have a people know their own strength." After the democrats had been defeated, John Locke wrote that "day-labourers and tradesmen, the spinsters and dairymaids" must be told what to believe; "The greatest part cannot know and therefore they must believe."[9]

These ideas have ample resonance until the present day.

Like John Milton and other civil libertarians of the period, Locke held a sharply limited conception of freedom of expression, barring those who "speak anything in their religious assembly irreverently or seditiously of the government or governors, or of state matters." The common people should be denied the right even to discuss the foundations of public affairs; Locke's Fundamental Constitution of Carolina provided that "all manner of comments and expositions on any part of these constitutions, or on any part of the common or statute laws of Carolines, are absolutely prohibited." In drafting reasons for Parliament to terminate censorship in 1694, Locke offered no defense of freedom of expression or thought, but only considerations of expediency and harm to commercial interests.[10] With the threat of democracy overcome and the libertarian rabble defeated, censorship was permitted to lapse in England, because the "opinion-formers...censored themselves. Nothing got into print which frightened the men of property," Christopher Hill observes. In a well-functioning state capitalist democracy like the United States, anything that might frighten the men of property is kept far from public eye—sometimes, with quite astonishing success.

The concerns aroused by the 17th century radical democrats were not new. As far back as Herodotus we can read how people who had struggled to gain their freedom "became once more subject to autocratic government" through the acts of able and ambitious leaders who "introduced for the first time the ceremonial of royalty," creating a legend that the leader "was a being of a different order from mere men" who must be shrouded in mystery, and leaving the secrets of government, which are not the affair of the vulgar, to those entitled to manage them.

In the 1650s, supporters of Parliament and the army against the people easily proved that the rabble could not be trusted with their own affairs. This was shown by their lingering monarchist sentiments and their reluctance to place their affairs in the hands of the gentry and the army, who were "truly the people," though the people in their foolishness did not agree. The mass of the people were described as "the giddy multitude," "beasts in men's shapes." It is proper to suppress them, just as it is proper "to save the life of a lunatique or distracted person even against his will." If the people are so "depraved and corrupt" as to "confer places of power and trust upon wicked and undeserving men, they forfeit their power in this behalf unto those that are good, though but a few."[11] The good and few may be the gentry or industrialists, or the vanguard Party and the Central Committee, or the intellectuals who qualify as "experts" because they articulate the consensus of the powerful (to quote one of Henry Kissinger's insights). They manage the business empires, ideological institutions, and political structures, or serve them at various levels. Their task is to keep the giddy multitude in a state of implicit submission, and thus to bar the dread prospect of freedom and self-determination.

Similar ideas had been designed as the Spanish explorers set about what Tzvetan Todorov calls "the greatest genocide in human history" after they "discovered America" 500 years ago. They justified their acts of terror and oppression on the grounds that the natives are not "capable of governing themselves any more than madmen or even wild beasts and animals, seeing that their food is not any more agreeable and scarcely better than that of wild beasts" and their stupidity "is much greater than that of children and madmen in other countries." Therefore, intervention is legitimate "in order to exercise the rights of guardianship," Todorov comments, summarizing the basic thought.[12]

When English savages took over the task a few years later, they naturally adopted the same pose, as they tried to tame the wolves in the guise of men, as George Washington described the objects that stood in the way of the advance of civilization and had to be eliminated for their own good. The English colonists had already applied the same notions to the Celtic "wild men," for example, when Lord Cumberland, known as "the butcher," laid waste to the Scottish highlands before going on to pursue his craft in North America.

One hundred and fifty years later, their descendants had purged North America of this native scourge, reducing the lunatics from about 10 million to some 200,000 according to recent estimates, and they turned their eyes elsewhere, to civilize the wild beasts in the Philippines. The Indian fighters who were assigned the task managed to save the souls of hundreds of thousands of Filipinos, accelerating their ascent to heaven. They too were rescuing "misguided creatures" from their depravity by "slaughtering the natives in English fashion," as the New York press described their painful responsibility, adding that we must take "what muddy glory lies in the wholesale killing till they have learned to respect our arms," then moving on to "the more difficult task of getting them to respect our intentions."[13]

This is pretty much the course of history, as the deadly plague of European civilization devastated much of the world.

On the home front, the continuing problem was formulated plainly by 17th century political thinker Marchamont Nedham.[14] The proposals of the radical democrats, he wrote, would result in "ignorant Persons, neither of Learning nor Fortune, being put in Authority." Given their freedom, the "self-opinionated multitude" would elect "*the lowest of the People*" who would occupy themselves with "Milking and Gelding the Purses of the Rich," taking "the ready Road to all licentiousness, mischief, mere Anarchy and Confusion."

Apart from the rhetorical flourishes, the sentiments are standard features of contemporary political and intellectual discourse; increasingly so, in fact, as popular struggles did succeed, over the centuries, in realizing the proposals of the radical democrats, a consequence that required ever more sophisticated means to reduce their substantive content and institute new mechanisms of subjugation to authority.

Such problems regularly arise in periods of turmoil and social revolution. After the American revolution, rebellious and independent farmers had to be taught, by force, that the ideals expressed in the pamphlets of 1776 were not to be taken seriously. The common people were not to be represented by countrymen like themselves, that know the peoples' sores, but by gentry, merchants, lawyers, and others who hold or serve private power. The reigning doctrine, expressed by the Founding Fathers, is that "the people who own the country ought to govern it," in John Jay's words. The rise of corporations in the 19th century, and the legal structures devised to grant them dominance over private and public life, established the victory of the Federalist opponents of popular democracy in a new and powerful form.

Quite regularly, revolutionary struggles pit aspirants to power against one another though united in opposition to radical democratic tendencies among the common people. Lenin and Trotsky, shortly after seizing state power in 1917, moved to dismantle organs of popular control, including factory councils and Soviets, thus proceeding to deter and overcome socialist tendencies. An orthodox Marxist, Lenin did not regard socialism as a viable option in this backward and underdeveloped country; until his last days, it remained for him an "elementary truth of Marxism, that the victory of socialism requires the joint efforts of workers in a number of advanced countries," notably Germany.[15] In what has always seemed to me his greatest work, Orwell described a similar process in Spain, where the fascists, Communists, and liberal democracies were united in opposition to the libertarian revolution that swept over much of the country, turning to the conflict over the spoils only when the radical popular forces were safely suppressed. There are many other examples, often crucially influenced by great power and violence.

This is particularly true in the Third World. A persistent concern of western elites is that popular organizations might lay the basis for meaningful democracy and social reform, threatening the prerogatives of the privileged. Those who seek "to raise the rascal multitude" and "draw them into associations and combinations with one another" against "the men of best quality" must, therefore, be repressed or eliminated. It comes as no surprise that Archbishop Romero should be assassinated shortly after pleading with President Carter to withhold support for the military junta, which will use it to "sharpen the repression that has been unleashed against the people's organizations fighting to defend their most fundamental human rights"; or that the media and intellectual opinion in the West should disregard the atrocity and conceal the complicity of the armed forces and the civilian government established by the U.S. as a cover for their necessary work in carrying out the task that the Archbishop described.

162

Worse still, "the rot may spread," in the terminology of U.S. government leaders; there may be a demonstration effect of successful independent development in a form that attends to the peoples' sores. Internal government planning documents, and even the public record, reveal that a driving concern of U.S. planners has been the fear that the "virus" of democracy and social reform might spread, "infecting" regions beyond. Examples include the first major postwar counterinsurgency operation in Greece in the late 1940s, the undermining of the labor movement in Europe at the same time, the U.S. invasion of South Vietnam, the overthrow of the democratic governments of Guatemala and Chile, the attack against Nicaragua and the popular movements elsewhere in Central America, and many other examples.

Similar fears were expressed by European statesman with regard to the American revolution. This might "lend new strength to the apostles of sedition," Metternich warned; it might spread "the contagion and the invasion of vicious principles" such as "the pernicious doctrines of republicanism and popular self-rule," one of the Czar's diplomats explained. A century later, the cast of characters was reversed. Woodrow Wilson's Secretary of State Robert Lansing warned that if the Bolshevik disease were to spread, it would leave the "ignorant and incapable mass of humanity dominant in the earth"; the Bolsheviks, he continued, were appealing "to the ignorant and mentally deficient, who by their numbers are urged to become masters,...a very real danger in view of the process of social unrest throughout the world." As always, it is democracy that is the awesome threat. When soldiers' and workers' councils made a brief appearance in Germany, Woodrow Wilson feared that they would inspire dangerous thoughts among "the American negro [soldiers] returning from abroad." Already, negro laundresses were demanding more than the going wage, saying that "money is as much mine as it is yours," Wilson had heard. Businessmen might have to adjust to having workers on their boards of directors, he feared, among other disasters if the Bolshevik virus were not exterminated.

163

With these dire consequences in mind, the Western invasion of the Soviet Union was justified on defensive grounds, in defense against "the Revolution's challenge...to the very survival of the capitalist order," as a highly-regarded contemporary diplomatic historian puts it approvingly. And it was also necessary to defend the civilized order against the popular enemy at home. Secretary of State Lansing explained that force must be used to prevent "the leaders of Bolshevism and anarchy" from proceeding to "organize or preach against government in the United States." The repression launched by the Wilson administration successfully undermined democratic politics, unions, freedom of the press, and independent thought, in the interest of corporate power and the state authorities who represented its interests, all with the general approval of the media and elites generally, all in self-defense against the ignorant rabble.

Much the same story was re-enacted after World War II, again under the pretext of a Soviet threat, in reality, to restore submission to the rulers.[16]

When political life and independent thought revived in the 1960s, the problem arose again, and the reaction was the same. The Trilateral Commission, bringing together liberal elites from Europe, Japan, and the United States, warned of an impending "crisis of democracy" because the "excess of democracy" was posing a threat to the unhampered rule of privileged elites—what is called "democracy" in political theology. The problem was the usual one: the rabble were trying to arrange their own affairs, gaining control over their communities and entering the political arena to press their demands. There were organizing efforts among young people, ethnic minorities, women, social activists, and others, encouraged by the struggles of benighted masses elsewhere for freedom and independence. More "moderation in democracy" would be required, the Commission concluded, a return to the good old days when "Truman had been able to govern the country with the cooperation of a relatively small number of Wall Street lawyers and bankers," as the American rapporteur commented with more than a trace of nostalgia.

At another point on the political spectrum, the conservative contempt for democracy is succinctly articulated by Sir Lewis Namier, who writes that "there is no free will in the thinking and actions of the masses, any more than in the revolutions of planets, in the migrations of birds, and in the plunging of hordes of lemmings into the sea." Only disaster would ensue if the masses were permitted to enter the arena of decision-making in a meaningful way. The leading neo-conservative intellectual Irving Kristol adds that "insignificant nations, like insignificant people, can quickly experience delusions of significance." These delusions must be driven from their tiny minds by force, he continues: "In truth, the days of 'gunboat diplomacy' are never over…Gunboats are as necessary for international order as police cars are for domestic order."[17]

These ideas bring us to the Reagan administration, which established a state propaganda agency that was by far the most extensive in American history, much to the delight of the advocates of a powerful and interventionist state who are called "conservatives" in one of the current Orwellian perversions of political discourse. The Office of Public Diplomacy, as it was called, was largely dedicated to mobilizing support for U.S. terror states in Central America and to "demonizing the Sandinistas," as one administration official put it. When the program was exposed, another high official described it as the kind of operation carried out in "enemy territory"—an apt phrase, expressing standard elite attitudes towards the public: an enemy, who must be subdued.

In this case, the enemy was not completely subdued. Popular movements have deepened their roots and spread into new sectors of the population since the 1960s, contrary to much propaganda, and they were able to drive the state underground to clandestine terror instead of more efficient forms of overt violence that John F. Kennedy could undertake before the public had been aroused.

As elites pondered the rising threat of democracy at home in the post-Vietnam period, they also had to deal with the spread of rot and cancers abroad. The mechanisms of thought-control at home, and the real reasons for subversion and state terror abroad, are brought out with great clarity in one of the most spectacular achievements of the Reagan administration propaganda operation—which was, incidentally, strictly illegal, as Congress irrelevantly determined. Virtually as a reflex, the propaganda system concocted the charge that the current enemy, in this case Nicaragua, was planning to conquer the hemisphere. But it went on to provide actual proof: the evil Communists had openly declared a "Revolution without Borders." This charge—which aroused no ridicule among the disciplined educated classes—was based on a speech by Sandinista leader Tomás Borge, in which he explained that Nicaragua cannot "export our revolution" but can only "export our example" while "the people themselves of these countries…must make their revolutions"; in this sense, he said, the Nicaraguan revolution "transcends national boundaries." The hoax was exposed at once, even noted marginally in the press. But it was too useful to abandon, and it was eagerly accepted by Congress, the media, and political commentators. The phrase is used as the title for a major State Department propaganda document, and it was brilliantly exploited by Reagan's speechwriters to stampede Congress into providing $100 million of aid to the contras in response to the World Court judgment calling upon the United States to terminate its "unlawful use of force" and illegal embargo against Nicaragua.

The crucial point is that lying behind the hoax there is a valid insight, which explains its wide appeal among the educated classes. Early Sandinista successes in instituting social reforms and production for domestic needs set the alarm bells ringing in Washington and New York. These successes aroused the same fears that agitated Metternich and the Czar, the people of best quality since the 17th century, all those who expect to dominate by right: the rot might spread, the virus might infect others, and the foundations of privilege might crumble.

Despite all efforts to contain them, the rabble continue to fight for their rights, and over time, libertarian ideals have been partially realized or have even become common coin. Many of the outrageous ideas of the 17th century radical democrats, for example, seem tame enough today, though other early insights remain beyond our current moral and intellectual reach.

The struggle for freedom of speech is an interesting case, and a very crucial one, since it lies at the heart of a whole array of freedoms and rights.[18] The central question is when, if ever, the state may act to interdict the content of communications. One critical element is seditious libel, the idea that the state can be criminally assaulted by speech, "the hallmark of closed societies throughout the world," legal historian Harry Kalven observes. A society that tolerates seditious libel is not free, whatever its other characteristics. In late 17th century England, men were castrated, disemboweled, quartered and beheaded for the crime. Through the 18th century, there was a general consensus that established authority could be maintained only by silencing subversive discussion, and "any threat, whether real or imagined, to the good reputation of the government" must be barred by force (Leonard Levy). "Private men are not judges of their superiors...[for] This wou'd confound all government," one editor wrote. Truth was no defense: true charges are even more criminal than false ones, because they tend even more to bring authority into disrepute. Treatment of dissident opinion, incidentally, follows a similar model in our more libertarian era. False and ridiculous charges are no real problem; it is the unconscionable people who reveal unwanted truths from whom society must be protected.

The doctrine of seditious libel was also upheld in the American colonies. The intolerance of dissent during the revolutionary period is notorious. The leading American libertarian, Thomas Jefferson, agreed that punishment was proper for "a traitor in thought, but not in deed," and authorized internment of political suspects. He and other Founders agreed that "traitorous or disrespectful words" against the authority of the national state or any of its component states was criminal. "During the Revolution," historian Leonard Levy observes, "Jefferson, like Washington, the Adamses, and Paine, believed that there could be no toleration for serious differences of political opinion on the issue of independence, no acceptable alternative to complete submission to the patriot cause. Everywhere there was unlimited liberty to praise it, none to criticize it." At the outset of the Revolution, the Continental Congress urged the states to enact legislation to prevent the people from being "deceived and drawn into erroneous opinion." It was not until the Jeffersonians were themselves subjected to repressive measures in the late 1790s that they developed a body of more libertarian thought for self-protection—reversing course, however, when they gained power themselves.[19]

Until World War I, there was only a slender basis for freedom of speech in the United States, and it was not until 1964 that the law of seditious libel was struck down by the Supreme Court. In 1969, the Court finally protected speech apart from "incitement to imminent lawless action." Two centuries after the revolution, the Court at last adopted the position that had been advocated in 1776 by Jeremy Bentham, who argued that a free government must permit "malcontents" to "communicate their sentiments, concert their plans, and practice every mode of opposition short of actual revolt, before the executive power can be legally justified in disturbing them."[20] The 1969 Supreme Court decision formulated a libertarian standard which, I believe, is unique in the world. In Canada, for example, people are still imprisoned for promulgating "false news," recognized as a crime in 1275 to protect the King.

166

In Europe, the situation is still more primitive. England has only limited protection for freedom of speech, and even tolerates such a disgrace as a law of blasphemy. The reaction to the Salmon Rushdie affair, most dramatically on the part of those who absurdly described themselves as "conservatives," was particularly noteworthy.[21] Doubtless many would agree with Conor Cruise O'Brien, who, when Minister for Posts and Telegraphs in Ireland, amended the Broadcasting Authority Act to permit the Authority to refuse to broadcast any matter that, in the judgment of the minister, "would tend to undermine the authority of the state."[22]

We should also bear in mind that the right to freedom of speech in the United States was not established by the First Amendment to the Constitution, but only through committed efforts over a long term by the labor movement, the civil rights and anti-war movements of the 1960s, and other popular forces. James Madison pointed out that a "parchment barrier" will never suffice to prevent tyranny. Rights are not established by words, but won and sustained by struggle.

It is also worth recalling that victories for freedom of speech are often won in defense of the most depraved and horrendous views. The 1969 Supreme Court decision was in defense of the Ku Klux Klan from prosecution after meeting with hooded figures, guns, and a burning cross, calling for "burying the nigger" and "sending the Jews back to Israel." With regard to freedom of speech there are basically two positions: you defend it vigorously for views you hate, or you reject it and prefer Stalinist/fascist standards. It is unfortunate that it remains necessary to stress these simple truths.[23]

The fears expressed by the men of best quality in the 17th century have become a major theme of intellectual discourse, corporate practice, and the academic social sciences. They were clearly expressed by the influential moralist and foreign affairs adviser Reinhold Niebuhr, who was revered by George Kennan, the Kennedy intellectuals, and many others. He wrote that "rationality belongs to the cool observers" while the common person follows not reason but faith. The cool observers, he explained, must recognize "the stupidity of the average man," and must provide the "necessary illusions" and the "emotionally potent oversimplifications" that will keep the naive simpletons on course. As in 1650, it remains necessary to protect the "lunatic or distracted person," the ignorant rabble, from their own "depraved and corrupt" judgments, just as one does not allow a child to cross the street without supervision.

In accordance with the prevailing conceptions, there is no infringement on democracy if a few corporations control the information system: in fact, that is the essence of democracy. In the *Annals of the American Academy of Political and Social Science*, the leading figure of the public relations industry, Edward Bernays, explained that "the very essence of the democratic process" is "the freedom to persuade and suggest," what he calls "the engineering of consent."

If the freedom to persuade happens to be concentrated in a few hands, we must recognize that such is the nature of a free society. From the early 20th century, the public relations industry has devoted vast resources to "educating the American people about the economic facts of life" to ensure a favorable climate for business. Its task is to control "the public mind," which is "the only serious danger confronting the company," an AT&T executive observed eighty years ago. And today, the *Wall St. Journal* describes with enthusiasm the "concerted efforts" of corporate America "to change the attitudes and values of workers" on a vast scale with "New Age workshops" and other contemporary devices of indoctrination and stupefaction designed to convert "worker apathy into corporate allegiance."[24] The agents of Reverend Moon and Christian evangelicals employ similar devices to bar the threat of peasant organizing and to undermine a church that serves the poor in Latin America—with the help of the Vatican, unfortunately. They are amply funded for these activities by the intelligence agencies of the U.S. and its clients and the closely-linked international organizations of the ultra-right.

Bernays expressed the basic point in a public relations manual of 1928: "The conscious and intelligent manipulation of the organized habits and opinions of the masses is an important element in democratic society...It is the intelligent minorities which need to make use of propaganda continuously and systematically." Given its enormous and decisive power, the highly class conscious business community of the United States has been able to put these lessons to effective use. Thus, Bernays' advocacy of propaganda is cited by Thomas McCann, head of public relations for the United Fruit Company, for which Bernays provided signal service in preparing the ground for the overthrow of Guatemalan democracy in 1954, a major triumph of business propaganda with the willing compliance of the media.[25]

The intelligent minorities have understood that this is their function. The dean of U.S. journalists, Walter Lippman, described a "revolution" in "the practice of democracy" as "the manufacture of consent" has become "a self-conscious art and a regular organ of popular government." This is a natural development when "the common interests very largely elude public opinion entirely, and can be managed only by a specialized class whose personal interests reach beyond the locality," the "men of best quality," who are capable of social and economic management.

These doctrines of sociology and psychology having been established by the device of authoritative pronouncement, it follows that there are two kinds of political roles that must be clearly distinguished, as Lippman goes on to explain. First, there is the role assigned to the specialized class, the "insiders," the "responsible men," who have access to information and understanding. Ideally, they should have a special education for public office, and should master the criteria for solving the problems of society; "In the degree to which these criteria can be made exact and objective, political decision," which is their domain, "is actually brought into relation with the interests of men." The "public men" are, furthermore to "lead opinion" and take the responsibility for "the formation of a sound public opinion." Tacitly assumed is that the specialized class serve the public interest—what is called "the national interest" in the webs of mythology and mystification spun by the academic social sciences.

The second role is "the task of the public," which should be very limited. It is not for the public, Lippman observes to "pass judgment on the intrinsic merits" of an issue or to offer analysis or solutions, but merely, on occasion, to place "its force at the disposal" of one or another group of "responsible men" from the specialized class. The public "does not reason, investigate, invent, persuade, bargain or settle." Rather, "the public acts only by aligning itself as the partisan of someone in a position to act executively," once he has given the matter at hand sober and disinterested thought. "The public must be put in its place," so that we "may live free of the trampling and the roar of a bewildered herd." The herd "has its function": to be "the interested spectators of action," not the participants; that is the duty of "the responsible man."[26]

These ideas, regarded as a progressive "political philosophy for liberal democracy," have an unmistakable resemblance to the Leninist idea of a vanguard party that leads the stupid masses to a better life that they cannot conceive or construct on their own. In fact, the transition from one position to the other, from Leninist enthusiasm to "celebration of America," has proven quite an easy one over the years. This is not surprising, since the doctrines are similar at their root, the difference lying primarily in an assessment of the prospects for power: through exploitation of mass popular struggle, or service to the interests of the current masters.

There is, transparently enough, an unspoken assumption behind the proposals of Lippman and others: the specialized class are offered the opportunity to manage public affairs by virtue of their subservience to those with real power—in our societies, dominant business interests—a crucial fact that is, not surprisingly, ignored in the self-praise of the elect.

Lippman's thinking on these matters dates from shortly after World War I, when the liberal intellectual community was much impressed with its success in serving as "the faithful and helpful interpreters of what seems to be one of the greatest enterprises ever undertaken by an American president" (*New Republic*). The enterprise was Woodrow Wilson's interpretation of his electoral mandate for "peace without victory" as the occasion for pursuing victory without peace, with the assistance of the liberal intellectuals, who later praised themselves for having "impose[d] their will upon a reluctant or indifferent majority," with the aid of propaganda fabrications about Hun atrocities and other such devices. They were serving, often unwittingly, as instruments of the British Ministry of Information, which secretly defined its task as "to direct the thought of most of the world."[27]

Fifteen years later, the influential political scientist Harold Lasswell explained in the *Encyclopaedia of the Social Sciences* that we should not succumb to "democratic dogmatisms about men being the best judges of their own interests." They are not; the best judges are the elites, who must, therefore, be ensured the means to impose their will, for the common good. When social arrangements deny them the requisite force to compel obedience, it is necessary to turn to "a whole new technique of control, largely through propaganda," because of the "ignorance and superstition [of]...the masses." Others have developed similar ideas, and put them into practice in the ideological institutions: the schools, the universities, the popular media, the elite journals, and so on.

Such doctrines are entirely natural in any society in which power is narrowly concentrated but formal mechanisms exist by which ordinary people may, in theory, play some role in shaping their own affairs—a threat that plainly must be barred.

The techniques of manufacture of consent are most finely honed in the United States, a more advanced business-run society than its allies and one that is in many ways more free than elsewhere, so that the ignorant and stupid masses are potentially more dangerous. But the same concerns remain standard in Europe, as in the past. In August 1943, South African Prime Minister Jan Christian Smuts warned his friend Winston Churchill that "with politics let loose among those peoples, we may have a wave of disorder and wholesale Communism set going all over those parts of Europe." Churchill's conception was that "the government of the world" should be in the hands of "rich men dwelling at peace within their habitations," who had "no reason to seek for anything more" and thus would keep the peace, excluding those who were "hungry" and "ambitious." The same precepts apply at home. Smuts was referring specifically to southern Europe, though the concerns were far broader. With conservative elites discredited by their association with fascism and radical democratic ideas in the air, it was necessary to pursue a worldwide program to crush the anti-fascist resistance and its popular base and to restore the traditional order, to ensure that politics would not be let loose among those peoples; this campaign, conducted from Korea to western Europe, would be the topic of the first chapter of any serious work on post-World War II history.[28]

The same problems arise today. In Europe, they are heightened by the fact that, unlike the United States, its variety of state capitalism has not yet largely eliminated labor unions and restricted politics to factions of the business party, so that some impediments remain to rule by people of the best quality. These persistent concerns help explain the ambivalence of European elites towards détente, which brings with it the loss of a technique of social control through fear of the great enemy.

The basic problem, recognized throughout, is that as the state loses the capacity to control the population by force, privileged sectors must find other methods to ensure that the public is marginalized and removed from the public arena. And the insignificant nations must be subjected to the same practices as the insignificant people. The dilemma was explained by Robert Pastor, Latin American specialist of the Carter Administration, at the extreme liberal and dovish end of the political spectrum. Defending U.S. policy over many years, he writes that "the United States did not want to control Nicaragua or other nations in the region, but it also did not want to allow developments to get out of control. It wanted Nicaraguans to act independently, *except* when doing so would affect U.S. interests adversely."[29] In short, Nicaragua and other countries should be free—free do what we want them to do—and should choose their course independently, as long as their choice conforms to our interests. If they use the freedom we accord them unwisely, then naturally we are entitled to respond in self-defense. The ideas expressed are a close counterpart to the prevailing liberal conception of democracy at home as a form of population control. At the other extreme of the spectrum, we find the "conservatives" with their preference for quick resort to Kristol's methods: gunboats and police cars.

A properly functioning system of indoctrination has a variety of tasks, some rather delicate. One of its targets is the stupid and ignorant masses. They must be kept that way, diverted with emotionally potent oversimplifications, marginalized, and isolated. Ideally, each person should be alone in front of the TV screen watching sports, soap operas, or comedies, deprived of organizational structures that permit individuals lacking resources to discover what they think and believe in interaction with others, to formulate their own concerns and programs, and to act to realize them. They can then be permitted, even encouraged, to ratify the decisions made by their betters in periodic elections. The "rascal multitude" are the proper targets of the mass media and a public education system geared to obedience and training in needed skills, including the skill of repeating patriotic slogans on timely occasions.

The problem of indoctrination is a bit different for those expected to take part in serious decision-making and control: the business, state, and cultural managers, and articulate sectors generally. They must internalize the values of the system and share the necessary illusions that permit it to function in the interests of concentrated power and privilege. But they must also have a certain grasp of the realities of the world, or they will be unable to perform their tasks effectively. The elite media and educational systems must find a way to deal with these dilemmas, not an easy task. It is intriguing to see in detail how it is done, but that is beyond the scope of these remarks.

I would like to end by stressing again one crucial point. The instinct for freedom can be dulled, and often is, but it has yet to be killed. The courage and dedication of people struggling for freedom, their willingness to confront extreme state terror and violence, is often amazing. There has been a slow growth of consciousness over many years and goals have been achieved that were considered utopian or scarcely contemplated in earlier eras. An inveterate

171

optimist can point to this record and express the hope that with a new decade, and soon a new century, humanity may be able to overcome some of its dire social maladies; others might draw a different lesson from recent history. It is hard to see rational grounds for affirming one or the other perspective. As in the case of many of the natural beliefs that guide our lives, we can do no better than to make a kind of Pascal's wager: by denying the instinct for freedom, we will only prove that humans are a lethal mutation, an evolutionary dead end; by nurturing it, if it is real, we may find ways to deal with dreadful human tragedies and problems that are awesome in scale.

Discussion Section

Opening Comments: Common Sense and Freedom

I am torn between two conflicting impulses. A sense of duty leads me to want to speak about the topic I've been asked to address. But I also feel a good deal of sympathy with sentiments expressed at the plenary session by many people who felt that there is something quite unsatisfying about general and abstract discussion of questions of deep human significance—such as self-determination and power—unless it is brought to bear quite directly upon concrete and substantive problems of daily life: what we should do about specific circumstances of injustice and oppression?

If we pursue the second course, we have to be serious about it. However much insight we might hope to develop in general terms about self-determination, freedom, and justice, it would still leave us far from the task of designing a specific course of action in particular conditions and situations, historical or personal. We might draw a lesson from the history of the sciences. It was not until the 19th century that practical engineering work could expect to draw much from fundamental science, and we need hardly stress that in the domains that we are concerned with today, we are very far from even much more primitive stages of scientific understanding.

To be serious about real historical situations we have to come to understand their particularities and to apply judgments that are by no means firmly based. Take the question of national self-determination, which has arisen several times. If we want to say something sensible about particular cases—say, Northern Ireland, the Ibos and Kurds, the Israeli-Palestinian conflict—then we have to understand these situations. General precepts may be helpful, but only in a limited way, and the human problems are too important for glib proposals to be warranted or even tolerable.

The same is true with regard to other questions that arose in the plenary session, such as educational policy, or political democracy under state capitalism, or democratization of the media.

So it seems that I have two choices: to keep to the general issues of freedom and common sense (as dictated by a sense of duty); or to discuss specific questions of power, justice, and human rights. If I were to take the latter course, I'd have to keep to questions to which I've given some thought and study. Thus in the case of national self-determination, I would feel able to discuss the question of Israel-Palestine, but not that of Northern Ireland. In the former case, what I have to say might be right or wrong, smart or stupid, but at least it would be based on inquiry and thought.

At a conference like this one, the second course seems to me the appropriate one for group sessions or for the general discussion that will follow. For the introductory comment such as these, the general issues seem a more proper choice. So, I'll follow the sense of duty and keep to some general remarks about these—but limited ones, so that we can turn the discussion of more concrete and urgent matters without undue delay.

On the matter of common sense and freedom, there is a rich tradition that develops the idea that people have intrinsic rights. Accordingly, any authority that infringes upon these rights is illegitimate. These are natural rights, rooted in human nature, which is part of the natural world, so that we should be able to learn about it by rational inquiry. But social theory and action cannot be held in abeyance while science takes its halting steps towards establishing truths about human nature, and philosophy seeks to explain the connection, which we all sense exists, between human nature and rights deriving from it. We therefore are compelled to take an intuitive leap, to make a posit as to what is essential to human nature, and on this basis to derive, however inadequately, a conception of a legitimate social order. Any judgment about social action (or inaction) relies upon reasoning of this sort. A person of any integrity will select a course of action on grounds that the likely consequences will accord with human rights and needs, and will explore the validity of these grounds as well as one can.

According to one traditional idea, it is a fundamental human need—and hence a fundamental human right—to inquire and to create, free of external compulsion. This is a basic doctrine of classical liberalism in its original 18th century version, for example, in the work of Wilhelm von Humboldt, who inspired Mill. Obvious consequences were immediately drawn. One is that whatever does not spring from free choice, but only from compulsion or instruction or guidance, remains alien to our true nature. If a worker labors under the threat of force or of need, or a student produces on demand, we may admire what they do, but we despise what they are. Institutional structures are legitimate insofar as they enhance the opportunity to freely inquire and create, out of inner need; otherwise, they are not.

For people with any faith in the worth and dignity of human beings, this is an attractive vision. We can proceed to draw from it a whole range of conclusions about legitimate institutions and social action.

This picture contrasts with a conflicting one that has dominated much intellectual discourse: the view that people are empty organisms, malleable, products of their training and cultural environment, their minds a blank slate on which experience writes what it will. Human nature is, then, a historical and cultural product, with no essential properties beyond the weak and general organizing principles with which the largely vacuous system may be endowed. If so, there are few moral barriers to compulsion, shaping of behavior, or manufacture of consent. From these assumptions, we derive a different conception of a legitimate social order, one that is familiar in our daily lives. This too is an attractive view—from the standpoint of those who claim the right to exercise authority and control.

Looked at in this way, the empty organism view is conservative, in that it tends to legitimate structures of hierarchy and domination. At least in its Humboldtian version, the classical liberal view, with its strong innatist roots, is radical in that, consistently pursued, it challenges the legitimacy of established coercive institutions. Such institutions face a heavy burden of proof: it must be shown that under existing conditions, perhaps because of some overriding consideration of deprivation or threat, some form of authority, hierarchy, and domination is justified, despite the prima facie case against it—a burden that can rarely be met. One can understand why there is such a persistent attack on Enlightenment ideals, with their fundamentally subversive content.

174

I should add that this is far from the usual way of framing the issues, but I think it is defensible and proper.

Apart from preferences and hopes, which of these conceptions, or which alternative to them, leads us towards the truth about human nature? To answer such questions, one must refine and elaborate the framework of ideas. That has been done to a limited extent, and when it is, we can raise questions of truth and falsity. It is, I think, a fair conclusion that in any domain where we know anything, the empty organism thesis, or any of its variants, is demonstrably false. It is therefore tenable only beyond the reach of our current understanding, a conclusion that is certainly suggestive.

Nevertheless, the thesis that lacks empirical support has always been widely accepted. Why should this be the case? One speculation derives from the question: who benefits? We have already seen a plausible answer: the beneficiaries are those whose calling is to manage and control, who face no serious moral barrier to their pursuits if empty organism doctrines are correct. The beneficiaries are a certain category of intellectuals, who can offer a service to systems of power and domination. But on average, it is this group that will attain reward and respectability, hence be recognized for their intellectual contributions. Pursuing this logic, we can see at least one reason why ideas about the mutability and essential vacuity of human nature should gain status and become entrenched, however slight their merit.

In a few domains, it has been possible to pose the question of fact in a serious way, and inquiry has borne some fruit. In these domains, it has been possible seriously to face the question of what we "innately know," a question raised in the announcement for this meeting. It has been possible to gain some understanding of those parts of our knowledge that come from the original hand of nature, in Hume's terms—from genetic endowment, in the modern version. We quickly learn that these components of our knowledge and understanding are far beyond anything that Hume envisioned. His predecessors appear to have been far closer to the mark: Lord Herbert of Cherbury and the Cambridge Platonists of the 17th century, and the continental rationalists of the same era.

The more we investigate, the more we discover that basic elements of thought and language derive from an invariant intellectual endowment, a structure of concepts and principles that provides the framework for experience, interpretation, judgment and understanding. The more we learn about these matters, the more it seems that training is an irrelevance and learning an artefact, except at the margins. It seems that mental structures grow in the mind along their natural, intrinsically determined path, triggered by experience and partially modified by it, but apparently only in fairly superficial ways. This should not be a surprising conclusion. If true, it means that mental organs are like bodily organs—or more accurately, like *other* bodily organs, for these are organs of the body as well. Despite conventional empiricist and behaviorist dogma, we should not be startled to discover that the mind and brain are like everything else in the natural world, and that it is a highly specific initial endowment that permits the mind to develop rich and articulated systems of knowledge, understanding and judgment, largely shared with others, vastly beyond the reach of any determining experience.

Where does this leave us with respect to social theory and action? Still pretty far away, I am afraid. There is a large gap between what we must establish to ground the choice of action, and what we grasp with any confidence and understanding. Whether the gap can be filled is not clear. No one knows how to do it now, and we are left with the unavoidable necessity to act on the basis of intuition and hope. Mine is that something like the classical liberal doctrine is correct, and that there is no legitimacy to the commissar, the corporate or cultural manager, or any of those who claim the right to manipulate and control us, typically on specious grounds.

NOTES

This talk was delivered in Glasgow, Scotland, in January 1990 at the "Glasgow Conference on Self-Determination and Power: Life Task, Political Task."

1. Davie, *The Democratic Intellect* (Edinburgh Univeristy Press, 1961), pp. 274f.

2. Marchamont Nedham, 1650, cited by Edmund S. Morgan, *Inventing the People* (Norton, 1988), p. 79; Hume, p. 1, cited with the qualification just noted.

3 Diego Ribadeneira, *Boston Globe*, January 1, 1990.

4 Galeano, *Days and Nights of Love and War* (Monthly Review, 1983).

5 For sources and discussion, see my *Problems of Knowledge and Freedom*, memorial lectures for Russell delivered at Trinity College, Cambridge (Pantheon, 1971).

6 James Harris, Ralph Cudworth. See my *Cartesian Linguistics* (Harper & Row, 1966), and for further discussion, Chapter 2 of this book ("Language and Freedom") and in James Peck, ed., *The Chomsky Reader* (Pantheon, 1987).

7 See my *Turning the Tide* (South End, 1985), chapter 5; Thomas Ferguson and Joel Rogers, *Right Turn* (Hill & Wang, 1986); Ferguson, "By Invitation Only," *Socialist Review*, 19.4, 1989.

8 Margaret Judson, cited by Leonard W. Levy, *Emergence of a Free Press* (Oxford Univeristy Press, 1985), p. 91.

9 Christopher Hill, *The World Turned Upside Down* (Penguin, 1975). "At least Locke," Hill adds, "did not intend that priests should do the telling; that was for God himself."

10 Levy, *op. cit.* On the "massive intolerance" of Milton's *Areopagitica*, mistakenly believed to be a libertarian appeal, see John Illo, *Prose Studies* (May 1988, no. 1). Milton himself explained that the purpose of the tract was "so that the determination of true and false, of what should be published and what should be suppressed, might not be under control of...unlearned men of mediocre judgment," but only "an appointed officer" of the right persuasion, who will have the authority to ban work he finds to be "mischievous or libelous," "erroneous and scandalous," "impious or evil absolutely against faith or manners," "popery" and "open superstition."

11 Morgan, *op. cit.*

12 Todorov, *The Conquest of America* (Harper & Row, 1983), pp. 5, 150, quoting professor and theologian Francisco de Vitoria, "one of the pinnacles of Spanish humanism in the sixteenth century."

13 See *Turning the Tide*, p. 162.

14 *Ibid.*

15 Lenin, 1922, cited by Moshe Lewin, *Lenin's Last Struggle* (Pantheon, 1968). Lewin's interpretation of Lenin's goals and efforts is far from what I have indicated here, however.

[16] For references here and below, where not otherwise cited, see my *Turning the Tide* (Boston: South End, 1985); *Necessary Illusions* (South End Press, 1989). For Lansing and Wilson, Lloyd Gardner, *Safe for Democracy* (Oxford Uiversity Press, 1987), pp. 157, 161, 261, 242.

[17] *Wall Street Journal*, December 13, 1973.

[18] For further discussion and references, see *Necessary Illusions*, appendix V, section 8.

[19] Levy, *op. cit.*, pp. 178–9, 297, 337ff.; Levy, *Jefferson and Civil Liberties: the Darker Side* (Harvard University Press, 1963; Ivan Dee, 1989, pp. 25f.).

[20] Cited by Levy, *Ibid.*, 45.

[21] See Christopher Frew, "Craven evasion on the threat to freedom," *Scotsman*, Aug. 3, 1989, referring to the shameful behavior of Paul Johnson and Hugh Trevor-Roper—who were, unfortunately, far from alone. Rushdie was charged with seditious libel and blasphemy in the courts, but the High Court ruled that the law of blasphemy extended only to Christianity, not Islam, and that only verbal attack "against Her Majesty or Her Majesty's Government or some other institution of the state" counts as seditious libel (*New York Times*, April 10, 1990). Thus the Court upheld the basic doctrines of the Ayatollah Khomeini, Stalin, Goebbels, and other opponents of freedom, while recognizing that English law, like that of its counterparts, protects only domestic power from criticism.

[22] Quoted in *British Journalism Review*, Vol. 1, No. 2, Winter 1990.

[23] Levy, *Emergence*, pp. xvii, 6, 9, 102; Harry Kalven, *A Worthy Tradition* (Harper & Row, 1988), pp. 63, 227f., 121f.

[24] Cited by Herbert Schiller, *The Corporate Takeover of Public Expression* (Oxford University Press, 1989).

[25] McCann, *An American Company* (Crown, 1976), p. 45. On the ludicrous performance of the media, see also my *Turning the Tide* (South End, 1985), pp. 164f. See also William Preston and Ellen Ray, "Disinformation and mass deception: democracy as a cover story," in Richard O. Curry, ed., *Freedom at Risk* (Temple University Press, 1988).

[26] Clinton Rossiter & James Lare, *The Essential Lippman: a Political Philosophy for Liberal Democracy* (Vintage, 1965).

[27] Cited from secret documents by R.R.A. Marlin, "Propaganda and the Ethics of Persuasion," *International Journal of Moral and Social Studies*, Spring 1989. For more on these matters, see my "Intellectuals and the State," Huizinga lecture, Leiden, December 1977; reprinted in my *Towards a New Cold War* (Pantheon, 1982).

[28] For some details, see my article "Democracy in the Industrial Societies," *Z Magazine*, January 1989, and sources cited.

[29] Pastor, *Condemned to Repetition* (Princeton University Press, 1987, p. 32), his emphasis.

SEVEN
ANARCHISM, MARXISM AND HOPE FOR THE FUTURE (1995)

First off, Noam, for quite a time now you've been an advocate for the anarchist idea. Many people are familiar with the introduction you wrote in 1970 to Daniel Guérin's Anarchism, *but more recently, for instance in the film* Manufacturing Consent, *you took the opportunity to highlight again the potential of anarchism and the anarchist idea. What is it that attracts you to anarchism?*

ANARCHISM: PLACING THE BURDEN OF PROOF ON AUTHORITY

I was attracted to anarchism as a young teenager, as soon as I began to think about the world beyond a pretty narrow range, and haven't seen much reason to revise those early attitudes since. I think it only makes sense to seek out and identify structures of authority, hierarchy, and domination in every aspect of life, and to challenge them; unless a justification for them can be given, they are illegitimate, and should be dismantled, to increase the scope of human freedom. That includes political power, ownership and management, relations among men and women, parents and children, our control over the fate of future generations (the basic moral imperative behind the environmental movement, in my view), and much else. Naturally this means a challenge to the huge institutions of coercion and control: the state, the unaccountable private tyrannies that control most of the domestic and international economy, and so on. But not only these.

That is what I have always understood to be the essence of anarchism: the conviction that the burden of proof has to be placed on authority, and that it should be dismantled if that burden cannot be met. Sometimes the burden can be met. If I'm taking a walk with my grandchildren and they dart out into a busy street, I will use not only authority but also physical coercion to stop them. The act should be challenged, but I think it can readily meet the challenge. And there are other cases; life is a complex affair, we understand very little about humans and society, and grand pronouncements are generally more a source of harm than of benefit. But the perspective is a valid one, I think, and can lead us quite a long way.

Beyond such generalities, we begin to look at cases, which is where the questions of human interest and concern arise.

It's true to say that your ideas and critique are now more widely known than ever before. It should also be said that your views are widely respected. How do you think your support for anarchism is received in this context? In particular, I'm interested in the response you receive from people who are getting interested in politics for the first time and who may, perhaps, have come across your views. Are such people surprised by your support for anarchism? Are they interested?

The general intellectual culture, as you know, associates "anarchism" with chaos, violence, bombs, disruption, and so on. So people are often surprised when I speak positively of anarchism and identify myself with leading traditions within it. But my impression is that among the general public, the basic ideas seem reasonable when the clouds are cleared away. Of course, when we turn to specific matters (say, the nature of families, or how an economy would work in a society that is more free and just), questions and controversy arise. But that is as it should be. Physics can't really explain how water flows from the tap in your sink. When we turn to vastly more complex questions of human significance, understanding is very thin, and there is plenty of room for disagreement, experimentation, both intellectual and real-life exploration of possibilities, to help us learn more.

Perhaps, more than any other idea, anarchism has suffered from the problem of misrepresentation. Anarchism can mean many things to many people. Do you often find yourself having to explain what it is that you mean by anarchism? Does the misrepresentation of anarchism bother you?

All misrepresentation is a nuisance. Much of it can be traced back to structures of power that have an interest in preventing understanding, for pretty obvious reasons. It's well to recall David Hume's *First Principles of Government.* He expressed surprise that people ever submitted to their rulers. He concluded that since "Force is always on the side of the governed, the governors have nothing to support them but opinion. 'Tis therefore, on opinion only that government is founded; and this maxim extends to the most despotic and most military governments, as well as to the most free and most popular." Hume was very astute (and incidentally, hardly a libertarian by the standards of the day). He surely underestimates the efficacy of force, but his observation seems to me basically correct, and important, particularly in the more free societies, where the art of controlling opinion is therefore far more refined. Misrepresentation and other forms of befuddlement are a natural concomitant.

So does misrepresentation bother me? Sure, but so does rotten weather. It will exist as long as concentrations of power engender a kind of commissar class to defend them. Since they are usually not very bright, or are bright enough to know that they'd better avoid the arena of fact and argument, they'll turn to misrepresentation, vilification, and other devices that are available to those who know that they'll be protected by the various means available to the powerful. We should understand why all this occurs, and unravel it as best we can. That's part of the project of liberation—of ourselves and others, or more reasonably, of people working together to achieve these aims.

Sounds simple-minded, and it is. But I have yet to find much commentary on human life and society that is not simple-minded, when absurdity and self-serving posturing are cleared away.

How about in more established left-wing circles, where one might expect to find greater familiarity with what anarchism actually stands for? Do you encounter any surprise here at your views and support for anarchism?

If I understand what you mean by "established left-wing circles," there is not too much surprise about my views on anarchism, because very little is known about my views on anything. These are not the circles I deal with. You'll rarely find a reference to anything I say or write. That's not completely true of course. Thus in the U.S. (but less commonly in the UK or elsewhere), you'd find some familiarity with what I do in certain of the more critical and independent sectors of what might be called "established left-wing circles," and I have personal friends and associates scattered here and there. But have a look at the books and journals, and you'll see what I mean. I don't expect what I write and say to be any more welcome in these circles than in the faculty club or editorial board room—again, with exceptions.

The question arises only marginally, so much so that it's hard to answer.

A number of people have noted that you use the term "libertarian socialist" in the same context as you use the word "anarchism." Do you see these terms as essentially similar? Is anarchism a type of socialism to you? The description has been used before that anarchism is equivalent to socialism with freedom. Would you agree with this basic equation?

The introduction to Guérin's book that you mentioned opens with a quote from an anarchist sympathizer a century ago, who says that "anarchism has a broad back," and "endures anything." One major element has been what has traditionally been called "libertarian socialism." I've tried to explain there and elsewhere what I mean by that, stressing that it's hardly original; I'm taking the ideas from leading figures in the anarchist movement whom I quote, and who rather consistently describe themselves as socialists, while harshly condemning the "new class" of radical intellectuals who seek to attain state power in the course of popular struggle and to become the vicious "red bureaucracy" of which Bakunin warned; what's often called "socialism." I rather agree with Rudolf Rocker's perception that these (quite central) tendencies in anarchism draw from the best of Enlightenment and classical liberal thought, well beyond what he described. In fact, as I've tried to show they contrast sharply with Marxist-Leninist doctrine and practice, the "libertarian" doctrines that are fashionable in the U.S. and UK particularly, and other contemporary ideologies, all of which seem to me to reduce to advocacy of one or another form of illegitimate authority, quite often real tyranny.

In the past, when you have spoken about anarchism, you have often emphasized the example of the Spanish Revolution. For you there would seem to be two aspects to this example. On the one hand, the experience of the Spanish Revolution is, you say, a good example of "anarchism in action." On the other, you have also stressed that the Spanish Revolution is a good example of what workers can achieve through their own efforts using participatory democracy. Are these two aspects—anarchism in action and participatory democracy—one and the same thing for you? Is anarchism a philosophy for people's power?

GRASSROOTS DEMOCRACY VERSUS PARLIAMENTARY DEMOCRACY

I'm reluctant to use fancy polysyllables like "philosophy" to refer to what seems ordinary common sense. And I'm also uncomfortable with slogans. The achievements of Spanish workers and peasants, before the revolution was crushed, were impressive in many ways. The term "participatory democracy" is a more recent one, which developed in a different context, but there surely are points of similarity. I'm sorry if this seems evasive. It is. But that's because I don't think either the concept of anarchism or of participatory democracy is clear enough to be able to answer the question whether they are the same.

One of the main achievements of the Spanish Revolution was the degree of grassroots democracy established. In terms of people, it is estimated that over three million were involved. Rural and urban production was managed by workers themselves. Is it a coincidence to your mind that anarchists, known for their advocacy of individual freedom, succeeded in this area of collective administration?

No coincidence at all. The tendencies in anarchism that I've always found most persuasive seek a highly organized society, integrating many different kinds of structures (workplace, community, and manifold other forms of voluntary association), but controlled by participants, not by those in a position to give orders (except, again, when authority can be justified, as is sometimes the case, in specific contingencies).

Anarchists often expend a great deal of effort at building up grassroots democracy. Indeed they are often accused of taking democracy to extremes. Yet, despite this, many anarchists would not readily identify democracy as a central component of anarchist philosophy. Anarchists often describe their politics as being about "socialism" or being about "the individual"—they are less likely to say that anarchism is about democracy. Would you agree that democratic ideas are a central feature of anarchism?

Criticism of "democracy" among anarchists has often been criticism of parliamentary democracy, as it has arisen within societies with deeply repressive features. Take the U.S., which has been as free as any, since its origins. American democracy was founded on the principle, stressed by James Madison in the Constitutional Convention in 1787, that the primary function of government is "to protect the minority of the opulent from the majority." Thus he warned that in England, the only quasi-democratic model of the day, if the general population were allowed a say in public affairs, they would implement agrarian reform or other atrocities, and that the American system must be carefully crafted to avoid such crimes against "the rights of property," which must be defended (in fact, must prevail). Parliamentary democracy within this framework does merit sharp criticism by genuine libertarians, and I've left out many other features that are hardly subtle—slavery, to mention just one, or the wage slavery that was bitterly condemned by working people who had never heard of anarchism or communism right through the 19th century, and beyond.

The importance of grassroots democracy to any meaningful change in society would seem to be self evident. Yet the Left has been ambiguous about this in the past. I'm speaking generally, of social democracy, but also of Bolshevism—traditions on the left that would seem to have more in common with elitist thinking than with strict democratic practice. Lenin, to use a well-known example, was skeptical that workers could develop anything more than trade union consciousness (by which, I assume, he meant that workers could not see far beyond their immediate predicament). Similarly, the Fabian socialist, Beatrice Webb, who was very influential in the Labor Party in England, had the view that workers were only interested in horse racing odds! Where does this elitism originate and what is it doing on the left?

THE SPANISH REVOLUTION VERSUS THE BOLSHEVIK COUP

I'm afraid it's hard for me to answer this. If the Left is understood to include "Bolshevism," then I would flatly dissociate myself from the Left.

Lenin was one of the greatest enemies of socialism, in my opinion, for reasons I've discussed. The idea that workers are only interested in horse-racing is an absurdity that cannot withstand even a superficial look at labor history or the lively and independent working-class press that flourished in many places, including the manufacturing towns of New England not many miles from where I'm writing—not to speak of the inspiring record of the courageous struggles of persecuted and oppressed people throughout history, until this very moment. Take the most miserable corner of this hemisphere, Haiti, regarded by the European conquerors as a paradise and the source of no small part of Europe's wealth, now devastated, perhaps beyond recovery. In the past few years, under conditions so miserable that few people in the rich countries can imagine them, peasants and slum-dwellers constructed a popular demo-cratic movement based on grassroots organizations that surpasses just about anything I know of elsewhere; only deeply committed commissars could fail to collapse with ridicule when they hear the solemn pronouncements of American intellectuals and political leaders about how the U.S. has to teach Haitians the lessons of democracy. Their achievements were so substantial and frightening to the powerful that they had to be subjected to yet another dose of vicious terror, with considerably more U.S. support than is publicly acknowledged, and they still have not surrendered. Are they interested only in horse-racing?

I'd suggest some lines I've occasionally quoted from Rousseau: "when I see multitudes of entirely naked savages scorn European voluptuousness and endure hunger, fire, the sword, and death to preserve only their independence, I feel that it does not behoove slaves to reason about freedom."

Speaking generally again, your own work (Deterring Democracy, Necessary Illusions, *etc.*) *has dealt consistently with the role and prevalence of elitist ideas in societies such as our own. You have argued that within "Western" (or parliamentary) democracy there is a deep antagonism to any real role or input from the mass of people, lest it threaten the uneven distri-bution in wealth which favors the rich. Your work is quite convincing here, but, this aside, some have been shocked by your assertions. For instance, you compare the politics of President John F. Kennedy with Lenin, more or less equating the two. This, I might add, has shocked supporters of both camps! Can you elaborate a little on the validity of the comparison?*

THE "NEW CLASS": TOTALITARIAN TO NEOLIBERAL

I haven't actually "equated" the doctrines of the liberal intellectuals of the Kennedy administration with Leninists, but I have noted striking points of similarity—rather as predicted by Bakunin a century earlier in his perceptive commentary on the "new class." For example, I quoted passages from

McNamara on the need to enhance managerial control if we are to be truly "free," and about how the "undermanagement" that is "the real threat to democracy" is an assault against reason itself. Change a few words in these passages, and we have standard Leninist doctrine. I've argued that the roots are rather deep, in both cases. Without further clarification about what people find "shocking," I can't comment further. The comparisons are specific, and I think both proper and properly qualified. If not, that's an error, and I'd be interested to be enlightened about it.

Specifically, Leninism refers to a form of Marxism that developed with V. I. Lenin. Are you implicitly distinguishing the works of Marx from the particular criticism you have of Lenin when you use the term "Leninism"? Do you see a continuity between Marx's views and Lenin's later practices?

Bakunin's warnings about the "Red bureaucracy" that would institute "the worst of all despotic governments" were long before Lenin, and were directed against the followers of Mr. Marx. There were, in fact, followers of many different kinds; Pannekoek, Luxemburg, Mattick and others are very far from Lenin, and their views often converge with elements of anarcho-syndicalism. Korsch and others wrote sympathetically of the anarchist revolution in Spain, in fact. There are continuities from Marx to Lenin, but there are also continuities to Marxists who were harshly critical of Lenin and Bolshevism. Teodor Shanin's work in the past years on Marx's later attitudes towards peasant revolution is also relevant here. I'm far from being a Marx scholar, and wouldn't venture any serious judgement on which of these continuities reflects the "real Marx," if there even can be an answer to that question.

Recently, we obtained a copy of your own "Notes on Anarchism" (re-published last year by Discussion Bulletin *in the U.S.). In this you mention the views of the early Marx, in particular his development of the idea of alienation under capitalism. Do you generally agree with this division in Marx's life and work—a young, more libertarian socialist but, in later years, a firm authoritarian?*

THE EARLY MARX AS A FIGURE OF THE LATE ENLIGHTENMENT

The early Marx draws extensively from the milieu in which he lived, and one finds many similarities to the thinking that animated classical liberalism, aspects of the Enlightenment and French and German Romanticism. Again, I'm not enough of a Marx scholar to pretend to an authoritative judgement. My impression, for what it is worth, is that the early Marx was very much a figure of the late Enlightenment, and the later Marx was a highly authoritarian activist, and a critical analyst of capitalism, who had little to say about socialist alternatives. But those are impressions.

From my understanding, the core part of your overall view is informed by your concept of human nature. In the past the idea of human nature was seen, perhaps, as something regressive, even limiting. For instance, the unchanging aspect of human nature is often used as an argument for why things can't be changed fundamentally in the direction of anarchism. You take a different view? Why?

Moral Agents with Some Conception of Human Nature

The core part of anyone's point of view is some concept of human nature, however it may be remote from awareness or lack articulation. At least, that is true of people who consider themselves moral agents, not monsters. Monsters aside, whether a person who advocates reform or revolution, or stability or return to earlier stages, or simply cultivating one's own garden, takes stand on the grounds that it is "good for people." But that judgement is based on some conception of human nature, which a reasonable person will try to make as clear as possible, if only so that it can be evaluated. So in this respect I'm no different from anyone else.

You're right that human nature has been seen as something "regressive," but that must be the result of profound confusion. Is my granddaughter no different from a rock, a salamander, a chicken, a monkey? A person who dismisses this absurdity as absurd recognizes that there is a distinctive human nature. We are left only with the question of what it is—a highly non-trivial and fascinating question, with enormous scientific interest and human significance. We know a fair amount about certain aspects of it—not those of major human significance. Beyond that, we are left with our hopes and wishes, intuitions and speculations.

There is nothing "regressive" about the fact that a human embryo is so constrained that it does not grow wings, or that its visual system cannot function in the manner of [the visual system of] an insect, or that it lacks the homing instinct of pigeons. The same factors that constrain the organism's development also enable it to attain a rich, complex, and highly articulated structure, similar in fundamental ways to conspecifics, with rich and remarkable capacities. An organism that lacked such determinative intrinsic structure, which of course radically limits the paths of development, would be some kind of amoeboid creature, to be pitied (even if it could survive somehow). The scope and limits of development are logically related.

Take language, one of the few distinctive human capacities about which much is known. We have very strong reasons to believe that all possible human languages are very similar; a Martian scientist observing humans might conclude that there is just a single language, with minor variants. The reason is that the particular aspect of human nature that underlies the growth of language allows very restricted options. Is this limiting? Of course. Is it liberating?

185

Also of course. It is these very restrictions that make it possible for a rich and intricate system of expression of thought to develop in similar ways on the basis of very rudimentary, scattered, and varied experience.

What about the matter of biologically-determined human differences? That these exist is surely true, and a cause for joy, not fear or regret. Life among clones would not be worth living, and a sane person will only rejoice that others have abilities that they do not share. That should be elementary. What is commonly believed about these matters is strange indeed, in my opinion.

Is human nature, whatever it is, conducive to the development of anarchist forms of life or a barrier to them? We do not know enough to answer, one way or the other. These are matters for experimentation and discovery, not empty pronouncements.

To begin finishing off, I'd like to ask you briefly about some current issues on the left. I don't know if the situation is similar in the U.S. but here, with the fall of the Soviet Union, a certain demoralization has set in on the left. It isn't so much that people were dear supporters of what existed in the Soviet Union, but rather it's a general feeling that with the demise of the Soviet Union the idea of socialism has also been dragged down. Have you come across this type of demoralization? What's your response to it?

My response to the end of Soviet tyranny was similar to my reaction to the defeat of Hitler and Mussolini. In all cases, it is a victory for the human spirit. It should have been particularly welcome to socialists, since a great enemy of socialism had at last collapsed. Like you, I was intrigued to see how people—including people who had considered themselves anti-Stalinist and anti-Leninist—were demoralized by the collapse of the tyranny. What it reveals is that they were more deeply committed to Leninism than they believed.

FROM TWO SUPERPOWERS TO ONE: REASONS TO BE CONCERNED

There are, however, other reasons to be concerned about the elimination of this brutal and tyrannical system, which was as much "socialist" as it was "democratic" (recall that it claimed to be both, and that the latter claim was ridiculed in the West, while the former was eagerly accepted, as a weapon against socialism—one of the many examples of the service of Western intellectuals to power).

One reason has to do with the nature of the Cold War. In my view, it was in significant measure a special case of the "North-South conflict," to use the current euphemism for Europe's conquest of much of the world. Eastern Europe had been the original "Third World," and the Cold War from 1917 had no slight resemblance to the reaction of attempts by other parts of the Third World to pursue an independent course, though in this case differences of scale gave the conflict a life of its own. For this reason, it was only reasonable to expect the region to return pretty much to its earlier status: parts of the West, like the Czech Republic or Western Poland, could be expected to rejoin it, while others revert to the traditional service role, the ex-Nomenklatura becoming the standard Third World elite (with the approval of Western state-corporate power, which generally prefers them to alternatives). That was not a pretty prospect, and it has led to immense suffering.

Another reason for concern has to do with the matter of deterrence and non-alignment. Grotesque as the Soviet empire was, its very existence offered a certain space for non-alignment, and for perfectly cynical reasons, it sometimes provided assistance to victims of Western attack. Those options are gone, and the South is suffering the consequences.

A third reason has to do with what the business press calls "the pampered Western workers" with their "luxurious lifestyles." With much of Eastern Europe returning to the fold, owners and managers have powerful new weapons against the working-classes and the poor at home. GM and VW can not only transfer production to Mexico and Brazil (or at least threaten to, which often amounts to the same thing), but also to Poland and Hungary, where they can find skilled and trained workers at a fraction of the cost. They are gloating about it, understandably, given the guiding values.

We can learn a lot about what the Cold War (or any other conflict) was about by looking at who is cheering and who is unhappy after it ends. By that criterion, the victors in the Cold War include Western elites and the ex-Nomenklatura, now rich beyond their wildest dreams, and the losers include a substantial part of the population of the East along with working people and the poor in the West, as well as popular sectors in the South that have sought an independent path.

Such ideas tend to arouse near hysteria among Western intellectuals, when they can even perceive them, which is rare. That's easy to show. It's also understandable. The observations are correct, and subversive of power and privilege; hence hysteria.

In general, the reactions of an honest person to the end of the Cold War will be more complex than just pleasure over the collapse of a brutal tyranny, and prevailing reactions are suffused with extreme hypocrisy, in my opinion.

In many ways the Left today finds itself back at its original starting point in the last century. Like then, it now faces a form of capitalism that is in the ascendancy. There would seem to be greater "consensus" today, more than at any other time in history, that capitalism is the only valid form of economic organization possible, this despite the fact that wealth inequality is widening. Against this backdrop, one could argue that the Left is unsure of how to go forward. How do you look at the current period? Is it a question of "back to basics"? Should the effort now be towards bringing out the libertarian tradition in socialism and towards stressing democratic ideas?

CORPORATE MERCANTILISM ("CAPITALISM"): UNACCOUNTABLE PRIVATE TYRANNIES

This is mostly propaganda, in my opinion. What is called "capitalism" is basically a system of corporate mercantilism, with huge and largely unaccountable private tyrannies exercising vast control over the economy, political systems, and social and cultural life, operating in close cooperation with powerful states that intervene massively in the domestic economy and international society. That is dramatically true of the United States, contrary to much illusion. The rich and privileged are no more willing to face market discipline than they have been in the past, though they consider it just fine for the general population.

Merely to cite a few illustrations: the Reagan administration, which reveled in free market rhetoric, also boasted to the business community that it was the most protectionist in post-war U.S. history—actually, more than all others combined. Newt Gingrich, who leads the current crusade, represents a super-rich district that receives more federal subsidies than any other suburban region in the country, outside of the federal system itself. The "conservatives" who are calling for an end to school lunches for hungry children are also demanding an increase in the budget for the Pentagon, which was established in the late 1940s in its current form because (as the business press was kind enough to tell us) high-tech industry cannot survive in a "pure, competitive, unsubsidized, 'free enterprise' economy," and the government must be its "savior." Without the "savior," Gingrich's constituents would be poor working people (if they were lucky). There would be no computers (electronics, generally), aviation industry, metallurgy, automation, etc., etc., right down the list. Anarchists, of all people, should not be taken in by these traditional frauds.

OMINOUS PORTENT—AND SIGNS OF GREAT HOPE

More than ever, libertarian socialist ideas are relevant, and the population is very much open to them. Despite a huge mass of corporate propaganda, outside of educated circles, people still maintain pretty much their traditional attitudes. In the U.S., for example, more than 80 percent of the population regard the economic system as "inherently unfair" and the political system as a fraud, which serves the "special interests," not "the people." Overwhelming majorities think working people have too little voice in public affairs (the same is true in England), that the government has the responsibility of assisting people in need, that spending for education and health should take precedence over budget-cutting and tax cuts, that the current Republican proposals that are sailing through Congress benefit the rich and harm the general population, and so on.

Intellectuals may tell a different story, but it's not all that difficult to find out the facts.

To a point anarchist ideas have been vindicated by the collapse of the Soviet Union (the predictions of Bakunin have proven to be correct). Do you think that anarchists should take heart from this general development and from the perceptiveness of Bakunin's analysis? Should anarchists look to the period ahead with greater confidence in their ideas and history?

I think (at least hope) that the answer is implicit in the above. I think the current era has ominous portent—and signs of great hope. Which result ensues depends on what we make of the opportunities.

Lastly, Noam, a different sort of question. We have a pint of Guinness on order for you here. When are you going to come and drink it?

Keep the Guinness ready. I hope it won't be too long.

Less jocularly, I'd be there tomorrow, if we could. We (my wife came along with me, unusual for these constant trips) had a marvelous time in Ireland, and would love to come back. Why don't we? Won't bore you with the sordid details, but demands are extraordinary, and mounting—a reflection of the conditions I've been trying to describe.

This interview was conducted in May 1995 by Kevin Doyle for *Red & Black Revolution: A Magazine of Libertarian Communism*, No. 2 (1995–1996), and published in Noam Chomsky, *Language and Politics*, expanded ed., edited by C. P. Otero (Oakland: AK Press, 2004), pp. 775–85.

EIGHT
Goals and Visions
(1996)

In referring to goals and visions, I have in mind a practical rather than a very principled distinction. As is usual in human affairs, it is the practical perspective that matters most. Such theoretical understanding as we have is far too thin to carry much weight.

By visions, I mean the conception of a future society that animates what we actually do, a society in which a decent human being might want to live. By goals, I mean the choices and tasks that are within reach, that we will pursue one way or another guided by a vision that may be distant and hazy.

An animating vision must rest on some conception of human nature, of what's good for people, of their needs and rights, of the aspects of their nature that should be nurtured, encouraged and permitted to flourish for their benefit and that of others. The concept of human nature that underlies our visions is usually tacit and inchoate, but it is always there, perhaps implicitly, whether one chooses to leave things as they are and cultivate one's own garden, or to work for small changes, or for revolutionary ones.

This much, at least, is true of people who regard themselves as moral agents, not monsters—who care about the effects of what they do or fail to do.

On all such matters, our knowledge and understanding are shallow; as in virtually every area of human life, we proceed on the basis of intuition and experience, hopes and fears. Goals involve hard choices with very serious human consequences. We adopt them on the basis of imperfect evidence and limited understanding, and though our visions can and should be a guide, they are at best a very partial one. They are not clear, nor are they stable, at least for people who care about the consequences of their acts. Sensible people will look forward to a clearer articulation of their animating visions and to the critical evaluation of them in the light of reason and experience. So far, the substance is pretty meager, and there are no signs of any change in that state of affairs. Slogans are easy, but not very helpful when real choices have to be made.

GOALS VERSUS VISIONS

Goals and visions can appear to be in conflict, and often are. There's no contradiction in that, as I think we all know from ordinary experience. Let me take my own case, to illustrate what I have in mind.

My personal visions are fairly traditional anarchist ones, with origins in the Enlightenment and classical liberalism. Before proceeding, I have to clarify what I mean by that. I do not mean the version of classical liberalism that has been reconstructed for ideological purposes, but the original, before it was broken on the rocks of rising industrial capitalism, as Rudolf Rocker put it in his work on anarcho-syndicalism 60 years ago—rather accurately, I think.[1]

As state capitalism developed into the modern era, economic, political and ideological systems have increasingly been taken over by vast institutions of private tyranny that are about as close to the totalitarian ideal as any that humans have so far constructed. "Within the corporation," political economist Robert Brady wrote half a century ago, "all policies emanate from the control above. In the union of this power to determine policy with the execution thereof, all authority necessarily proceeds from the top to the bottom and all responsibility from the bottom to the top. This is, of course, the inverse of 'democratic' control; it follows the structural conditions of dictatorial power." "What in political circles would be called legislative, executive, and judicial powers" is gathered in "controlling hands" which, "so far as policy formulation and execution are concerned, are found at the peak of the pyramid and are manipulated without significant check from its base." As private power "grows and expands," it is transformed "into a community force ever more politically potent and politically conscious," ever more dedicated to a "propaganda program" that "becomes a matter of converting the public...to the point of view of the control pyramid." That project, already substantial in the period Brady reviewed, reached an awesome scale a few years later as American business sought to beat back the social democratic currents of the postwar world, which reached the United States as well, and to win what its leaders called "the everlasting battle for the minds of men," using the huge resources of the Public Relations industry, the entertainment industry, the corporate media, and whatever else could be mobilized by the "control pyramids" of the social and economic order. These are crucially important features of the modern world, as is dramatically revealed by the few careful studies.[2]

The "banking institutions and moneyed incorporations" of which Thomas Jefferson warned in his later years—predicting that if not curbed, they would become a form of absolutism that would destroy the promise of the democratic revolution—have since more than fulfilled his most dire expectations. They have become largely unaccountable and increasingly immune from popular interference and public inspection while gaining great and expanding control over the global order. Those inside their hierarchical command structure take orders from above and send orders down below. Those outside may try to rent themselves to the system of power, but have little other relation to it (except by purchasing what it offers, if they can). The world is more complex than any simple description, but Brady's is pretty close, even more so today than when he wrote.

It should be added that the extraordinary power that corporations and financial institutions enjoy was not the result of popular choices. It was crafted by courts and lawyers in the course of the construction of a developmental state that serves the interests of private power, and extended by playing one state against another to seek special privileges, not hard for large private institutions. That is the major reason why the current Congress, business-run to an unusual degree, seeks to devolve federal authority to the states, more easily threatened and manipulated. I'm speaking of the United States, where the process has been rather well studied in academic scholarship. I'll keep to that case; as far as I know, it is much the same elsewhere.

We tend to think of the resulting structures of power as immutable, virtually a part of nature. They are anything but that. These forms of private tyranny only reached something like their current form, with the rights of immortal persons, early in this century. The grants of rights and the legal theory that lay behind them are rooted in much the same intellectual soil as nourished the other two major forms of 20th century totalitarianism, fascism and Bolshevism. There is no reason to consider this tendency in human affairs to be more permanent than its ignoble brethren.[3]

Conventional practice is to restrict such terms as "totalitarian" and "dictatorship" to political power. Brady is unusual in not keeping to this convention, a natural one, which helps to remove centers of decision-making from the public eye. The effort to do so is expected in any society based on illegitimate authority— any actual society, that is. That is why, for example, accounts in terms of personal characteristics and failings, vague and unspecific cultural practices, and the like, are much preferred to the study of the structure and function of powerful institutions.

When I speak of classical liberalism, I mean the ideas that were swept away, in considerable measure, by the rising tides of state capitalist autocracy. These ideas survived (or were reinvented) in various forms in the culture of resistance to the new forms of oppression, serving as an animating vision for popular struggles that have considerably expanded the scope of freedom, justice, and rights. They were also taken up, adapted, and developed within libertarian left currents. According to this anarchist vision, any structure of hierarchy and authority carries a heavy burden of justification, whether it involves personal relations or a larger social order. If it cannot bear that burden— sometimes it can—then it is illegitimate and should be dismantled. When honestly posed and squarely faced, that challenge can rarely be sustained. Genuine libertarians have their work cut out for them.

State power and private tyranny are prime examples at the outer limits, but the issues arise pretty much across the board: in relations among parents and children, teachers and students, men and women, those now alive and the future generations that will be compelled to live with the results of what we do, indeed just about everywhere. In particular, the anarchist vision, in almost every variety, has looked forward to the dismantling of state power. Personally, I share that vision, though it runs directly counter to my goals. Hence the tension to which I referred.

My short-term goals are to defend and even strengthen elements of state authority which, though illegitimate in fundamental ways, are critically necessary right now to impede the dedicated efforts to "roll back" the progress that has been achieved in extending democracy and human rights. State authority is now under severe attack in the more democratic societies, but not because it conflicts with the libertarian vision. Rather the opposite: because it offers (weak) protection to some aspects of that vision. Governments have a fatal flaw: unlike the private tyrannies, the institutions of state power and authority offer to the despised public an opportunity to play some role, however limited, in managing their own affairs. That defect is intolerable to the masters, who now feel, with some justification, that changes in the international economic and political order offer the prospects of creating a kind of "utopia for the masters," with dismal prospects for most of the rest. It should be unnecessary to spell out here what I mean. The effects are all too obvious even in the rich societies, from the corridors of power to the streets, countryside, and prisons. For reasons that merit attention but that lie beyond the scope of these remarks, the rollback campaign is currently spearheaded by dominant sectors of societies in which the values under attack have been realized in some of their most advanced forms, the English-speaking world; no small irony, but no contradiction either.

It is worth bearing in mind that fulfillment of the utopian dream has been celebrated as an imminent prospect from early in the 19th century (I'll return briefly to that period). By the 1880s, the revolutionary socialist artist William Morris could write:

> I know it is at present the received opinion that the competitive or "Devil take the hindmost" system is the last system of economy which the world will see; that it is perfection, and therefore finality has been reached in it; and it is doubtless a bold thing to fly in the face of this opinion, which I am told is held even by the most learned men.

If history is really at an end, as confidently proclaimed, then "civilization will die," but all of history says it is not so, he added. The hope that "perfection" was in sight flourished again in the 1920s. With the strong support of liberal opinion generally, and of course the business world, Woodrow Wilson's Red Scare had successfully undermined unions and independent thought, helping to establish an era of business dominance that was expected to be permanent. With the collapse of unions, working people had no power and little hope at the peak of the automobile boom. The crushing of unions and workers' rights, often by violence, shocked even the right-wing British press. An Australian visitor, astounded by the weakness of American unions, observed in

1928 that "Labour organization exists only by the tolerance of employers...It has no real part in determining industrial conditions."

Again, the next few years showed that the hopes were premature. But these recurrent dreams provide a model that the "control pyramids" and their political agents seek to reconstitute today.[4]

In today's world, I think, the goals of a committed anarchist should be to defend some state institutions from the attack against them, while trying at the same time to pry them open to more meaningful public participation—and ultimately, to dismantle them in a much more free society, if the appropriate circumstances can be achieved.

Right or wrong—and that's a matter of uncertain judgment— this stand is not undermined by the apparent conflict between goals and visions. Such conflict is a normal feature of everyday life, which we somehow try to live with but cannot escape.

THE "HUMANISTIC CONCEPTION"

With this in mind, I'd like to turn to the broader question of visions. It is particularly pertinent today against the background of the intensifying attempt to reverse, undermine, and dismantle the gains that have been won by long and often bitter popular struggle. The issues are of historic importance, and are often veiled in distortion and deceit in campaigns to "convert the public to the point of view of the control pyramid." There could hardly be a better moment to consider the ideals and visions that have been articulated, modified, reshaped, and often turned into their opposite as industrial society has developed to its current stage, with a massive assault against democracy, human rights, and even markets, while the triumph of these values is being hailed by those who are leading the attack against them — a process that will win nods of recognition from those familiar with what used to be called "propaganda" in more honest days. It is a moment in human affairs that is as interesting intellectually as it is ominous from a human point of view.

Let me begin by sketching a point of view that was articulated by two leading 20th century thinkers, Bertrand Russell and John Dewey, who disagreed on a great many things, but shared a vision that Russell called "the humanistic conception"—to quote Dewey, the belief that the "ultimate aim" of production is not production of goods, but "of free human beings associated with one another on terms of equality." The goal of education, as Russell put it, is "to give a sense of the value of things other than domination," to help create "wise citizens of a free community" in which both liberty and "individual creativeness" will flourish, and working people will be the masters of their fate, not tools of production. Illegitimate structures of coercion must be unraveled; crucially, domination by "business for private profit through private control of banking, land, industry, reinforced by command of the press, press agents and

194

other means of publicity and propaganda" (Dewey). Unless that is done, Dewey continued, talk of democracy is largely beside the point. Politics will remain "the shadow cast on society by big business, [and] the attenuation of the shadow will not change the substance." Democratic forms will lack real content, and people will work "not freely and intelligently, but for the sake of the work earned," a condition that is "illiberal and immoral." Accordingly, industry must be changed "from a feudalistic to a democratic social order" based on workers' control, free association, and federal organization, in the general style of a range of thought that includes, along with many anarchists, G. D. H. Cole's guild socialism and such left Marxists as Anton Pannekoek, Rosa Luxemburg, Paul Mattick, and others. Russell's views were rather similar, in this regard.[5]

Problems of democracy were the primary focus of Dewey's thought and direct engagement. He was straight out of mainstream America, "as American as apple pie," in the standard phrase. It is therefore of interest that the ideas he expressed not many years ago would be regarded today in much of the intellectual culture as outlandish or worse, if known, even denounced as "Anti-American" in influential sectors.

The latter phrase, incidentally, is interesting and revealing, as is its recent currency. We expect such notions in totalitarian societies. Thus in Stalinist days, dissidents and critics were condemned as "anti-Soviet," an intolerable crime; Brazilian neo-Nazi Generals and others like them had similar categories. But their appearance in much more free societies, in which subordination to power is voluntary, not coerced, is a far more significant phenomenon. In any milieu that retains even the memory of a democratic culture, such concepts would merely elicit ridicule. Imagine the reaction on the streets of Milan or Oslo to a book entitled *Anti-Italianism* or *The Anti-Norwegians*, denouncing the real or fabricated deeds of those who do not show proper respect for the doctrines of the secular faith. In the Anglo-American societies, however—including Australia, so I've noticed—such performances are treated with solemnity and respect in respectable circles, one of the signs of a serious deterioration of ordinary democratic values.

The ideas expressed in the not very distant past by such outstanding figures as Russell and Dewey are rooted in the Enlightenment and classical liberalism, and retain their revolutionary character: in education, the workplace, and every other sphere of life. If implemented, they would help clear the way to the free development of human beings whose values are not accumulation and domination, but independence of mind and action, free association on terms of equality, and cooperation to achieve common goals. Such people would share Adam Smith's contempt for the "mean" and "sordid pursuits" of "the masters of mankind" and their "vile maxim": "All for ourselves, and nothing for other people," the guiding principles we are taught to admire and revere, as traditional values are eroded under unremitting attack. They would readily

195

understand what led a pre-capitalist figure like Smith to warn of the grim consequences of division of labor, and to base his rather nuanced advocacy of markets in part on the belief that under conditions of "perfect liberty" there would be a natural tendency towards equality, an obvious desideratum on elementary moral grounds.

The "humanistic conception" that was expressed by Russell and Dewey in a more civilized period, and that is familiar to the libertarian left, is radically at odds with the leading currents of contemporary thought: the guiding ideas of the totalitarian order crafted by Lenin and Trotsky, and of the state capitalist industrial societies of the West. One of these systems has fortunately collapsed, but the other is on a march backwards to what could be a very ugly future.

"The New Spirit of the Age"

It is important to recognize how sharp and dramatic is the clash of values between this humanistic conception and what reigns today, the ideals denounced by the working class press of the mid-19th century as "the New Spirit of the Age: Gain Wealth, forgetting all but Self," Smith's "vile maxim," a demeaning and shameful doctrine that no decent person could tolerate. It is remarkable to trace the evolution of values from a pre-capitalist figure like Smith, with his stress on sympathy, the goal of liberty with equality, and the basic human right to creative and fulfilling work, to those who celebrate "the New Spirit of the Age," often shamelessly invoking Smith's name. Let's put aside the vulgar performances that regularly deface the ideological institutions. Consider instead someone who can at least be taken seriously, say, Nobel Prize-winning economist James Buchanan, who tells us that "the ideal society is anarchy, in which no one man or group of men coerces another." He then offers the following gloss, stated authoritatively as fact:

> any person's ideal situation is one that allows him full freedom
> of action and inhibits the behavior of others so as to force adherence to his own desires. That is to say, each person seeks mastery
> over a world of slaves,[6]

a thought that Adam Smith would have considered pathological, as would Wilhelm von Humboldt, John Stuart Mill, or anyone even close to the classical liberal tradition—but that is your fondest dream, in case you hadn't noticed.

One intriguing illustration of the state of the intellectual culture and its prevailing values is the commentary on the difficult problems we face in uplifting the people of Eastern Europe, now at last liberated, so that we can extend to them the loving care we have lavished on our wards elsewhere for several hundred years. The consequences seem rather clear in an impressive array of horror chambers around the world, but miraculously—and most fortunate-

196

ly—they teach no lessons about the values of our civilization and the principles that guide its noble leaders; only "anti-Americans" and their ilk could be so demented as to suggest that the consistent record of history might merit a side glance, perhaps. Now there are new opportunities for our beneficence. We can help the people released from Communist tyranny to reach, or at least approach, the blessed state of Bengalis, Haitians, Brazilians, Guatemalans, Filipinos, indigenous peoples everywhere, African slaves, and on, and on.

In late 1994, the *New York Times* ran a series of articles on how our pupils are doing. The one on East Germany opens by quoting a priest who was a leader of the popular protests against the Communist regime. He describes his growing concerns about what is happening in his society: "brutal competition and the lust for money are destroying our sense of community. Almost everyone feels a level of fear or depression or insecurity," as they master the lessons we provide to the backward peoples of the world. But their reaction carries no lessons for us.[7]

The showcase that everyone is proud of is Poland, where "capitalism has been kinder" than elsewhere, Jane Perlez reports under the headline "Fast and Slow Lanes on the Capitalist Road": some Poles are getting the point, but others are slow learners.[8]

Perlez gives examples of both types. The good student is the owner of a small factory that is a "thriving example" of the best in modern capitalist Poland. Thanks to interest-free government loans in this now-flourishing free market society, her factory produces "glamorous beaded dresses" and "intricately designed wedding gowns," sold mostly to rich Germans, but to wealthy Poles as well. Meanwhile, the World Bank reports, poverty has more than doubled since the reforms were instituted while real wages dropped 30 percent, and by the end of 1994 the Polish economy was expected to recover to 90 percent of its pre-1989 gross domestic product. But "capitalism has been kinder": hungry people can appreciate the "signs of sudden consumption," admiring the wedding gowns in the windows of elegant shops, the "foreign cars with Polish license plates" roaring down the Warsaw-Berlin road, and the "nouveau riche women with $1300 cellular telephones tucked in their pocketbooks."

"People have to be taught to understand they must fight for themselves and can't rely on others," a job counselor in the Czech Republic explains. Concerned about "the creation of an entrenched underclass," she is running a training class to teach proper attitudes to people who had "egalitarian values drilled into their minds" in the days when "the proud slogan used to be: 'I am a miner, who else is better?'" The fast learners now know the answer to that question: the ex-Nomenklatura, rich beyond their wildest dreams as they become the agents of foreign enterprises, which naturally favor them because of their skills and experience; the bankers set up in business through the "old boy network"; the Polish women enjoying consumer delights; the government-

197

assisted manufacturers of elegant dresses for export to other rich women. In brief, the right kind of people.

Those are the successes of American values. Then there are the failures, still on the slow lane. Perlez selects as her example a 43-old coal miner, who "sits in his wood-paneled living room admiring the fruits of his labor under Communism—a television set, comfortable furniture, a shiny, modern kitchen," now unemployed after 27 years in the mines and thinking about the years before 1989. They "were great," he says, and "life was secure and comfortable." A slow learner, he finds the new values "unfathomable," and cannot understand "why he is at home, jobless and dependent on welfare payments," worrying about his 10 children, lacking the skill to "Gain Wealth, forgetting all but Self."

It is understandable, then, that Poland should find its place on the shelf alongside the other trophies, inspiring further pride and self-acclaim.

The region is plagued with other slow learners, a problem reviewed in a "global report" of *Christian Science Monitor* correspondents in the former Communist world. One entrepreneur complained that "he offered a fellow Ukrainian $100 a month to help him grow roses in a private plot" (in translation: to work for him). "Compared with the $4 that the man earned on a collective farm, it was a fortune. But the offer was rejected." The fast learner attributes the irrationality to "a certain mentality" that lingers on even after the victory of freedom: "He thinks, '*Nyet*, I'm not going to leave the collective and be your slave.'" American workers had long been infected with the same unwillingness to become someone's slave, until properly civilized; I'll return to that.

Tenants in an apartment building in Warsaw suffer from the same malady. They do not want to hand over their apartments to an industrialist who claims ownership of the building from before World War II, asking "Why should people profit from something they don't have a right to?" There has been "significant reform progress" in overcoming such retrograde attitudes, the report continues, though "there is still great reluctance to let foreigners buy and sell land." The coordinator of US-sponsored agricultural initiatives in Ukraine explains that "You'll never have a situation where 100 percent of the land is in private hands. They've never had democracy." True, anti-democratic passions do not run as high as in Vietnam, where a February 1995 decree "set the clock back": "In a tribute to Marx, the decree aims to help Vietnamese by squeezing rent from the privileged few who have land certificates for businesses," granted in an effort to attract foreign investment. If only foreign investors and a tiny domestic elite were allowed to buy up the country, the natives could work for them (if they are lucky), and we'd have freedom and "democracy" at last, as in Central America, the Philippines, and other paradises liberated long ago.[9]

Cubans have long been berated for the same kinds of backwardness. Outrage peaked during the Pan-American games held in the United States, when Cuban athletes failed to succumb to a huge propaganda campaign to induce them to defect, including lavish financial offers to become professionals; they felt a commitment to their country and its people, they told reporters. Fury knew few bounds over the devastating impact of Communist brainwashing and Marxist doctrine.

Fortunately, Americans are protected from the fact that even under the conditions of poverty imposed by US economic warfare, Cubans still refuse to accept dollars for domestic service, so visitors report, not wanting to be "your slave." Nor are they likely to be subjected to the results of a 1994 Gallup poll, considered to be the first independent and scientific survey, published in the Miami Spanish-language press but apparently not elsewhere: that 88 percent said they were "proud of being Cuban" and 58 percent that "the revolution's successes outstrip its failures," 69 percent identified themselves as "revolutionaries" (but only 21 percent as "Communist" or "socialist"), 76 percent said they were "satisfied with their personal life," and 3 percent said that "political problems" were the key problems facing the country.

If such Communist atrocities were to be known, it might be necessary to nuke Havana instead of simply trying to kill as many people as possible from starvation and disease to bring "democracy." That became the new pretext for strangling Cuba after the fall of the Berlin wall, the ideological institutions not missing a beat as they shifted gears. No longer was Cuba an agent of the Kremlin, bent on taking over Latin America and conquering the United States, trembling in terror. The lies of 30 years can be quietly shelved: terror and economic warfare have always been an attempt to bring democracy, in the revised standard version. Therefore we must tighten the embargo that "has contributed to an increase in hunger, illness, death and to one of the world's largest neurological epidemics in the past century," according to health experts writing in US medical journals in October 1994. The author of one says, "Well, the fact is that we are killing people," by denying them food and medicines, and equipment for manufacturing their own medical products.

Clinton's "Cuban Democracy Act"—which President Bush at first vetoed because it was so transparently in violation of international law, and then signed when he was outflanked from the right by Clinton during the election campaign—cut off trade by US subsidiaries abroad, 90 percent of it food, medicine and medical equipment. That contribution to democracy helped to bring about a considerable decline in Cuban health standards, an increase in mortality rates, and "the most alarming public health crisis in Cuba in recent memory," a neurological disease that had last been observed in tropical prison camps in Southeast Asia in World War II, according to the former chief of neuro-epidemiology at the National Institute of Health, the author of one of the articles. To illustrate the effects, a Columbia University Professor of

Medicine cites the case of a Swedish water filtration system that Cuba had purchased to produce vaccines, barred because some parts are produced by an American-owned company, so life-saving vaccines can be denied to bring "democracy" to the survivors.[10]

The successes in "killing people" and making them suffer are important. In the real world, Castro's Cuba was a concern not because of a military threat, human rights abuses, or dictatorship. Rather, for reasons deeply rooted in American history. In the 1820s, as the takeover the continent was proceeding apace, Cuba was regarded by the political and economic leadership as the next prize to be won. That is "an object of transcendent importance to the commercial and political interests of our Union," the author of the Monroe Doctrine, John Quincy Adams, advised, agreeing with Jefferson and others that Spain should keep sovereignty until the British deterrent faded, and Cuba would fall into US hands by "the laws of political...gravitation," a "ripe fruit" for harvest, as it did a century ago. By mid-twentieth century, the ripe fruit was highly valued by US agricultural and gambling interests, among others. Castro's robbery of this US possession was not taken likely. Worse still, there was a danger of a "domino effect" of development in terms that might be meaningful to suffering people elsewhere—the most successful health services in Latin America, for example. It was feared that Cuba might be one of those "rotten apples" that "spoil the barrel," a "virus" that might "infect" others, in the terminology favored by planners, who care nothing about crimes, but a lot about demonstration effects.

But respectable people do not dwell on such matters or even the elementary facts about the campaign to restore the ripe fruit to its rightful owner since 1959, including its current phase. Few Americans were exposed to the subversive material in the October 1994 medical journals, or even the fact that in the same month, the UN General Assembly passed a resolution calling for an end to the illegal embargo by a vote of 101 to 2, the US able to rely only on Israel, now abandoned even by Albania, Romania, and Paraguay, which had briefly joined Washington in its crusade for democracy in earlier years.

The standard story is that Eastern Europe, liberated at last, can now join the wealthy societies of the West. Perhaps, but then one wonders why that hadn't happened during the preceding half millennium, as much of Eastern Europe steadily declined relative to the West, well into this century, becoming its original "Third World." A different prospect that might be imagined is that the status quo ante will be more or less restored: parts of the Communist empire that had belonged to the industrial West— western Poland, the Czech Republic, some others—will gradually rejoin it, while others revert to something like their earlier status as service areas for the rich industrial world, which, of course, did not get that way merely because of its unique virtue. As Winston Churchill observed in a paper submitted to his Cabinet colleagues in January 1914, we are not a young people with *an innocent record* and a scanty inheritance. We have engrossed to ourselves...an *altogether disproportionate* share of the wealth and traffic of the world. We have got all we want in territory, and our claim to be left in the unmolested enjoyment of vast and splendid possessions, *mainly acquired by violence, largely maintained by force*, often seems less reasonable to others than to us.

To be sure, such honesty is rare in respectable society, though the passage would be acceptable without the italicized phrases, as Churchill understood. He did make the paper public in the 1920s, in *The World Crisis*, but with the offending phrases removed.[11]

It is also instructive to observe the framework in which the disaster of Communism is portrayed. That it was a monstrosity has never been in doubt, as was evident from the first moment to anarchists, people of independent mind like Russell and Dewey, and left Marxists—indeed predicted by many of them in advance. Nor could the collapse of the tyranny be anything but an occasion for rejoicing for anyone who values freedom and human dignity. But consider a narrower question: the standard proof that the command economy was a catastrophic failure, demonstrating the superior merits of capitalism: Simply compare West Germany, France, England, and the United States to the Soviet Union and its satellites. QED. The argument is scarcely more than an intellectual reflex, considered so obviously valid as to pass unnoticed, the presupposition of all further inquiry.

It is an interesting argument, with broad applicability. By the same logic, one can, for example, demonstrate the colossal failure of the kindergartens in Cambridge Massachusetts, and the grand success of MIT: Simply ask how well children entering first grade understand quantum physics as compared with MIT PhDs. QED.

Someone who put forth that argument might be offered psychiatric treatment. The fallacy is trivially obvious. To conduct a sane evaluation, one would have to compare the graduates of the Cambridge kindergartens with children who entered the system at the same level. The same elementary rationality dictates that to evaluate the Soviet command economy as compared with the capitalist alternative, we must compare Eastern European countries to others that were like them when the "experiment" with the two development models began. Obviously not the West; one has to go back half a millennium to a find a time when it was similar to Eastern Europe. A proper comparison might be Russia and Brazil, or Bulgaria and Guatemala, though that would be unfair to the Communist model, which never had anything remotely like the advantages of the US satellites. If we undertake the rational comparison, we conclude, indeed, that the Communist economic model was a disaster; and the Western one an even more catastrophic failure. There are nuances and complexities, but the basic conclusions are rather solid.

It is intriguing to see how such elementary points cannot be understood, and to observe the reaction to attempts to explore the issue, which also cannot be understood. The exercise offers some useful lessons about the ideological systems of the free societies.[12]

What is happening now in much of Eastern Europe in part recapitulates the general record of regions of the world that were driven to a service role, in which many remain, with exceptions that are instructive. It also falls into place alongside of a long, interesting, and important strand of the history of the industrial societies themselves. Modern America was "created over its workers' protests," Yale University labor historian David Montgomery points out, protests that were vigorous and outspoken, along with "fierce struggles." There were some hard-won victories, interspersed with forced accommodation to "a most undemocratic America," notably in the 1920s, he observes, when it seemed that "the house of labor" had "fallen."

The voice of working people was clearly and vividly articulated in the labor and community press that flourished from the mid-19th century until World War II, and even beyond, finally destroyed by state and private power. As recently as the 1950s, 800 labor newspapers were still reaching 20-30 million people, seeking—in their words—to combat the corporate offensive to "sell the American people on the virtues of big business"; to expose racial hatred and "all kinds of antidemocratic words and deeds"; and to provide "antidotes for the worst poisons of the kept press," the commercial media, which had the task of "damning labor at every opportunity while carefully glossing over the sins of the banking and industrial magnates who really control the nation."[13]

VOICES OF RESISTANCE

The popular movements of resistance to state capitalist autocracy, and their eloquent voices, have a good deal to teach us about the goals and visions of ordinary people, their understanding and aspirations. The first major study of the mid-19th century labor press (and to my knowledge still the only one) was published 70 years ago by Norman Ware. It makes illuminating reading today, or would, if it were known. Ware focuses on the journals established and run by mechanics and "factory girls" in industrial towns near Boston, "the Athens of America" and home of its greatest universities. The towns are still there, largely demoralized and in decay, but no more so than the animating visions of the people who built them and laid the foundation for American wealth and power.

The journals reveal how alien and intolerable the value systems demanded by private power were to working people, who stubbornly refused to abandon normal human sentiments. "The New Spirit of the Age" that they bitterly condemned "was repugnant to an astonishingly large section of the earlier American community," Ware writes. The primary reason was "the decline of the industrial worker as a person," the "psychological change," the "loss of dignity and independence" and of democratic rights and freedoms, as the values of industrial capitalism were imposed by state and private power, by violence when necessary.

Workers deplored the "degradation and the loss of that self-respect which had made the mechanics and laborers the pride of the world," the decline of culture, skill and attainment and even simple human dignity, as they were subjected to what they called "wage slavery," not very different from the chattel slavery of southern plantations, they felt, as they were forced to sell *themselves*, not what they produced, becoming "menials" and "humble subjects" of "despots." They described the destruction of "the spirit of free institutions," with working people reduced to a "state of servitude" in which they "see a moneyed aristocracy hanging over us like a mighty avalanche threatening annihilation to every man who dares to question their right to enslave and oppress the poor and unfortunate." And they could hardly be unaware of the material conditions at home or in nearby Boston, where life expectancy for Irish was estimated at 14 years in 1849.

Particularly dramatic, and again relevant to the current onslaught against democracy and human rights, was the sharp decline in high culture. The "factory girls" from the farms of Massachusetts had been accustomed to spend their time reading classics and contemporary literature, and the independent craftsmen, if they had a little money, would hire a boy to read to them while they were working. It has been no small task to drive such thoughts from people's minds, so that today, a respected commentator can dismiss with derision ideas about democratizing the internet to allow access by the less privileged:

> One would imagine that the poor get about all the information they want as things stand now and in many cases, even resist the efforts of schools, libraries and the information media to make them better informed. Indeed, that resistance often helps explain why they are poor

—along with their defective genes, no doubt. The insight was considered so profound that it was highlighted in a special box by the editors.[14]

The labor press also condemned what it called the "bought priesthood" of the media, the universities, and the intellectual class, apologists for power who sought to justify the despotism that was strengthening its grip and to instill its demeaning values. "They who work in the mills ought to own them," working people wrote without the benefit of radical intellectuals. In that way they would overcome the "monarchical principles" that were taking root "on democratic soil." Years later, that became a rallying cry for the organized labor movement, even its more conservative sectors. In a widely circulated address at a trade union picnic, Henry Demarest Lloyd declared that the "mission of the labour movement is to free mankind from the superstitions and sins of the market, and to abolish the poverty which is the fruit of those sins. That goal can be attained by extending to the direction of the economy the principles of democratic politics." "It is by the people who do the work that the hours of labour, the conditions of employment, the division of the produce is to be determined," he urged in what David Montgomery calls "a clarion call to the 1893 AFL convention." It is by the workers themselves, Lloyd continued, that "the captains of industry are to be chosen, and chosen to be servants, not masters. It is for the welfare of all that the coordinated labour of all must be directed.... This is democracy."[15]

These ideas are, of course, familiar to the libertarian left, though radically counter to the doctrines of the dominant systems of power, whether called "left," "right," or "center" in the largely meaningless terms of contemporary discourse. They have only recently been suppressed, not for the first time, and can be recovered, as often before.

Such values would also have been intelligible to the founders of classical liberalism. As in England earlier, reactions of workers in the industrial towns of New England illustrate the acuity of Adam Smith's critique of division of labor. Adopting standard Enlightenment ideas about freedom and creativity, Smith recognized that "The understandings of the greater part of men are necessarily formed by their ordinary employments." Hence:

> the man whose life is spent in performing a few simple operations, of which the effects too are, perhaps, always the same, or very nearly the same, has no occasion to exert his understanding...and generally becomes as stupid and ignorant as it is possible for a human creature to be.... But in every improved and civilized society this is the state into which the labouring poor, that is, the great body of the people, must necessarily fall, unless government takes pains to prevent it,

as must be done to bar the destructive impact of economic forces, he felt. If an artisan produces a beautiful object on command, Wilhelm von Humboldt wrote in classic work that inspired Mill, "we may admire what he does, but we despise what he is": not a free human being, but a mere device in the hands of others. For similar reasons, "the labourer who tends a garden is perhaps in a truer sense its owner than the listless voluptuary who enjoys its fruits." Genuine conservatives continued to recognize that market forces will destroy what is of value in human life, unless sharply constrained. Alexis de Tocqueville, echoing Smith and von Humboldt a half century earlier, asked rhetorically what "can be expected of a man who has spent twenty years of his life in making heads for pins?" "The art advances, the artisan recedes," he commented. Like Smith, he valued equality of condition, recognizing it to be the foundation of American democracy, and warning that if "permanent inequality of conditions" ever becomes established, "the manufacturing aristocracy which is growing up under our eyes," and which "is one of the harshest that has ever existed in the world," might escape its confines, spelling the end of democracy. Jefferson also took it as a fundamental proposition that "widespread poverty and concentrated wealth cannot exist side by side in a democracy."[16]

It was only in the early 19th century that the destructive and inhuman market forces that the founders of classical liberalism condemned were elevated to objects of veneration, their sanctity established with the certainty of "the principles of gravitation" by Ricardo and other classical economists as their contribution to the class war that was being fought in industrializing England—doctrines now being resurrected as "the everlasting battle for the minds of men" is waged with renewed intensity and cruelty.

It should be noted that in the real world, these economic counterparts to Newton's laws were heeded in practice much as they are today. The rare studies of the topic by economic historians estimate that about half the industrial sector of New England would have closed down had the economy been opened to the much cheaper products of British industry, itself established and sustained with ample resort to state power. Much the same is true today, as will quickly be discovered by anyone who sweeps aside the fog of rhetoric and looks at the reality of "economic liberalism" and the "entrepreneurial values" it fosters.

John Dewey and Bertrand Russell are two of the 20th century inheritors of this tradition, with its roots in the Enlightenment and classical liberalism, captured most vividly, I think, in the inspiring record of the struggle, organization and thinking of working men and women as they sought to maintain and expand the sphere of freedom and justice in the face of the new despotism of state-supported private power.

One basic issue was formulated by Thomas Jefferson in his later years, as he observed the growth of the new "manufacturing aristocracy" that alarmed de Tocqueville. Much concerned with the fate of the democratic experiment, he drew a distinction between "aristocrats" and "democrats." The "aristocrats" are "those who fear and distrust the people, and wish to draw all powers from them into the hands of the higher classes." The democrats, in contrast, "identify with the people, have confidence in them, cherish and consider them as the honest & safe...depository of the public interest," if not always "the most wise." The aristocrats of his day were the advocates of the rising capitalist state, which Jefferson regarded with dismay, recognizing the obvious contradiction between democracy and capitalism—or more accurately, "really existing capitalism," linked closely to state power.

Jefferson's description of the "aristocrats" was developed further by Bakunin, who predicted that the "new class" of intellectuals would follow one of two parallel paths. They might seek to exploit popular struggles to take state power into their own hands, becoming a "Red bureaucracy" that will impose the most cruel and vicious regime of history. Or they might perceive that power lies elsewhere and offer themselves as its "bought priesthood," serving the real masters either as managers or apologists, who "beat the people with the people's stick" in the state capitalist democracies.

That must be one of the few predictions of the social sciences to have come true so dramatically. It deserves a place of honor in the famous canon for that reason alone, though we will wait a long time for that.

"TOUGH LOVE"

There is, I think, an eerie similarity between the present period and the days when contemporary ideology—what is now called "neoliberalism" or "economic rationalism"—was being fashioned by Ricardo, Malthus, and others. Their task was to demonstrate to people that they have no rights, contrary to what they foolishly believe. Indeed, that is proven by "science." The grave intellectual error of pre-capitalist culture was the belief that people have a place in the society and a right to it, perhaps a rotten place, but at least something. The new science demonstrated that the concept of a "right to live" was a simple fallacy. It had to be patiently explained to misguided people that they have no rights, other than the right to try their luck in the market. A person lacking independent wealth who cannot survive in the labor market "has no claim of right to the smallest portion of food, and, in fact, has no business to be where he is," Malthus proclaimed in influential work. It is a "great evil" and violation of "natural liberty" to mislead the poor into believing that they have further rights, Ricardo held, outraged at this assault against the principles of economic science and elementary rationality, and the moral principles that are no less exalted. The message is simple. You have a free choice: the labor market, the workhouse prison, death, or go somewhere else—as was possible when vast spaces were opening thanks to the extermination and expulsion of indigenous populations, not exactly by market principles.

The founders of the science were surpassed by none in their devotion to the "happiness of the people," and even advocated some extension of the franchise to this end: "not indeed, universally to all people, but to that part of them which cannot be supposed to have any interest in overturning the right of property," Ricardo explained, adding that still heavier restrictions would be appropriate if it were shown that "limiting the elective franchise to the very narrowest bounds" would guarantee more "security for a good choice of representatives." There is an ample record of similar thoughts to the present day.[17]

It is useful to remember what happened when the laws of economic rationalism were formulated and imposed—in the familiar dual manner: market discipline for the weak, but the ministrations of the nanny state, when needed, to protect the wealthy and privileged. By the 1830s, the victory of the new ideology was substantial, and it was established more fully a few years later. There was a slight problem, however. People couldn't seem to get it into their heads that they had no intrinsic rights. Being foolish and ignorant, they found it hard

206

to grasp the simple truth that they have no right to live, and they reacted in all sorts of irrational ways. For some time, the British army was spending a good part of its energies putting down riots. Later things took a more ominous turn. People began to organize. The Chartist movement and later the labor movement became significant forces. At that point, the masters began to be a bit frightened, recognizing that *we* can deny them the right to live, but *they* can deny us the right to rule. Something had to be done.

Fortunately, there was a solution. The "science," which is somewhat more flexible than Newton's, began to change. By mid-century, it had been substantially reshaped in the hands of John Stuart Mill and even such solid characters as Nassau Senior, formerly a pillar of orthodoxy. It turned out that the principles of gravitation now included the rudiments of what slowly became the capitalist welfare state, with some kind of social contract, established through long and hard struggle, with many reverses, but significant successes as well.

Now there is an attempt to reverse the history, to go back to the happy days when the principles of economic rationalism briefly reigned, gravely demonstrating that people have no rights beyond what they can gain in the labor market. And since now the injunction to "go somewhere else" won't work, the choices are narrowed to the workhouse prison or starvation, as a matter of natural law, which reveals that any attempt to help the poor only harms them—the poor, that is; the rich are miraculously helped thereby, as when state power intervenes to bail out investors after the collapse of the highly-touted Mexican "economic miracle," or to save failing banks and industries, or to bar Japan from American markets to allow domestic corporations to reconstruct the steel, automotive, and electronics industry in the 1980s (amidst impressive rhetoric about free markets by the most protectionist administration in the postwar era and its acolytes). And far more; this is the merest icing on the cake. But the rest are subject to the iron principles of economic rationalism, now sometimes called "tough love" by those who allocate the benefits.

Unfortunately, this is no caricature. In fact, caricature is scarcely possible. One recalls Mark Twain's despairing comment, in his (long-ignored) anti-imperialist essays, on his inability to satirize one of the admired heroes of the slaughter of Filipinos: "No satire of Funston could reach perfection, because Funston occupies that summit himself...[he is] satire incarnated."

What is being reported blandly on the front pages would elicit ridicule and horror in a society with a genuinely free and democratic intellectual culture. Take just one example. Consider the economic capital of the richest country in the world: New York City. Its Mayor, Rudolph Giuliani, finally came clean about his fiscal policies, including the radically regressive shift in the tax burden: reduction in taxes on the rich ("all of the Mayor's tax cuts benefit business," the *New York Times* noted in the small print) and increase in taxes on the poor (concealed as rise in transit fares for school children and working people, higher tuition at city schools, etc.). Coupled with severe cutbacks in public funds that serve public needs, these policies should help the poor go somewhere else, the Mayor explained. These measures would "enable them to move freely around the country," the report in the *Times* elaborated, under the headline: "Giuliani Sees Welfare Cuts Providing a Chance to Move."[18]

In short, those who were bound by the welfare system and public services are at last liberated from their chains, much as the founders of the doctrines of classical liberalism advised in their rigorously demonstrated theorems. And it is all for their benefit, the newly-reconstituted science proves. As we admire the imposing edifice of rationality incarnated, the compassion for the poor brings tears to the eyes.

Where will the liberated masses go? Perhaps to *favelas* on the outskirts, so they can be "free" to find their way back somehow to do the dirty work for those who are entitled to enjoy the richest city in the world, with inequality greater than Guatemala and 40 percent of children already below the poverty line before these new measures of "tough love" are instituted.

Bleeding hearts who cannot comprehend the favors being lavished on the poor should at least be able to see that there is no alternative. "The lesson of the next few years may be that New York is simply not wealthy or economically vital enough to afford the extensive public sector that it has created over the post great Depression period," we learn from an expert opinion featured in another *Times* front-page story.

The loss of economic vitality is real enough, in part a result of "urban development" programs that eliminated a flourishing manufacturing base in favor of the expanding financial sector. The city's wealth is another matter. The expert opinion to which the *Times* turned is the report to investors of the J. P. Morgan investment firm, fifth in the ranking of commercial banks in the 1995 *Fortune* 500 listing, suffering from a mere $1.2 billion in profits in 1994. To be sure, it was not a great year for J. P. Morgan as compared with the "stunning" profit increase of 54 percent for the 500 with a mere 2.6 percent increase of employment and 8.2 percent sales gain in "one of the most profitable years ever for American business," as *Fortune* reported exultantly. The business press hailed another "banner year for U.S. corporate profits," while "U.S. household wealth seems to have actually fallen" in this fourth straight year of double-digit profit growth and 14th straight year of decline in real wages. The *Fortune* 500 have attained new heights of "economic might," with revenues close to two-thirds of gross domestic product, a good bit more than Germany or Britain, not to speak of their power over the global economy—an impressive concentration of power in unaccountable private tyrannies. and another welcome blow against democracy and markets.[19]

We live in "lean and mean times," and everyone has to tighten their belts; so the mantra goes. In reality, the country is awash in capital, with "surging profits" that are "overflowing the coffers of Corporate America," *Business Week*

208

exulted even before the grand news came in about the record-breaking final quarter of 1994, with a "phenomenal 71 percent advance" for the 900 companies in *Business Week*'s "Corporate Scoreboard." And with times so tough all over, what choice is there but to "provide a chance to move" to the now-liberated masses?[20]

"Tough love" is just the right phrase: love for the rich and privileged, tough for everyone else.

The rollback campaign on the social, economic, political, and ideological fronts exploits opportunities afforded by significant shifts of power in the past 20 years, into the hands of the masters. The intellectual level of prevailing discourse is beneath contempt, and the moral level grotesque. But the assessment of prospects that lies behind them is not unrealistic. That is, I think, the situation in which we now find ourselves, as we consider goals and visions.

As always in the past, one can choose to be a democrat in Jefferson's sense, or an aristocrat. The latter path offers rich rewards, given the locus of wealth, privilege and power, and the ends it naturally seeks. The other path is one of struggle, often defeat, but also rewards that cannot be imagined by those who succumb to "the New Spirit of the Age: Gain Wealth, forgetting all but Self."

Today's world is far from that of Thomas Jefferson or mid–19th century workers. The choices it offers, however, have not changed in any fundamental way.

209

NOTES

First published in Noam Chomsky, *Powers and Prospects: Reflections on Human Nature and the Social Order* (St Leonards, New South Wales: Allen & Unwin, 1996; Boston: South End Press, 1996), pp. 70–93, 222–23.

1 Rudolph Rocker, *Anarcho-syndicalism* (London: Secker & Warburg, 1938); "Anarchism and Anarcho-syndicalism," appended essay in P. Eltzbacher (London: Freedom Press, 1960). [Republished in 2004 by AK Press as *Anarcho-Syndicalism: Theory and Practice*]

2 Brady, *Business as a System of Power* (New York: Columbia University Press, 1943). On corporate propaganda, see particularly the pioneering work of Alex Carey, some now collected in his *Taking the Risk out of Democracy* (Urbana: University of Illinois Press, 1997); and on postwar America, Elizabeth Fones-Wolf, *Selling Free Enterprise: The Business Assault on Labor and Liberalism, 1945-1960* (Urbana: University of Illinois Press, 1995), the first American academic study of the general topic. See also William Puette, *Through Jaundiced Eyes: How the Media View Organized Labor* (Ithaca: Cornell University Press, 1992); William Solomon and Robert McChesney, eds., *New Perspectives in U.S. Communication History* (Minneapolis: University of

Minnesota Press, 1993); McChesney, *Telecommunications, Mass Media and Democracy* (New York: Oxford University Press, 1993).

3 Particularly illuminating on these matters is the work of Harvard legal historian Morton Horwitz, including *The Transformation of American Law, 1870–1960*, vol. II (New York: Oxford University Press, 1992).

4 Gary Zabel, ed., *Art and Society: Lectures and Essays by William Morris* (Boston: George's Hill, 1993). Hugh Grant Adams, cited by Ronald Edsforth, *Class Conflict and Cultural Consensus* (New Brunswick: Rutgers University Press, 1987), p. 29. See also Patricia Cayo Sexton, *The War on Labor and the Left* (Boulder, CO: Westview Press, 1991).

5 See my Russell memorial lectures, *Problems of Knowledge and Freedom* (New York: New Press, 2003), for discussion. On Dewey, see particularly Robert Westbrook, *John Dewey and American Democracy* (Ithaca: Cornell University Press, 1991).

6 James Buchanan, *The Limits of Liberty: Between Anarchy and Leviathan* (Chicago: University of Chicago Press, 1975), p. 92.

7 Stephen Kinzer, *New York Times*, October 14, 1994.

8 Jane Perlez, *New York Times*, October 7, 1994.

9 Justin Burke, et al., *Christian Science Monitor*, July 26, 1995.

10 Poll, Maria Lopez Vigil, *Envío* (Jesuit University of Central America, Managua), June 1995. Colum Lynch, *Boston Globe*, September 15, 1994; apparently the only report in the mainstream press. See also Alexander Cockburn, *The Nation*, November 7, 1994.

11 Clive Ponting, Churchill (London: Sinclair-Stevenson 1994), p. 132.

12 For some efforts at comparison, and review of the meager literature on the topic, see my *Year 501* (Boston: South End Press. 1993); also *World Orders, Old and New*, 2nd ed. (New York: Columbia University Press, 1994). I'll skip the reaction, though it is of some interest.

13 Montgomery, *The Fall of the House of Labor* (New Haven: Yale University Press, 1987), p, 7; Jon Bekken, in Solomon and McChesney, eds., *New Perspectives in U.S. Communication History*; Fones-Wolf, *Selling Free Enterprise*. On similar developments in England a few years later, see Edward Herman and Noam Chomsky, *Manufacturing Consent*, 2nd ed. (New York: Pantheon, 2002), chapter 1.2.

14 George Melloan, *Wall Street Journal*, May 16, 1994.

15 Ware, *The Industrial Worker* 1840–1860 (Chicago: Ivan Dee, 1990, reprint of 1924 edition); Montgomery, *Citizen Worker* (Cambridge: Cambridge University Press, 1993).

16 Von Humboldt, see my *Cartesian Linguistics* (New York: Harper & Row, 1966), "Language and Freedom," 1969, reprinted in *For Reasons of State* (New York: Pantheon, 1973) and James Peck, ed., *The Chomsky Reader* (New York: Pantheon, 1987). Also *Problems of Knowledge and Freedom*. Smith, see Patricia Werhane, *Adam Smith and His Legacy for Modern Capitalism* (New York: Oxford University Press, 1991), and *Year 501*. De Tocqueville, Jefferson, see John Manley, "American

Liberalism and the Democratic Dream," *Policy Studies Review*, vol. 10. No. 1 (1990); "The American Dream," *Nature, Society, and Thought*, vol. 1, no. 4 (1988).

17 Rajani Kanth, *Political Economy and Laissez-Faire* (Boulder, CO: Rowman and Littlefield, 1986); see *World Orders*, for further discussion.

18 David Firestone, *New York Times*, April 29, 1995; tax cuts, Steven Lee Myers, *New York Times*, April 28, 1995.

19 *Fortune*, May 15, May 1, 1995; *Business Week*, March 6, 1995.

20 *Business Week*, January 30, 1995; May 15, 1995.

NINE
ANARCHISM, INTELLECTUALS AND THE STATE
(1996)

You were invited to Brazil as a linguistic scholar by the Brazilian Association of Linguists (ABRALIN). Why did you assign some time in your schedule to get in touch with local social movements?

I always do that. I think it's been 40 years since I've gone anywhere just to give linguistics talks. I always combine them. In fact, usually I go for the social/political movements and give linguistics talks on the side. So, if I give a talk in the United States to a social justice movement in Colorado or wherever, it usually takes place under the auspices of the linguistics department and they cover the travel. There is nothing unusual about this. In fact, the invitations came from many groups. So, it's normal.

ANARCHISM AND THE STATE

In an article ("Goals and Visions") in your new book Powers and Prospects, *you say that as an anarchist your long-term goal is to abolish the state, but your "short-term goals are to defend and even strengthen elements of state authority [...] to impede the dedicated efforts to "roll back" the progress that has been achieved in extending democracy and human rights." What do you mean by strengthening the state? Do you mean effective participation in the state, like voting for the Democrats or the Partido dos Trabalhadores? If not, where do you draw the line?*

This was a talk to an anarchist conference, and in my view the libertarian movements have been very shortsighted in pursuing doctrine in a rigid fashion without being concerned about the human consequences. So it's perfectly proper...I mean, in my view, and that of a few others, the state is an illegitimate institution. But it does not follow from that that you should not support the state. Sometimes there is a more illegitimate institution which will take over if you do not support this illegitimate institution. So, if you're concerned with the people, let's be concrete, let's take the United States. There is a state sector that does awful things, but it also happens to do some good things. As a result of centuries of extensive popular struggle there is a minimal welfare system that provides support for poor mothers and children. That's under attack in an effort to minimize the state. Well, anarchists can't seem to understand that they are to support that. So they join with the ultra-right in saying "Yes, we've got to minimize the state," meaning put more power into the hands of private tyrannies which are completely unaccountable to the public and purely totalitarian.

It's kind of reminiscent of an old Communist Party slogan back in the early thirties "The worse, the better." So there was a period when the Communist Party was refusing to combat fascism on the theory that if you combat fascism, you join the social democrats and they are not good guys, so "the worse, the better." That was the slogan I remember from childhood. Well, they got the worse: Hitler. If you care about the question of whether seven-year-old children have food to eat, you'll support the state sector at this point, recognizing that in the long term it's illegitimate. I know that a lot of people find that hard to deal with and personally I'm under constant critique from the left for not being principled. Principle to them means opposing the state sector, even though opposing the state sector at this conjuncture means placing power into the hands of private totalitarian organizations who would be delighted to see children starve. I think we have to be able to keep those ideas in our heads if we want to think constructively about the problems of the future. In fact, protecting the state sector today is a step towards abolishing the state because it maintains a public arena in which people can participate, and organize, and affect policy, and so on, though in limited ways. If that's removed, we'd go back to a [...] dictatorship or say a private dictatorship, but that's hardly a step towards liberation.

213

It seems that according to you we are in a position where if the state gains power, corporate power loses and vice-versa...

Pretty much.

I think you have not mentioned a third party in this competition of power: the organized people. Let me give you an example. In Brazil, the health system is state-run, partly by the federal government, partly by the local city government. Last year the mayor of São Paulo proposed a reformulation of the city health system that consisted of doctors, nurses and other health workers receiving their pay from the state, but running health centers on their own. However they are allowed to pass the management of the centers to private companies, if they feel they are not able to run it properly. The Left noticed immediately that that was a twisted way of privatizing the health system, which is forbidden by the Constitution. At the same time libertarian workers in the health system proposed, instead of privatizing or keeping it state-owned that the health system should be self-managed by workers and the local community. The equipment and buildings would be state-owned and the salaries would also come from the state, but workers and the community would determine policy, work, organization, and so on. In this case, you are extending democracy...

I understand, you don't have to go on.

And at the same time weakening the state...

No, it's not weakening the state, it's strengthening the state because notice what you put in there—the salaries will be paid by the state. The ownership will be by the state; that's strengthening the state sector. I'm very much in favor of that. I think there should be worker self-management, but I think that the funding should be socialized. For example, if you had added one thing to this, namely that the funding should come from the communities, that would have been a major gift to rich people. They'd love that. What they want is to eliminate the role of what there is of the tax system—it's not much, but there's something which places at least some burden on them to support welfare systems. They'd love to see that removed. So if you go as far as self-management, terrific, I think it's a great idea and that's not at all inconsistent with what I said. So, for example, consistent with what I said before are moves to have self-management in factories, worker self-management in factories. It's the same thing. That's still making sure that, under present circumstances, it's not the poor people who pay for it, that the costs are socialized. That means strengthening the state against private powers. So these are all perfectly consistent, it's not a third option; it's part of the second option I was describing. In fact, within the public arena that is preserved in parliamentary democracy that allows some role for the state, there's all kinds of opportunities for struggle. For example, the crucial ones, of which this is a small part, are eliminating management and ownership in the entire private system. That's within the system. That could actually be theoretically done by parliamentary means. It hasn't been done but at least the mechanisms are there. Anyway, one should always pursue the mechanisms to the limits. The reason why transnational corporations are so interested in the liberals is that, from their point of view, it is precisely liberals that minimize the state. And minimizing the state means strengthening the private sectors. It narrows the domain within which public influence can be expressed. That's not an anarchist goal. I mean people may be seduced by the words "minimize the state" and sort of trapped in them, but think what it means. It's minimizing the state and increasing an even worse power. That's not an anarchist goal.

Are you stressing this because many anarchists in the United States mistake the libertarian party for a party that defends anarchist ideals or something close to anarchism. Is that the reason why...?

214

That's sort of related. That's a peculiarly Anglo-Saxon phenomenon, in the English speaking world and the United States. One dream of anarchism—and the only kind that survived—was ultra-right anarchism, which you see in the libertarian party, which is just loved by the big corporations and the investment firms and so on. Not that they believe in it. They know perfectly well that they'll never get rid of the state because they need it for their own purposes, but they love to use this as an ideological weapon against everyone else. So the libertarian party is very warmly accepted within mainstream business circles who really ridicule it privately because they know perfectly well that they're not going to survive without a massive state subsidy, so they want a powerful state. But they like the libertarian ideology which they can use as a battering ram against everyone else. If you actually pursued the ideals of the libertarian party you would create the worst totalitarian monster that the world has ever seen. Actually, I have lots of personal friends there. For years, the only journals I could write in were ultra-right libertarian journals because we agree on a lot of things. For example, we agree on the opposition to American imperialism. For example, nobody would publish the first article that I was able to write on East Timor. They published it, back in the late seventies. That's the only article that appeared in the United States on the subject in the seventies. They also published many other things and we remained personal friends. Although there is a big area of difference.

There was a left anarchist movement, too—the working class anarchist movement. They were pretty much destroyed by force. That's when people like Emma Goldman and Alexander Berkman were jailed and thrown out of the country. So the working class, left libertarian movement was mostly smashed, but the right libertarian movement was applauded. Not because people in power believe it, but because it's a useful battering ram. Lots of anarchists are very much confused by this. The United States has a tradition of individualist anarchism. "I'll go off into the woods and work by myself," that kind of anarchism. Which is sort of a thing that develops in that kind of a society, a very business-run society, with lots of space. It takes many forms. One of the forms it takes is the kind of militias, who are very anti-statist. I mean, if I talk to groups where there is strong support for the ultra-right militias, we agree on a lot of things. They're distributing my books. You go to the militia conferences, my books are there. They think we are on the same side because we're both attacking the state. Just as anarchists think we're on different sides because I do something to preserve the state. If you think these things through a little bit, I mean, one slogan doesn't give you the answer. You have to put the slogan in the context of a more complicated reality.

It's funny for us that Americans make such a gross confusion between the far right and the far left...

It's not unusual, look at history, where Mussolini comes from.

SPECIALIZATION AND THE INTELLECTUAL DIVISION OF LABOR

You mentioned somewhere [Language and Responsibility] *the role of the intellectual in mantaining social order and defending the interest of the elite, and then criticized the idea that social knowledge (history, international politics, etc.) requires special tools (theory, methodology) that ordinary people don't and can't have. At the same time, the criticism that denounces this perverse specialization of social knowledge is itself specialized, in the sense that it demands a great deal of effort that only a professional intellectual or a hard working dilettante can do. How can the critical intellectual escape this dilemma of criticizing specialization and being a specialist himself?*

I think that you have to be honest. If you were to ask me, could I explain to you what I teach in my graduate courses in linguistics in five minutes, I'd say "no" because it requires too much background, there's too much understanding, and there's technical knowledge required and so on. But if you asked me to explain Brazil's debt crisis in five minutes I'd say "yes" because it's relatively straightforward. And in fact virtually everything in social and political affairs is right on the surface. Nobody understands very much in the sciences: when you get beyond big molecules it becomes pretty descriptive. The areas in which there is significant, non-superficial knowledge are pretty rare. If it's there, you respect that it's there, so I'm not going to give a talk in quantum physics because I don't know any.

On the other hand, these questions are really accessible to everybody. One of the things that intellectuals do is make them inaccessible, for various reasons, including the reasons of domination and personal privilege. It's very natural for intellectuals to try to make simple things look difficult. It's like when the medieval church was creating mysteries to maintain it's importance. Read *The Grand Inquisitor* by Dostoyevsky—it says it beautifully. The Grand Inquisitor explains that you have to create mysteries because otherwise the common people will be able to understand things. They have to be subordinated so you have to make things look mysterious and complicated. That's the test of the intellectual. It's also good for them: then you're an important person, talking big words which nobody can understand. Sometimes it gets kind of comical, say in post-modern discourse. Especially around Paris, it has become a comic strip, I mean it's all gibberish. But it's very inflated, a lot of television cameras, a lot of posturing. They try to decode it and see what is the actual meaning behind it, things that you could explain to an eight-year old child. There's nothing there. But these are the ways in which contemporary intellectuals, including those on the Left, create great careers for themselves, power for themselves, marginalize people, intimidate people and so on. In the

United States, for example, and indeed much of the Third World, lots of young radical activists are simply intimidated by the incomprehensible gibberish that comes out of left-wing intellectual movements—often radical feminists, or this or that—which is just impossible to understand. It makes people feel they're not going to do anything because, unless I somehow understand the latest version of post-modern this and that, I can't go out in the streets and organize people, because I'm not bright enough. It may not be intended this way but the effect is a technique of marginalization and control and self-interest. Because the people themselves become prestigious and travel around and live in high circles and so forth. Paris is maybe the extreme version of it. There it has become almost a comic strip, but you find it elsewhere.

On the other hand, the question you have to ask yourself in regard to this query is "Well, if there is some theory or set of principles or doctrines that are too complicated to understand and you have to really study them, then show me something that can't be said in simple words." If somebody can show you that, then take it seriously. Ask a person in physics, they can do it. [But] there's a difference. For example, if there's something that comes out in a physics experiment which I don't understand, which often happens, I can go to my friends in the physics department and I can ask them to explain it to me. I'd tell them the level at which I can understand and they can do it. Just as I can explain to them something happening at a post-graduate linguistics seminar in whatever terms they want to understand, with the details. They'll get the idea. Try asking somebody to explain to you the latest essay of Derrida or somebody in terms that you can understand. They can't do it. At least they can't do it to me: I don't understand. And I think you must ask yourself very carefully what great leap in evolution has taken place that enables people to have these fantastic insights that they can't convey to ordinary people about topics that no one understands very much about. One should be very skeptical about that, that's another technique by which intellectuals dominate people in my opinion.

CONSCIENCE AND VANGUARD

You just mentioned Derrida. There has been much discussion lately on relativism. It has led many to a kind of position where passivity is justified by a respect for cultural diversity. It seems to me that this discussion is two-sided. It has a liberal side, which is multiculturalism, but it also has a leftist side, a discussion that goes from Gramsci to Paulo Freire. In the latter (and most interesting) side, it is a discussion that has emphasized how the dichotomy between an enlightened vanguard and the narrow-minded pro-

letariat has led to authoritarianism. What position should be taken to avoid both general passivity and authoritarianism?

Vanguard ideas are easy to understand; they are ways for people to justify their own power, such as right-wing libertarianism. It gives an ideological justification for me to have power and have no other value. People who are serious will work with people. When you teach you don't stand there and make statements that people are supposed to copy down. You work with people. That's true whether you're teaching six-year old children or post-graduate school. You're working together, trying to enlighten yourselves. Often the person that's teaching learns more than the student. So you're using whatever knowledge and resources and privilege you have to help other people and to learn from them and so on. That's what respectable intellectual work is. It doesn't mean there is any vanguard; in fact, the intellectual is a servant working together with other people to try and gain better understanding. There is really nothing more to say about this. I mean, in fact, it's kind of remarkable that the place where it is completely understood is in the hard sciences. If you go to topics that really have a lot of substantive content—like, say, higher mathematics or advanced physics or even our graduate courses in linguistics— This is exactly what they are. It's not a matter of a professor standing there and people taking notes, people would laugh at that. It's an interchange. You talk about the work you are doing, some of the students get up and say that's wrong, it's a different way, you should think about that. Then you work again at the problem. It's no different when you are talking to working class people in slums and they are trying to figure out what their problems are. I mean, you have certain knowledge, they have certain knowledge, you have experience, they have experience. Try to put them together and see if it can be used constructively. I'm not trying to be super-modest or anything. I know perfectly well that when I give a talk to striking workers or welfare mothers and so on, there are things I know that they don't know. And there are things they know that I don't know and we put that together and have a common intergrowth.

In "Democracy and Markets in the New World Order" [Powers and Prospects] you say that over 80 percent of American people "think that workers have too little influence—though only 20 percent feel that way about unions and 40 percent consider them too influential, another sign of the effects of the propaganda system in inducing confusion". There (but not only there) you make two uses of statistical evidence: one, to demonstrate the "real" interest of the people, and another to demonstrate the manipulative effect of the media. If what people say and think is no certain sign of what is their interest, how can we determine that interest?

Well, we know what they think; what they think is very straightforward. They think that working people should have more say in what goes on and they think that unions should have less say. And both assumptions are reasonable based on the information available to them. People make judgements on the basis of the information available. The information available to them is that unions are a weapon against working people. Did you see *On the Waterfront*, a famous film years ago? Sort of a model, a model that the media has been presenting like a battering ram for fifty years. The idea is that the unions are the enemy of the workers and the simple worker has to rise up and overthrow the union. You can understand why the entertainment industry, which is just a huge corporate system, would try to prevent the idea of unions. And to some extent they've succeeded. So people honestly believe that working people have to liberate themselves from unions, and that's one of the ways in which working people will have more say in what goes on. There's of course a factual error there. It's not that we don't know what people believe. They believe a false fact, namely that unions are the enemy of the working people. Sometimes it's true incidentally, like any propaganda. The craziest propaganda is always based on some elements of truth. And there's elements of truth here too. Unions have been enemies of workers, but they are also probably the most democratic form of organization that exists in our highly undemocratic society. There can be and often have been associations within which workers can free themselves and extend the sphere of social justice. But the media are not going to tell you that, so the answer to the dilemma is to get people to understand what unions are or could be, to learn working class history. Nobody knows working class history, nobody studies it. In fact, just take a look at the media you find all over the world. There are business sections, have you ever seen a labor section? I don't know a single newspaper that has a labor section. Every single one has a business section. There's a business press, is there a labor press? If you look here, I don't know, but in the United States, try to find a reporter who's assigned to the labor movement. There are maybe two working in the whole country. That means the whole population doesn't get covered. What gets covered is the business world and it's a reflection of power. Unless people are able to unravel that system of propaganda they're not going to be able to liberate themselves. So that's part of the job, to overcome these differences.

219

It's the same with welfare. Overwhelmingly, the population thinks that the government, meaning the organized public, has a responsibility to provide people with minimal standards of living, health, and so on. On the other hand, they're opposed to welfare, which does exactly that. The reason: the image of welfare is a rich, black mother having children over and over again so that we'll pay for them, riding in a Cadillac to the welfare office to pick up her check. That's what people think welfare is, so you can understand why they're opposed to welfare. Why should I work to pay for her? So they're opposed to welfare. On the other hand, they say "Well, there's that poor woman over there who can't take care of her child. She should have support." It's not a contradiction, it's just a false assumption built in by heavy indoctrination. And the answer is unravel the indoctrination. It's like saying that Brazil has to pay it's debt. That's indoctrination. Who has to pay the debt? The people who took the money and sent it back to New York to make more money? They're the ones who should pay the debt, if anybody should. That's not Brazil. You have to talk about these things, so people can understand them. They're not very hard, you don't have to talk about them in post-modern rhetoric. You can talk about them in very simple words because they're very simple points and people easily understand. The only people who don't understand them are intellectuals. But of course, they have a vested interest in not understanding them. If they understand them, then their own powers are lost. So they're not going to understand them, they're going to cloud them in mysteries.

This interview was conducted in Brazil in November 1996 by Pablo Ortellado and André Ryoki Inoue. It originally appeared in a special issue (on Democracy and Self-management) of *Temporaes*, the review of the History students of the University of São Paulo (São Paulo: Humanitas, 1999). It was later published in a collection of Chomsky's articles and interviews on anarchism: *Notas sobre o Anarquismo*, Felipe Correa (ed), São Paulo: Imaginário/Sedição, 2004.

TEN
INTERVIEW WITH BARRY PATEMAN (2004)

Thank you for seeing us today, as you know we want to talk about the ideas of anarchism and your thoughts on anarchism. And it's going to be a rather wandering chat but hopefully we'll get somewhere.

In the middle 1990s in an interview that you gave you talked about one of the problems with anarchism was that maybe it was too negative, that it criticized but didn't offer a positive...

Well, if I said that I shouldn't have because I don't agree with it. In fact you can take a look at the shelf up there. [Pointing, laughter] There are anarchist studies which offer proposals for society in such meticulous detail that they go beyond anything plausible in my view. Diego Abad de Santillan is a famous case who in 1936 wrote a critique of the anarchist revolution in Spain. He was an Argentinian anarchist who was in Spain. It was called *After the Revolution* and he laid out a very detailed program for what a largely anarcho-syndicalist vision of Spanish society, or for that matter any society, ought to be like. And there are many other proposals. I think the question for detailed planning for the future isn't so much "can we do it?" Sure we can do it, but it's whether we know enough about human beings, about society, institutions, the effects of introducing institutional structures into human life. Do we know enough about that to be able to plan in any detail what a society should look like? Or should it be experimental, guided by certain general ideas about liberty, equality, authority and domination and let people explore different ways of working through this maze and see what comes natural to them? How much variety should there be? What are you going to do with people who don't want to work or people with criminal tendencies or people who don't want to go to meetings? There are millions of questions that come up. To what extent do you want to interchange jobs or delegate responsibility on the basis of interest and talent? If somebody wants to be a carpenter, a nuclear physicist or a pianist and someone else wants to be an administrator do you necessarily require that they interchange jobs as a matter of principle, even if they are all happier if they don't? I don't think we know, there are both positive and negative comments you can make about that, but I don't think we know the answers.

I was reading Isaac Puente the Spanish libertarian communist theorist who was arguing rather like that. He was arguing that "Well, if one becomes a teacher one learns by experience, and if one becomes a doctor one learns by experience." It wasn't one isn't a doctor when one is 22 but you learn and maybe that is how anarchism ought to be seen.

At a very general level I think we would all agree. People in the rough range of those who call themselves anarchists—which is pretty broad—there would at least be a general agreement that, whatever social structures and arrange- ments are developed, they ought to maximize the possibilities for people to pursue their own creative potential and you can't make a formula for that. People are too different and they ought to be different and the differences ought to be encouraged. It's just like with raising children, you want them to find their own paths. You don't say here's the rigid framework—lots of people do, but they shouldn't—here is the framework you are supposed to follow. My own view, and I differ with some of my close friends on this, is that we should be cautious in trying to sketch out the nature of the future society in too much detail. It's not that it can't be done. It can be done in interesting and different ways—and it has been done—but I think the real question is to what is extent is it important to do it and to what extent is it important to just try and exper- iment and chip away at existing structures?

Actually, another problem which I think must be faced is that at any par- ticular point in human history people have not understood what oppression is. It's something you learn. If I go back to, say, my parents or grandmother, she didn't think she was oppressed by being in a super patriarchal family where the father would walk down the street and not recognize his daughter when she came because—not because he didn't know who she was, but because you don't nod to your daughter. It didn't feel like oppression. It just felt like the way life works. I mean, what psychic effects it had internally—well, that's a complicat- ed question. But, as anyone involved in any kind of activism knows—say the women's movement—one of the first tasks is to get people to understand that they are living under conditions of oppression and domination. It isn't obvi- ous, and who knows what forms of oppression and domination we are just accepting without even noticing them. At some further stage of self-enlighten- ment and communal understanding we will recognize that those are the things we have to deal with and we can't plan for them if we don't know about them.

Linked to that then, Emma Goldman, as she grew older and feared the fact that there might not be an immediate revolution, became very influenced by Gustav Landauer who said the state isn't just out there. It's inside us and that we have to become ourselves—as free as we can be in capitalism. In fact she was always worried that there may be a chance that people won't be ready for revolution and that there is a way of developing the politics of the personal so maybe more people could be ready to experience that life that is possible.

I think that's quite true, and in fact the people who understand this the best are those who are carrying out the control and domination in the more free societies, like the U.S. and England, where popular struggles have have won a lot of freedoms over the years and the state has limited capacity to coerce. It is very striking that it's precisely in those societies that elite groups—the business world, state managers and so on—recognized early on that they are going to have to develop massive methods of control of attitude and opinion, because you cannot control people by force anymore and therefore you have to modify their consciousness so that they don't perceive that they are living under conditions of alienation, oppression, subordination and so on. In fact, that's what probably a couple trillion dollars are spent on each year in the U.S., very self-consciously, from the framing of television advertisements for two-year olds to what you are taught in graduate school economics programs. It's designed to create a consciousness of subordination and it's also intended specifically and pretty consciously to suppress normal human emotions.

Normal human emotions are sympathy and solidarity, not just for people but for stranded dolphins. It's just a normal reaction for people. If you go back to the classical political economists, people like Adam Smith, this was just taken for granted as the core of human nature and society. One of the main concentrations of advertising and education is to drive that out of your mind. And it's very conscious. In fact, it's conscious in social policy right in front of our eyes today. Take the effort to destroy Social Security. Well, what's the point of that? There's a lot of scam about financial problems, which is all total nonsense. And, of course, they want Wall Street to make a killing. Underlying it all is something much deeper. Social Security is based on a human emotion and it's a natural human emotion which has to be driven out of people minds, namely the emotion that you care about other people. You care. It's a social and community responsibility to care whether a disabled widow across town has enough food to eat, or whether a kid across the street can go to school. You have to get that out of people's heads. You have to make them say, "Look, you are a personal, rational wealth maximizer. If that disabled widow didn't prepare for her own future, it's her problem not your problem. It's not your fault she doesn't have enough to eat so why should you care?"

There is no such a thing as society then, is that what you are saying?

Yes. There is only you maximizing your own wealth and subordinating yourself to power and not thinking about anyone else. And that has an effect. You can see it in attitudes. Now, just to get back to your point, the same is true of those who are trying to change society to more decent forms. Yes, you are going to have to deal with people's consciousness and awareness and, as I say,

223

every organizer knows this. Take the women's movement, as a striking example. It begins with consciousness-raising groups. Where people talk to each other and bring out elements of their lives that they may not perceive very clearly. And it's true across the board for educational institutions, factories and everywhere else. It's very striking to see how this has worked over the years. Go back to the early days of the industrial revolution, right around here in Lowell, Lawrence, the places where the textile mills were being created. Among the people who were drawn into the early factories—young women from the farms, Irish artisans from the slums etc.—there was an extremely radical consciousness that was just natural. They didn't read Marx, weren't aware of European radicalism, had never heard of anarchism or anything else. It was just the natural assumption. They had a very free press—something that we have lost. The free press of those days just took for granted that wage labor was pretty much like slavery, that those who worked in the mills ought to own them— "Why do we need these bosses telling us what to do?"—and that "the factory system, industrial system is just crushing our cultural values and creative impulses; they are turning us into robots" and so forth. All of this was understood, taken for granted. You go out to a working class neighborhood today and you won't find it. But it's not that people have to be taught it: it has to be brought out from their inner nature where it has been suppressed by very conscious efforts.

224   It's striking to see how conscious this is. About a century ago Taylorism was introduced into industry—"Taylorism" for Frederick Taylor—basically to turn workers into robots so every emotion is controlled, so they don't have any choices and they become essentially robots. Like everything else it was initiated in the military system because there you can carry out experiments cost-free, at public cost and risk. Then it was transferred to industry, the mass production system and so on. Lenin was very enamored of it. He had about the same conceptions as capitalist managers and the idea was to robotize work. But it was quickly recognized in the 1920s that what they called "on-job control" could be extended to "off-job control." That is, controlling every other aspect of life in the same way. So why should people not be robots in their entire life? And to be a robot means to focus your attention on what were called the superficial things of life. Like fashionable consumption, not on care for one another, not on working together to create a decent environment, not on what the world will be like for your children. To turn you into a passive consumer, a person who pushes buttons every couple years and is taught that that is democracy. Follow orders, don't think. Identify your own value as a human being in the amount of useless consumption that you can carry out. That's "off-job control." It runs through all the institutions and it's a huge industry. And, yes, to overcome off-job control you have to make people realize that your value as a human being is not how deeply you can go in debt and how many credit cards you can max out to get commodities you want. That is not your value as a human being. You go to a mall over the weekend and see young kids who in

their spare time—young girls usually—what they do for fun is window shopping. I mean, if they want to do it you can't say don't do it—but what this tells you about how people's consciousness has been modified by "off-job control" is pretty frightening.

Linked to that as well, one of the things that I think is striking when you look at the history of anarchism, is that at its most popular it was almost an organic movement answering community needs, the Jewish anarchists in New York in the 1890s, Spain obviously, Argentina as you mentioned, France. Isn't community also being destroyed by things such as technology, where now there are more communities in cyberspace than maybe the type of community where you or I grew up? Myself in a coal mining community where you knew everyone and everyone knew you. Yes, there were tensions, but you had that sense of relationships. Isn't that going rather quickly and isn't technology helping that go?

In my view technology is a pretty neutral instrument. It could go in that direction or it could go in an opposite direction. Technology could in fact be used to help the workforce in a factory run it without any managers, by providing people at the workbench with real-time information that would enable them to join with others in making sensible decisions. That's another use of technology. Of course that technology doesn't get developed. In fact there are very interesting studies about how it does work. One of the most interesting studies was done by David Noble, who used to be here (at MIT), but he was a bit too radical. He did terrific work. One of the main topics he studied was called Numerical Control—computer controlled machine tool production— that kind of thing. That was developed in the military system at public cost, but it was designed so one way of using it could have been to eliminate managerial roles and put decision-making into the hands of skilled mechanics who knew what they were doing, and were usually people who knew more than those people in the offices upstairs. I'm sure it was true in the coal mining work. So put the decision-making into their hands and the technology could have been designed to do that. Studies were done showing that that would even increase profits. But it was done the opposite way, in ways that increase levels of management control, which is highly inefficient, to deskill mechanics and to turn them into robots who just push buttons. Well, that is a choice as to how to use technology and it's a kind of class warfare, but it has nothing to do with the inherent nature of technology. However, the point you make is an interesting one. I don't know what will come of it but it is true that there are virtual communities which are very real. I mean, I would say that I've never seen 95 percent of my close friends. We just interact all the time on the internet. And, at my age it seems perfectly reasonable, but when I see my grandchildren do it, I don't like it. I think they need to learn things about face-to-face communication.

My son does instant messaging. And he instant messages with people who, while he's at school, he can hardly talk to. It provides a neutral framework, but I worry enormously because I'd rather he spoke and interacted...

I agree with you. I don't know what kind of effect this is going to have on young kids growing up. I mean, they live in an imaginary world. And they are even interacting with people who are adopting false personalities. When kids used to play Dungeons and Dragons...I mean, okay, I didn't love it but I didn't see much wrong with it. On the other hand, when much of your life is in an imaginary world with characters who you have created, and who have created themselves, and you don't have face-to-face interactions with—that can have psychic effects which I don't think we understand. It could be pretty malevolent...

Taking another step forward, you certainly know that there is a tendency, certainly in the last 10 years in anarchism, that we call primitivism. They call it anarcho-primitivism and suggest that capitalism is so rotten, the technology involved in capitalism is so destructive, that we just ought get rid of the whole thing. It's so destructive, so corroding, so horrible that it's just damaging people, so let's get rid of it and step back, or forward in their eyes, to a more natural, organic world of nature. Is that possible?

You know, I sympathize with people who say that but I do not think that they are realizing that what they are calling for is the mass genocide of millions of people because of the way society is now structured and organized, urban life and so forth. If you eliminate these structures everybody dies. For example, I can't grow my own food. It's a nice idea, but it's not going to work, not in this world. And, in fact, none of us want to live a hunter-gatherer life. There are just too many things in life that the modern world offers us. In just plain terms of survival, what they are calling for is the worst mass genocide in human history. And, unless one thinks through these things, it's not really serious.

Yes, I agree. A lot of people in Europe know you through your introduction to Daniel Guérin's book Anarchism. *AK Press put out his* No Gods, No Masters *in English...*

Yes, it's right up there on the shelf.

It's a great book and it's obvious that Guérin was very keen to blend what he felt were the best aspects of anarchism and the best aspects of socialism into this Libertarian Socialism. Do you think that those two terms— Libertarian Socialism and Anarchism—are synonymous or do you think there are real differences between the two?

Well, I don't think we can really say, because the terms of political discourse aren't well defined. Capitalism, trade, the state, pick any one…they are pretty loose terms. Which is okay, but it doesn't make sense to try to define these terms carefully when you don't have an explanatory theory to embed them in. But the fact is we can't really answer the question, anarchism covers too many things, libertarian socialism covers too many things. But I sympathize with what he's trying to do. I think it's the right thing. If you look carefully they are really close, there are similarities and relationships. The more anti-statist, anti-vanguardist left elements of the socialist movement, Marxist movement in fact—folks like Anton Pannekoek and others—there are close similarities between them and some of the wings of the anarchist movement, like the anarcho-syndicalists. It's pretty hard to make much of a distinction between, say, Pannekoek's workers' councils and anarcho-syndicalist conceptions of how to organize society. There are some differences, but they are the kind of differences that ought to exist when people are working together in comradely relationships. So, yes, that's a sensible blend in my view. The much sharper distinction is between all these movements and the various forms of totalitarianism like Bolshevism, corporate capitalism and so on. There you have a real break. Totalitarian structures on the one hand and free societies on the other. In fact, I think there are significant similarities between libertarian socialism and anarchism, this blend, and even very mainstream thinkers like John Dewey—there are striking similarities.

227

I know he was quite influenced by Stelton and the Modern School and he took a lot of those ideas and thought about them…

His basic view was that unless we eliminate what he called political and industrial feudalism and turn it into industrial democracy—which means pretty much workers' control—then the whole formal democratic system doesn't really mean very much. And he comes straight out of mainstream American histories. He's as American as apple pie.

A couple of quick things. I know from reading you that you are very much impressed by Pannekoek, and Gorter, the left communist strand. I take it you don't see a danger of things like workers' councils or the work of Pannekoek or Gorter leading into another form of totalitarianism. Do you think that breaks from that…

No, I think there is plenty of danger, but there is also danger that participatory economics could lead to totalitarianism. Every one of us have been in movement meetings, we all know the dynamics. No matter what you are working on, putting up a traffic light on the corner or organizing resistance against the Vietnam war, or whatever it may be…there is a meeting of people and we differ in our levels of tolerance for boring activities. Some people just drop off really fast—like me for example, I just can't tolerate much of it. Other people really commit to, basically, controlling things and there is a natural dynamic in which in the most free, cooperative, libertarian structures can turn into an authoritarian one just by virtue of who is going to stick around, take enough control and finally make the decisions until others decide to go do something else. Those are always dangers.

The last person standing ends up making the decisions…

And we're all perfectly familiar with it; groups of friends, affinity groups working on something or the other. So, yes, those are always problems to deal with. There is no magic formula for preventing that from happening.

Linked to that, what do you feel about the role of class in social change and anarchism? There's no doubt certainly that in America there is a tendency in anarchism, among some new anarchists, to see class as belonging to the past. It really isn't the most relevant focus of change anymore.

How many of those people have worked in your coalmine or on a factory floor, or as a data processor in industry? I mean, if those are your jobs then you haven't any problems with class. You know who is the boss, and who gives the orders and who takes them. You understand the capital concentration that lies beyond the choice of who make the orders and who take the orders. And those are class differences. Off in some other domain you could say "I don't see it," but when you enter the real life of people who live and work in society, I don't think they have much problem discerning class differences and their significance. There is a huge difference between giving orders and taking them. And, even if it's true that the people who are giving orders are taking them from somewhere else, that is the nature of totalitarian systems. It's not that the top guy gives the orders to the bottom guy: there are levels of transmission for which orders are taken and given. Managerial supervision and levels of decision making of various kinds, and that leads to fundamental class difference. There are plenty of people who just take the orders or starve. There is no choice. And in fact we see class issues rising all the time.

Take real concrete issues, like outsourcing. What attitude should people take about outsourcing? There are conflicting values. First of all, outsourcing is a very misleading term. Outsourcing is internal to totalitarian systems. If GM outsources, that means they are transferring jobs to some firm under their control which is able to escape labor laws, environmental constraints and so on and to give them cheap inputs for the next stage of manufacturing. But that's all internal to command economies. Outsourcing is kind of like a pretense. It has something to do with the free market. It has to do with internal workings of command economies. But what should our attitudes be to it? If people here are losing their jobs because you can get a worker for 10 percent of the cost in, say, India or China, should we be for it or against it?

Well, the arguments go both ways, but I think both are highly misleading because they are accepting a framework that we shouldn't accept. I mean, if you accept the framework that says totalitarian command economies have the right to make these decisions, and if the wage levels and working conditions are fixed facts, then we have to make choices within those assumptions. Then you can make an argument that poor people here ought to lose their jobs to even poorer people somewhere else…because that increases the economic pie, and it's the usual story. Why make those assumptions? There are other ways of dealing with the problem. Take, for example rich people here. Take those like me who are in the top few percent of the income ladder. We could cut back our luxurious lifestyles, pay proper taxes, there are all sorts of things. I'm not even talking about Bill Gates, but people who are reasonably privileged. Instead of imposing the burden on poor people here and saying "well, you poor people have to give up your jobs because even poorer people need them over there," we could say "okay, we rich people will give up some small part of our ludicrous luxury and use it to raise living standards and working conditions elsewhere, and to let them have enough capital to develop their own economy, their own means." Then the issue will not arise. But it's much more convenient to say that poor people here ought to pay the burden under the framework of command economies—totalitarianism. But, if you think it through, it makes sense and almost every social issue you think about—real ones, live ones, ones right on the table—has these properties. We don't have to accept and shouldn't accept the framework of domination of thought and attitude that only allows certain choices to be made…and those choices almost invariably come down to how to put the burden on the poor. That's class warfare. Even by real nice people like us who think it's good to help poor workers, but within a framework of class warfare that maintains privilege and transfers the burden to the poor. It's a matter of raising consciousness among very decent people.

Here's a more grim question. Voltairine De Cleyre in the 1900s in an essay talks about the hope she has of a peaceful change into a better world, and then talks about the masters who are creating such a system that they are going to reap a horrible whirlwind. Are we still in this situation where a peaceful transition to a freer, better world is possible for us, or can we not say it's less likely as the years go on?

Actually no one knows. But my own subjective, low-credibility judgement is that the opportunities for peaceful change are considerably greater now than they have been in the past. The reason for that is that the repressive apparatus of state and corporate power has been reduced. You can't break up strikes with Pinkerton guards any more. You won't get away with it. You can't smash working class sovereign towns like Homestead, PA, with the National Guard. All that makes a difference. You can't get away with it now. Enough victories have been won so that repression has been reduced. Look at the simple question of how many workers get killed in labor actions. It used to be very high—it went up until the late 1930s. I can remember as a kid, workers getting killed in labor actions by security guards, Pinkertons and police, and that has stopped. Maybe occasionally it happens but it's a substantial change.

At the Emma Goldman Papers we look at the New York Times *or we get students to look at the daily papers from the 1890s. Every week there was a worker getting killed.*

I saw it as a kid. I have childhood memories of watching policemen wade into women strikers at a textile plant and beating the shit out of them. And, I don't think you'd get away with it now. Alright, and that generalizes. Just like it would be much harder now for the U.S. to institute a military coup in Brazil than it was 40 years ago. Much harder in fact, probably impossible. Because there have been just enough changes that people won't accept it anymore and the structures of power have dissolved. In fact, many of the structures of power are very fragile. A lot of them have shifted from direct coercion to indoctrination and thought and attitude control. It's bad enough to have your kids bombarded with horrendous television, but it's a lot different than having them beaten over the head by police and having torture chambers around. So those changes mean that there are many more options for peaceful change.

But it does make it more complex to fire back? At least if there is a Pinkerton guard you know who your enemy is.

Yes, you know who your enemy is. When it's your friendly executive from this awful corporation claiming to be on the same side you are on, it's harder, but it doesn't mean it's impossible. A couple days ago I was giving a talk—which I do every year—to a terrific group of mostly young labor activists at Harvard, which is run by a fantastic person, Elaine Bernard. She is a real dynamic, livewire labor activist, feminist, just terrific. This program for bringing the young labor leaders into Harvard was begun around 1940 as part of the corporate academic reaction to the perceived threat—real threat—of significant radical labor action that revolutionized the country. The sit-down strike was just one thought away from taking over the plant. It was really close. As part of the technique for undermining that, as it was becoming harder to use Pinkerton guards and police to break up this up, it became understood that what you have to do is socialize the rising young labor leadership, civilize them, teach them by bringing them to Harvard, and do what Harvard is good at. In fact, what it does with its own students: teach them how to have polite conversations, have class solidarity, drink the right wine, pick up the right attitudes and relations. Stick these young [labor activists] in the business schools and they'll see "we're all friends" and we're all doing the same things. And it went on like that for years. And then Elaine Bernard came along and took it over. And, since, it's become a center for radical international labor activists. And it's because all these ideas are just there, barely below the surface and when you puncture the surface it all just comes out. It's all so natural and obvious that it takes massive effort to beat it down. By now [the Harvard program] is completely different and has big effects throughout the world. And that can be done in all kinds of places, but those are modes of peaceful change. And in just Elaine's own lifetime they have led to very big changes.

The change has gone in both directions. On the one hand, you can't crush Homestead the way you could 100 years ago, while, on the other hand, the consciousness that led to Homestead is gone. So it's not just progress, but rebuilding that consciousness is the kind of peaceful activity that can be carried out and is in many respects a lot easier than fighting the National Guard.

A final question because I think we're running out of time. I have been working on Alexander Berkman's book, Now and Then: an ABC of Anarchism *because AK Press has just republished it as* What Is Anarchism? *In reading his letters in the 1920s when he was working on the book and he was finding it very difficult, one of the things that he was trying to come to grips with in the book is "Why haven't people come to this idea? This idea, which to me is just common sense…this natural instinct to solidarity and support? I've seen Russia and I've seen totalitarianism in action. Why haven't anarchist ideas had a greater impact in the world?" Now that was nearly 80 years ago and the question we're all still facing is we at least believe, as Emma Goldman says, "Anarchism is the only belief that shows men and women their true selves and who they can be." But we see that, and we know that instinctively, yet it has still had such a miniscule impact. Is that true?* 231

I do not think it's true that it's had a minuscule impact. A lot of the progressive social change of the past century isn't anarchist. Progressive taxations, Social Security isn't anarchist, but it's a reflection of attitudes and understandings which, if they go a little bit further, do reflect anarchist commitments. They are based on the idea that there really should be solidarity, community, mutual support, mutual aid and so forth—opportunities for creative action. They are all based on these. They are subdued, channeled and modified so they never take real libertarian forms, but they are there and they lead to social change.

Why hasn't it gone further? Well a large part of it is violence. Take for example Berkman's experience in Russia. He entered into a violent, totalitarian state. Up until the Bolshevik takeover—coup, revolution, whatever you want to call it—there were very signifigant popular libertarian, sometimes anarchist initiatives all over, from peasant anarchism in the Ukraine to workers' councils in the Soviets. They were simply smashed by force, by great violence. Lenin and Trotsky were totalitarian extremists and they had a theory behind it. They were dedicated Marxists who believed that a backward, primitive country like Russia can't go to socialism because the Master's principles tell us that. Therefore we have to drive the country by force through the stages of essentially state capitalist development and then ultimately something will happen. They weren't repeating the master accurately, this required the suppression of many years of Marx's later work—which were literally suppressed—his studies of peasant societies in Russia and so forth.

The point is they had the force. It wasn't easy to destroy it. Take Makhno's movement, Kronstadt, or the elimination of the Soviets: it wasn't a trivial operation but it was carried out. Berkman saw it and he saw the vicious totalitarian society arising very much the way anarchists had predicted. I mean, Bakunin spelled it all out. In fact even Trotsky in his early work, before he joined [the Bolsheviks], said it was going to happen, as did Rosa Luxemburg and others. But it happened and that's their variant. Our variant was different. Berkman was writing right after Wilson's Red Scare, which made the Patriot Act look like a tea party. It was a violent repression run by the "progressive" Woodrow Wilson and others, not just against the anarchists—not just Emma Goldman who was kicked out—but against people pretty much in the mainstream like Eugene Debs, who was the leading labor figure. Wilson was completely vindictive, tossed him in jail because he raised questions about the nobility of Wilsons' war, and he refused to grant him an amnesty when everyone else was granted an amnesty. All this really crushed independent thought and labor. It had a big effect.

Alongside the violence there is the rise of massive propaganda, the rise of the public relations industry, to try to control attitudes and beliefs. Apart from that, there is something quite simple: the disciplinary effects of the way life is organized. Take students today They are in some ways freer than they were 60 years ago in their attitudes and commitments and so on. On the other hand they are more disciplined. They are disciplined by debt. Part of the reasoning for arranging education so you come out with heavy debt is so you are disciplined. Take the last 20 years—the neo-liberal years roughly—a very striking part of what is called "globalization" is just aimed at discipline. It wants to eliminate freedom of choice and impose discipline. How do you do that? Well, if you're a couple in the U.S. now, each working 50 hours a week to put food on the table, you don't have time to think about how to become a libertarian socialist. When what you are worried about is "how can I get food on the table?" or "I've got kids to take care of, and when they are sick I've got to go to work and what's going to happen to them?" Those are very well-designed techniques of imposing discipline. And there are costs to trying to be independent. Take, say, trying to organize a labor union. If you are the organizer, there are gonna be costs to you. Maybe the work force will gain but there is a cost to you. We know there is, we know what that cost is—not just in energy and effort, but in punishment. People living in fragile circumstances make a reasonable calculation, they say "Why should I take the cost when I can just get by?" So there are many reasons why normal instincts and attitudes don't come out. Although over time they often do. After all that's how we have social change for the better.

Thank you so much for your time. It was great to meet you, thanks for your thoughts.

This interview was conducted in February, 2004 in Cambridge, MA by Barry Pateman, Associate Editor of the Emma Goldman Papers.

When somebody declares himself as an anarchist, he basically tells very little about his inspirations and aspirations—about the question of means and ends. This only confirms an old truth that we can not define anarchism as self-sufficient dot, but rather as a mosaic composed of many different dots or political views (and aspirations)—green, feminist, pacifist, etc. This question of means and ends is part of the fascination of anarchism in theory, but sometimes part its frustration in practice. Do you think that this diversity makes anarchism ineffective and an inconsequential body of ideas, or rather makes anarchism universally adaptable?

234

Anarchism is a very broad category; it means a lot of different things to different people. The main strains of anarchism have been very concerned with means. They have often tended to try to follow the idea that Bakunin expressed, that you should build the seeds of the future society within the existing one, and have been very extensively involved in educational work: organizing and forming collectives, small collectives and larger ones, and other kinds of organizations. There are other groups that call themselves anarchist, who are also mostly concerned about means—so, what kind of demonstrations should we carry out, what sort of direct actions are appropriate and so on and so forth. I don't think it is possible to ask whether it is effective or not. There are different ways of proceeding, effective in different circumstances. And there is no unified anarchist movement that has a position to talk about. There are just many conflicting strains that often disagree quite sharply. There have never been many anarchists, as far as I know, who object to carrying out what they call reformist measures within existing society—like improving women's rights, worker's health. There are other anarchists whose positions are primitivist, who want to eliminate technology and return to the soil...

In theoretical political science we can analytically identify two main conceptions of anarchism—a so-called collective anarchism with Bakunin, Kropotkin and Makhno as main figures and which is limited to Europe, and, on another hand, so-called individualistic anarchism which is limited to the U.S. Do you agree with this theoretical separation, and in this perspective, where do you see the historical origins of anarchism in the U.S.?

The individualistic anarchism that you are talking about, Stirner and others, is one of the roots of—among other things—the so-called "libertarian" movement in the U.S. This means dedication to free market capitalism, and has no connection with the rest of the international anarchist movement. In the European tradition, anarchists commonly called themselves libertarian socialists, in a very different sense of the term "libertarian." As far as I can see, the workers' movements, which didn't call themselves anarchist, were closer to the main strain of European anarchism than many of the people in the U.S. who called themselves anarchists. If we go back to the labor activism from the early days of the industrial revolution, to the working class press in 1850s, and so on, it's got a real anarchist strain to it. They never heard of European anarchism, never heard of Marx, or anything like that. It was spontaneous. They took for granted that wage labor is little different from slavery, that workers should own the mills, that the industrial system is destroying individual initiative, culture, and so on, that they have to struggle against the what they called "the new spirit of the age" in the 1850s: "Gain Wealth, Forgetting all but Self." Sounds rather familiar. And the same is true of other popular movements—let's take the New Left movements. Some strains related themselves to traditional collectivist anarchism, which always regarded itself as a branch of socialism. But U.S. and to some extent British libertarianism is quite a different thing and different development, in fact has no objection to tyranny as long as it is private tyranny. That is radically different from other forms of anarchism.

235

Where in a long and rich history of people's struggles in the U.S. do you see the main inspiration of contemporary anarchism in the U.S.? What is your opinion about the Transcendentalism as an inspiration in this perspective?

Maybe you'll discover something in your research on this topic, but my feeling is that the Transcendentalist movement, which was mostly intellectuals, may have had some influence on individualist anarchism, but didn't connect, to my knowledge, in any significant fashion with the working class popular movements, which much more resemble the anarchism of Bakunin, Kropotkin, the Spanish revolutionaries and others.

Most of the creative energy for radical politics—for the new movement of movements or so-called anti-capitalist, even anti-globalization movement— is nowadays coming from anarchism, but few of the people involved in the movement actually call themselves "anarchists." Where do you see the main reason for this?

I think it has always been true. Most activists, people in human rights struggles, women's struggles, labor struggles, and so on, didn't call themselves anarchists, they didn't draw from any knowledge or understanding of anarchist tradition. Maybe in the U.S. they heard of Emma Goldman, but they just developed out of their needs, concerns, instincts, natural commitments. I don't think we have to work very hard to bring ordinary people in the U.S., who never heard of authentic anarchism, to help them come to the kind of understanding that young women from the farms and workers from the urban slums had from the 1850s, also on their own. In the mid-19th century when the workers in the mills, in Lowell and in Salem, were developing a very lively and active working class culture, I doubt that they knew anything about the Transcendentalists, who were right from the same neighborhood and about the same period.

Ordinary people often confuse anarchism with chaos and violence, and do not know that anarchism (an archos) doesn't mean life or a state of things without rules, but rather a highly organized social order, life without a ruler, "principe." Is pejorative usage of the word anarchism maybe a direct consequence of the fact that the idea that people could be free was and is extremely frightening to those in power?

236　　　There has been an element within the anarchist movement that has been concerned with "propaganda by the deed," often with violence, and it is quite natural that power centers seize on it in an effort to undermine any attempt for independence and freedom, by identifying it with violence. But that is not true just for anarchism. Even democracy is feared. It is so deep-seated that people can't even see it. If we take a look at the *Boston Globe* on July 4th—July 4th is of course Independence Day, praising independence, freedom and democracy—we find that they had an article on George Bush's attempt to get some support in Europe, to mend fences after the conflict. They interviewed the foreign policy director of the "libertarian" Cato Institute, asking why Europeans are critical of the U.S. He said something like this: The problem is that Germany and France have weak governments, and if they go against the will of the population, they have to pay a political cost. This is the libertarian Cato Institute talking. The fear of democracy and hatred of it is so profound that nobody even notices it. In fact the whole fury about Old Europe and New Europe last year was very dramatic, particularly the fact that the criterion for membership in one or the other was somehow not noticed. The criterion was extremely sharp. If the government took the same position as the overwhelming majority of the population, it was bad: "Old Europe—bad guys." If the government followed orders from Crawford, Texas and overruled an even larger majority of the population, then it was the hope of the future and democracy: Berlusconi, Aznar, and other noble figures. This was pretty uniform across the spectrum, just taken for granted. The lesson was: if you have a very strong government you don't have to pay a political cost if you overrule the population. That's admirable. That's what governments are for—to overrule the population and work for the rich and powerful. It is so deep-seated that it wasn't even seen.

What is your opinion about the "dilemma" of means—revolution versus social and cultural evolution?

I don't really see it as a dilemma. It makes sense, in any system of domination and control, to try to change it as far as possible within the limits that the system permits. If you run up against limits that are impassable barriers, then it may be that the only way to proceed is conflict, struggle and revolutionary change. But there is no need for revolutionary change to work for improving safety and health regulations in factories, for example, because you can bring about these changes through parliamentary means. So you try to push it as far as you can. People often do not even recognize the existence of systems of oppression and domination. They have to try to struggle to gain their rights within the systems in which they live before they even perceive that there is repression. Take a look at the women's movement. One of the first steps in the development of the women's movement was so-called "consciousness-raising efforts." Try to get women to perceive that it is not the natural state of the world for them to be dominated and controlled. My grandmother couldn't join the women's movement, since she didn't feel any oppression, in some sense. That's just the way life was, like the sun rises in the morning. Until people can realize that it is not like the sun rising, that it can be changed, that you don't have to follow orders, that you don't have to be beaten, until people can perceive that there is something wrong with that, until that is overcome, you can't go on. And one of the ways to do that is to try to press reforms within the existing systems of repression, and sooner or later you find that you will have to change them.

Do you think that the change should be achieved through institutionalized (party) politics, or rather through other means such as disobedience, building parallel frameworks, alternative media, etc?

It is impossible to say anything general about it, because it depends on circumstances. Sometimes one tactic is right, sometimes another one. Talk of tactics sounds sort of trivial, but it is not. Tactical choices are the ones that have real human consequences. We can try to go beyond the more general strategic choices—speculatively and with open minds—but beyond that we descend into abstract generalities. Tactics have to do with decisions about what to do next, they have real human consequences. So for example, let's take the upcoming Republican National Convention. If a large group that calls itself anarchist acts in such a way as to strengthen the systems of power and antagonize the public, they will be harming their own cause. If they can find actions that will get people to understand why it makes sense to challenge systems of formal democracy without substance, then they picked the right tactic. But you cannot check or look in a textbook to find the answers. It depends on careful evaluation of the situation that exists, the state of public understanding, the likely consequences of what we do, and so on.

The United States has a very long history of Utopism—of different attempts towards alternative social orders. Transcendentalism was also famous because its Brook Farm and Fruitlands experiments. French thinker Proudhon once wrote that: "Freedom is the mother, not the daughter of order." Where do you see life after or beyond the (nation) state?

My feeling is that any interaction among human beings that is more than personal—meaning that takes institutional forms of one kind or another—in community, or workplace, family, larger society, whatever it may be, should be under direct control of its participants. So that would mean workers' councils in industry, popular democracy in communities, interaction between them, free associations in larger groups, up to organization of international society. You can spell out the details in many different ways, and I don't really see a lot a point in it. And here I disagree with some of my friends; I think spelling out in extensive detail the form of future society goes beyond our understanding. There surely will have to be plenty of experimentation—we don't know enough about human beings and societies, their needs and limitations. There is just too much we don't know, so lots of alternatives should be tried.

On many occasions activists, intellectuals, students, have asked you about your specific vision of anarchist society and about your very detailed plan to get there. Once, you answered that "we can not figure out what problems are going to arise unless you experiment with them." Do you also have a feeling that many left intellectuals are loosing too much energy with their theoretical disputes about the proper means and ends to even start "experimenting" in practice.

Many people find this extremely important and find that they cannot act as, let's say, organizers in their community unless they have a detailed vision of the future that they are going to try to achieve. OK, that's the way they perceive the world and themselves. I would not presume to tell them it's wrong. Maybe it is right for them, but it is not right for me. A lot of flowers have a right to bloom. People do things in different ways.

With the process of economic globalization getting stronger day after day, many on the left are caught in a dilemma—either one can work to reinforce the sovereignty of nation-states as a defensive barrier against the control of foreign and global capital; or one can strive towards a non-national alternative to the present form of globalization and that is equally global. What's your opinion about this riddle?

As usual, I don't see it as a conflict. It makes perfect sense to use the means that nation states provide in order to resist exploitation, oppression, domination, violence and so on, yet at the same time to try to override these means by developing alternatives. There is no conflict. You should use whatever methods are available to you. There is no conflict between trying to overthrow the state and using the means that are provided in a partially democratic society, the means that have been developed through popular struggles over centuries. You should use them and try to go beyond, maybe destroy the institution. It is like the media. I am perfectly happy to write columns that are syndicated by the *New York Times*, which I do, and to write in *Z Magazine*. It is no contradiction. In fact, let's take a look at this place (MIT). It has been a very good place for me to work; I've been able to do things I want to do. I have been here for fifty years, and have never thought about leaving it. But there are things about it that are hopelessly illegitimate. For example, it is a core part of the military-linked industrial economy. So you work within it and try to change it.

Many oppose "democracy" since it is still a form of tyranny—tyranny of the majority. They object to the notion of majority rule, noting that the views of the majority do not always coincide with the morally right one. Therefore we have an obligation to act according to the dictates of this conscience, even if the latter goes against majority opinion, the presiding leadership, or the laws of the society. Do you agree with this notion?

It is impossible to say. If you want to be a part of the society, you have to accept the majority decisions within it, in general, unless there is a very strong reason not to. If I drive home tonight, and there is a red light, I will stop, because that is a community decision. It doesn't matter if it is 3 a.m. and I may be able to go through it without being caught because nobody is around. If you are part of the community, you accept behavioral patterns that maybe you don't agree with. But there comes a point when this is unacceptable, when you feel you have to act under your own conscious choice and the decisions of the majority are immoral. But again, anyone looking for a formula about it is going be very disappointed. Sometimes you have to decide in opposition to your friends. Sometimes that would be legitimate, sometimes not. There simply are no formulas for such things and cannot be. Human life is too complex, with too many dimensions. If you want to act in violation of community norms, you have to have pretty strong reasons. The burden of proof is on you to show that you are right, not just: "My conscience says so." That is not enough of a reason.

What is your opinion about so-called "scientific" anarchism—attempts to scientifically prove Bakunin's assumption that human beings have an instinct for freedom. That we have not only a tendency towards freedom but also a biological need. Something that you were so successful in proving with universal grammar...

That is really a hope, it is not a scientific result. So little is understood about human nature that you cannot draw any serious conclusions. We can't even answer questions about the nature of insects. We draw conclusions—tentative ones—through a combination of our intuitions, hopes, some experiences. In that way we may draw the conclusion that humans have an instinct for freedom. But we should not pretend that it is derived from scientific knowledge and understanding. It isn't and can't be. There is no science of human beings and their interactions, or even of simpler organisms, that reaches anywhere near that far.

Last question. Henry David Thoreau opens his essay "Civil Disobedience" with the following sentence: "That government is the best that governs the least or doesn't govern at all." History teaches us that our freedom, labor rights, environmental standards have never been given to us by the wealthy and influential few, but have always been fought for by ordinary people—with civil disobedience. What should be in this respect our first steps toward another, better world?

There are many steps to achieve different ends. If we take the immediate problems in the U.S., probably the main domestic problem we face is the collapse of the health care system, which is a very serious problem. People can't get drugs, can't get medical care, costs are out of control, and it is getting worse and worse. That is a major problem. And that can be, in principle and I think in fact, dealt within the framework of parliamentary institutions. In some recent polls 80 percent of the population prefer much more reasonable programs, some form of national health insurance, which would be far cheaper and more efficient and would give them the benefits they want. But the democratic system is so corrupted that 80 percent of the population can't even put their position on the electoral agenda. But that can be overcome. Take Brazil, which has much higher barriers than here, but the population was able to force through legislation which made Brazil a leader in providing AIDS medication at a fraction of the cost elsewhere and in violation of international trade rules imposed by the U.S. and other rich countries. They did it. If Brazilian peasants can do it, we can do it. Instituting a reasonable health care system is one thing that should be done, and you can think of a thousand others. There is no way of ranking them; there is no first step. They should all be done. You can decide to be engaged in this one or that one or some other one, wherever your personal concerns, commitments and energy are. They are all interactive, mutually supportive. I do things I think are important, you do things you think are important, they do what they think is important, they can all be means for achieving more or less the same ends. They can assist one another, achievements in one domain can assist those in others. But who am I to say what the first step is?

Do you go to the polls? Do you vote?

Sometimes. Again, it depends on whether there is a choice worth making, whether the effect of voting is significant enough so it is worth the time and effort. On local issues I almost always vote. For example, there was recently a referendum in the town where I live that overrode ridiculous tax restrictions, and I voted on that. I thought it is important for a town to have schools, fire stations, libraries and so on and so forth. Usually the local elections make some kind of difference, beyond that it is… If this state (Massachusetts) were a swing state, I would vote against Bush.

And what about upcoming elections?

Since it is not a swing state, there are other choices. One might have reasons to vote for Ralph Nader, or for the Green Party, which also runs candidates apart from the presidency. There are a variety of possible choices, depending on one's evaluation of the significance.

241

This interview was conducted on July 14, 2004, in Cambridge, MA, by Ziga Vodovnik, Assistant/Young Researcher at the Department of Social Sciences, University of Ljubljana, Slovenia, Europe. A rough transcript was also published on Znet (www.zmag.org)

Ordering Information

AK Press
674-A 23rd Street,
Oakland, CA 94612-1163,
USA

Phone: (510) 208-1700
E-mail: akpress@akpress.org
URL: www.akpress.org
Please send all payments (checks, money orders, or cash at your own
risk) in U.S. dollars. Alternatively, we take VISA and MC.

AK Press
PO Box 12766,
Edinburgh, EH8 9YE,
Scotland

Phone: (0131) 555-5165
E-mail: ak@akedin.demon.co.uk
URL: www.akuk.com
Please send all payments (cheques, money orders, or cash at your own
risk) in U.K. pounds. Alternatively, we take credit cards.

For a dollar, a pound or a few IRC's, the same addresses would be
delighted to provide you with the latest complete AK catalog,
featuring several thousand books, pamphlets, zines, audio products and
stylish apparel published & distributed by AK Press. Alternatively, check
out our websites for the complete catalog, latest news and updates,
events, and secure ordering.

AK Press Books, CDs, & DVDs by Noam Chomsky

At War With Asia by Noam Chomsky
$18.95 ISBN 1 902593 89 8
In 1970, Noam Chomsky urged Americans to confront and avoid the dangers inherent in the American invasion of Southeast Asia. Looking back 30 years later, we still share Chomsky's concern: Will this new war lead us to an ever-expanding battle against the people of the world and increasing repression at home? *At War With Asia* is an indispensable guide to understanding not only the past, but the current logic of imperial force.

Language and Politics by Noam Chomsky edited by C.P. Otero
$28.00 ISBN 1 902593 82 0
An enormous chronological collection of over fifty interviews conducted with Chomsky beginning with his 1968 discussion of the US war on Vietnam and ending soon after the appearance of his best-selling book, *9-11*, and the start of America's War On Terror. Many of the pieces have never appeared in any other collection, some have never appeared in English, and more than one has been suppressed. The interviews add a personal dimension to the full breadth of Chomsky's impressive written canon—equally covering his analysis in linguistics, philosophy, and politics.

Radical Priorities by Noam Chomsky edited by C.P. Otero
$18.95 ISBN 1 902593 69 3
In *Radical Priorities*, C.P. Otero sets out to "provide relatively easy access to Chomsky's libertarian philosophy and political analysis". Taken from a wide variety of sources, many never widely published—some never in a book at all and spanning four decades, the reader is furnished with a truly comprehensive window into Chomsky's anarchist convictions. Convictions which, while ever-present in his analysis are left largely misunderstood or worse-ignored. In seeking to combat the great challenges facing humanity, Chomsky's analysis and the traditions that bore it must not be left in obscurity.

Distorted Morality DVD by Noam Chomsky
$25.00 ISBN 1 905293 76 6
Here Chomsky offers a devastating critique of America's current War on Terror—arguing that it is a logical impossibility for such a war to be taking place. Chomsky presents his reasoning with refreshing clarity, drawing from a wealth of historic knowledge and analysis. The DVD includes a shorter; more recent talk on the danger, cruelty, and stupidity of the U.S. and Israel's policy of Pre-emptive War and a lively Q&A session all in an easily searchable user friendly format.

The Emerging Framework of World Power CD by Noam Chomsky
$14.98 ISBN 1 902593 75 8
Chomsky's state-of-the-world address. America's leading foreign policy critic surveys the role of the U.S. in a post-911 world—and finds nothing has changed.

The New War on Terrorism: Fact and Fiction CD by Noam Chomsky
$14.98 ISBN 1 902593 62 6
"We certainly want to reduce the level of terror... There is one easy way to do that... stop participating in it."—Noam Chomsky, from the CD
What is terrorism? And how can we reduce the likelihood of such crimes, whether they are against us, or against someone else? With his vintage flair, penetrating analysis, and ironic wit, Chomsky, in perhaps his most anticipated lecture ever—delivered a month after 9/11, and his first public statement—makes sense of a world apparently gone mad.

An American Addiction: Drugs, Guerillas, Counterinsurgency—U.S. Intervention in Colombia
CD by Noam Chomsky
$13.98 ISBN 1 902593 44 8
"Colombia has been the leading recipient of US arms and training in the Western Hemisphere through the 1990s. It has also had the worst human rights record by far in the Western Hemisphere during these years. That correlation is one of the best correlations in contemporary history....It's a very important correlation that should be known and understood by the people who are paying for it. That's us. And it will get worse." (Noam Chomsky, from the CD)

Propaganda and Control of the Public Mind 2×CD by Noam Chomsky
$20.00 ISBN 1 873176 68 6
"The war against working people should be understood to be a real war. It's not a new war. It's an old war. Furthermore it's a perfectly conscious war everywhere, but specifically in the U.S... which happens to have a highly class-conscious business class... And they have long seen themselves as fighting a bitter class war, except they don't want anybody else to know about it." (Noam Chomsky, from the CD)

Case Studies In Hypocrisy: U.S. Human Rights Policy 2×CD by Noam Chomsky
$20.00 ISBN 1 902593 27 8
With the recent celebration of the fiftieth anniversary of the Universal Declaration Of Human Rights, and America's undisputed position as the world's only superpower, the contrast between the rhetoric and the reality of U.S. foreign policy has never been more stark. With his inimitable penetrating analysis and dry wit, Chomsky leads us through the murky blood-soaked reality of America's New World Order.

For A Free Humanity: For Anarchy 2×CD by Noam Chomsky/Chumbawamba
$18.00 ISBN 1 873176 74 0
A Double CD with Noam Chomsky and Chumbawamba. Disc One comprises the Noam Chomsky lecture "Capital Rules"—another articulate, and immediately accessible description of Corporate America's unrelenting attack on poor and working class people. Disc Two is Chumbawamba's best collection of live sounds—*Showbusiness!*, previously only available as an expensive import. Recorded live in '94. The double CD is accompanied by a 24 page booklet, with extensive interviews with both Noam Chomsky—discussing corporate structure as private tyranny, domestic surveillance of activists, and visions for a new society—and Chumbawamba discussing their past, politics, and anarchism.

Prospects For Democracy CD by Noam Chomsky
$14.98 ISBN 1 873176 38 4
Beginning with a broad review of democratic theory and political history, he argues that classical democrats such as Thomas Jefferson would be shocked at the current disrepair of American democracy. The enormous growth of corporate capitalism has already devastated democratic culture and government by concentrating power in the hands of the wealthy. And the future looks no brighter. In spite of this dark assessment, Chomsky maintains that any hope for democracy rests ultimately with you and me—on whether we can shake off our political malaise and build a democratic future.

Free Market Fantasies: Capitalism in the Real World CD by Noam Chomsky
$13.98 ISBN 1 873176 79 1
There is endless talk about the free market and its virtues. Entrepreneurs compete on level playing fields and the public benefits. The chasm between such fantasies and reality is acute and growing wider. Megamergers and monopolies are limiting competition. Fewer than 10 corporations control most of the global media. The existing free market depends heavily on taxpayer subsidies and bailouts. Corporate welfare far exceeds that which goes to the poor. Economic policy is based on the dictum: take from the needy, and give to the greedy. The captains of industry of today make the robber barons of the 19th century look like underachievers. The gap between CEO and worker salaries has never been sharper. One union leader put it this way, "Workers are getting the absolute crap kicked out of them."

OTHER AK TITLES...

Books

MARTHA **ACKELSBERG**	*Free Women of Spain*
KATHY **ACKER**	*Pussycat Fever*
MICHAEL **ALBERT**	*Moving Forward: Program for a Participatory Economy*
JOEL **ANDREAS**	*Addicted to War: Why the U.S. Can't Kick Militarism*
PAUL **AVRICH**	*Anarchist Voices: An Oral History of Anarchism in America (Unabridged)*
PAUL **AVRICH**	*The Modern School Movement: Anarchism and Education in the United States*
PAUL **AVRICH**	*The Russian Anarchists*
ALEXANDER **BERKMAN**	*What is Anarchism?*
ALEXANDER **BERKMAN**	*The Blast: The Complete Collection*
HAKIM **BEY**	*Immediatism*
JANET **BIEHL** & PETER **STAUDENMAIER**	*Ecofascism: Lessons From The German Experience*
BIOTIC BAKING BRIGADE	*Pie Any Means Necessary: The Biotic Baking Brigade Cookbook*
JACK **BLACK**	*You Can't Win*
MURRAY **BOOKCHIN**	*Anarchism, Marxism, and the Future of the Left*
MURRAY **BOOKCHIN**	*The Ecology of Freedom: The Emergence and Dissolution of Hierarchy*
MURRAY **BOOKCHIN**	*Post-Scarcity Anarchism*
MURRAY **BOOKCHIN**	*Social Anarchism or Lifestyle Anarchism: An Unbridgeable Chasm*
MURRAY **BOOKCHIN**	*Spanish Anarchists: The Heroic Years 1868–1936, The*
MURRAY **BOOKCHIN**	*To Remember Spain: The Anarchist and Syndicalist Revolution of 1936*
MURRAY **BOOKCHIN**	*Which Way for the Ecology Movement?*
MAURICE **BRINTON**	*For Workers' Power*
DANNY **BURNS**	*Poll Tax Rebellion*
MATT **CALLAHAN**	*The Trouble With Music*
CHRIS **CARLSSON**	*Critical Mass: Bicycling's Defiant Celebration*
JAMES **CARR**	*Bad*
NOAM **CHOMSKY**	*At War With Asia*
NOAM **CHOMSKY**	*Language and Politics*
NOAM **CHOMSKY**	*Radical Priorities*

WARD **CHURCHILL**	*On the Justice of Roosting Chickens: Reflections on the Consequences of U.S. Imperial Arrogance and Criminality*
WARD **CHURCHILL**	*Speaking Truth in the Teeth of Power: Lectures on Globalization, Colonialism, and Native North America*
HARRY **CLEAVER**	*Reading Capital Politically*
ALEXANDER **COCKBURN** & JEFFREY **ST. CLAIR** (ed.)	*Dime's Worth of Difference*
ALEXANDER **COCKBURN** & JEFFREY **ST. CLAIR** (ed.)	*Politics of Anti-Semitism, The*
ALEXANDER **COCKBURN** & JEFFREY **ST. CLAIR** (ed.)	*Serpents in the Garden*
DANIEL **COHN-BENDIT** & GABRIEL **COHN-BENDIT**	*Obsolete Communism: The Left-Wing Alternative*
EG **SMITH COLLECTIVE**	*Animal Ingredients A–Z (3rd edition)*
VOLTAIRINE **de CLEYRE**	*Voltarine de Cleyre Reader*
HOWARD **EHRLICH**	*Reinventing Anarchy, Again*
SIMON **FORD**	*Realization and Suppression of the Situationist International: An Annotated Bibliography 1972–1992*
YVES **FREMION** & **VOLNY**	*Orgasms of History: 3000 Years of Spontaneous Revolt*
LUIGI **GALLEANI**	*Anarchy Will Be! The Selected Writings of Luigi Galleani*
BERNARD **GOLDSTEIN**	*Five Years in the Warsaw Ghetto*
DANIEL **GUERIN**	*No Gods No Masters*
AGUSTIN **GUILLAMON**	*Friends Of Durruti Group, 1937–1939, The*
ANN **HANSEN**	*Direct Action: Memoirs Of An Urban Guerilla*
WILLIAM **HERRICK**	*Jumping the Line: The Adventures and Misadventures of an American Radical*
FRED **HO**	*Legacy to Liberation: Politics & Culture of Revolutionary Asian/Pacific America*
STEWART **HOME**	*Assault on Culture*
STEWART **HOME**	*Neoism, Plagiarism & Praxis*
STEWART **HOME**	*Neoist Manifestos / The Art Strike Papers*
STEWART **HOME**	*No Pity*
STEWART **HOME**	*Red London*
STEWART **HOME**	*What Is Situationism? A Reader*
KATHY **KELLY**	*Other Lands Have Dreams: From Baghdad to Pekin Prison*
JAMES **KELMAN**	*Some Recent Attacks: Essays Cultural And Political*
KEN **KNABB**	*Complete Cinematic Works of Guy Debord*

TOM **VAGUE**	*Televisionaries*
JAN **VALTIN**	*Out of the Night*
RAOUL **VANEIGEM**	*Cavalier History Of Surrealism, A*
FRANCOIS EUGENE **VIDOCQ**	*Memoirs of Vidocq: Master of Crime*
GEE **VOUCHER**	*Crass Art And Other Pre-Postmodern Monsters*
MARK J **WHITE**	*Idol Killing, An*
JOHN **YATES**	*Controlled Flight Into Terrain*
JOHN **YATES**	*September Commando*
BENJAMIN **ZEPHANIAH**	*Little Book of Vegan Poems*
BENJAMIN **ZEPHANIAH**	*School's Out*
HELLO	*2/15: The Day The World Said NO To War*
DARK STAR COLLECTIVE	*Beneath the Paving Stones: Situationists and the Beach, May 68*
DARK STAR COLLECTIVE	*Quiet Rumours: An Anarcha-Feminist Reader*
ANONYMOUS	*Test Card F*
CLASS WAR FEDERATION	*Unfinished Business: The Politics of Class War*

CDs

THE **EX**	*1936: The Spanish Revolution*
MUMIA **ABU JAMAL**	*175 Progress Drive*
MUMIA **ABU JAMAL**	*All Things Censored Vol.1*
MUMIA **ABU JAMAL**	*Spoken Word*
FREEDOM ARCHIVES	*Chile: Promise of Freedom*
FREEDOM ARCHIVES	*Prisons on Fire: George Jackson, Attica & Black Liberation*
JUDI **BARI**	*Who Bombed Judi Bari?*
JELLO **BIAFRA**	*Become the Media*
JELLO **BIAFRA**	*Beyond The Valley of the Gift Police*
JELLO **BIAFRA**	*High Priest of Harmful*
JELLO **BIAFRA**	*I Blow Minds For A Living*
JELLO **BIAFRA**	*If Evolution Is Outlawed*
JELLO **BIAFRA**	*Machine Gun In The Clown's Hand*
JELLO **BIAFRA**	*No More Cocoons*
NOAM **CHOMSKY**	*American Addiction, An*
NOAM **CHOMSKY**	*Case Studies in Hypocrisy*
NOAM **CHOMSKY**	*Emerging Framework of World Power*
NOAM **CHOMSKY**	*Free Market Fantasies*
NOAM **CHOMSKY**	*New War On Terrorism: Fact And Fiction*
NOAM **CHOMSKY**	*Propaganda and Control of the Public Mind*

DVDs